Control and Audit in Management Accounting

C I *m* A

Published in association with
the Chartered Institute of
Management Accountants

Other titles in the CIMA series

Stage 1

Economics for Accountants
Keith West

Quantitative Methods
Kevin Pardoe

Stage 2

Accounting Information Systems and Data Processing
Krish Bhaskar and Richard Housden

Cost Accounting
Mark Lee Inman

Financial Accounting
Peter Taylor and Brian Underdown

Management
Cliff Bowman

Stage 3

Advanced Financial Accounting
Peter Taylor and Brian Underdown

Company Law
Julia Bailey and Iain McCallum

Management Accounting Techniques
David Benjamin and Colin Biggs

Stage 4

Financial and Treasury Management
Paul Collier, Terry Cooke and John Glynn

Management Accounting: Strategic Planning and Marketing
Patrick McNamee

Revision Guides

Advanced Accounting Techniques Groups and Special Transactions Revision Guide
Peter Taylor and Brian Underdown

Business Law Revision Guide
Stan Marsh

Company Accounting Revision Guide
Peter Taylor and Brian Underdown

Cost Accounting Revision Guide
Colin Drury

Economics Revision Guide
Rob Dixon and Keith West

Quantitative Methods Revision Guide
Paul Goodwin

Control and Audit in Management Accounting

Stage 4

Jeff Coates, Colin Rickwood and Ray Stacey

Heinemann Professional Publishing

Heinemann Professional Publishing Ltd
Halley Court, Jordan Hill, Oxford OX2 8EJ

OXFORD LONDON MELBOURNE AUCKLAND SINGAPORE
IBADAN NAIROBI GABORONE KINGSTON

First published 1989

© Jeff Coates, Colin Rickwood and Ray Stacey 1989

British Library Cataloguing in Publication Data
Coates, Jeff
 Control and audit in management accounting
 1. Management accounting. For executives
 I. Title II. Rickwood, Colin
 III. Stacey, Ray
 658.1'511

ISBN 0 434 90268 3

Printed and bound in Great Britain by
Redwood Burn Limited, Trowbridge, Wiltshire.

Contents

Preface		ix
1	**Introduction**	1
	What is management accounting?	1
	Origins and development of management accounting	4
	Planning, control and audit	5
	References	9
2	**Control theory and MIS**	10
	The systems views	10
	Organizational theory and structure	17
	Organizational goals	17
	Behavioural considerations and motivation	20
	Summary	22
	References	22
	Further reading	23
	Questions	23
3	**Budgets and planning**	25
	Planning – budgets and standards	25
	Constraints on resources	32
	Setting standards	33
	Revision of budgets and standards	36
	References	42
	Questions	43
4	**Budgets and control**	47
	Introduction	47
	Collection and presentation of budget information for control purposes	48
	Measurement and control of staff performance	52
	Variance analysis	53

vi *Contents*

	Managerial participation in budget planning and control	62
	Conclusion	64
	References	64
	Questions	65
5	**Budgeting in not-for-profit (NFP) organizations**	**67**
	Introduction	67
	Budgeting in local authorities	69
	Zero-base budgeting (ZBB)	70
	Planning, programming and budgeting systems (PBBS)	75
	Value for money (VFM) audit	80
	The Cambridgeshire Experiment	93
	General conclusions	94
	References	94
6	**Assessing performance in businesses**	**96**
	Introduction	96
	Objectives, rewards, measurement and motivation	96
	Inter-firm comparisons	99
	References	105
	Questions	105
7	**Assessing segmental performance**	**109**
	Centralization and decentralization	109
	Divisionalization and segmentalization	111
	Segments large and small	114
	Responsibility centres	115
	Assessment criteria	120
	Annuity depreciation	126
	Valuing assets at net present value	129
	Accounting conventions and policies	130
	Asset hire or ownership	133
	Apportionments, attributability and controllability	134
	Short-term measures, long-term goals	140
	Profit centres	141
	Non-financial criteria	146
	References	148
	Questions	149
8	**Assessing performance – expense and service centres**	**158**
	Introduction	158
	Effectiveness and efficiency	158
	Expense or cost centres	159
	Cost centres and control	160
	Revenue centres	165
	Budgeted performance measures	165
	References	166
	Questions	166

9 Assessing performance in public sector organizations — 167
Introduction — 167
The significance of the public sector — 169
Ratio analysis — 170
Nationalized industries — 172
Local authorities — 181
Central government — 187
Summary — 189
References — 189
Appendix 9.1　Thames Water Authority — 190
Appendix 9.2　Performance ratios — 196
Appendix 9.3　The Water Authorities (Return on Assets) Order 1985 — 200

10 Internal audit and control — 202
Internal control — 202
Internal audit and the internal auditor — 205
Principles of internal audit — 208
Management of internal audit — 213
Performance audits — 217
Summary — 221
References — 221
Further reading — 222
Questions — 222

11 Auditing techniques and procedures — 224
Introduction — 224
System documentation — 225
Testing internal systems — 225
The level of substantive testing — 230
Recording and appraising the system — 231
Statistical sampling — 235
Direct selection of account balances — 241
Procedures for applications — 242
Summary of applications' procedure — 247
References — 248
Questions — 248

12 Systems evaluation and audit — 251
Introduction — 251
Information system evaluation — 252
System development controls — 254
Computer security and protection — 259
Computer audit — 264
Conclusion — 267
References — 267
Further reading — 268
Questions — 268

13 Investigations and special audits 271
Acquisitions of businesses 272
Disposals of businesses and management buy-outs 277
Raising debt finance 278
Investigation of fraud 279
References 280
Further reading 280
Questions 280

14 Conclusion 283
References 288

Appendix: linear programming 289

Index 293

Preface

There are no regulations creating formal boundaries on the scope of management accounting. In meeting the information needs of management, it is extended in form, diversity and function according to the requirements of the organization in which it operates. Within this potentially wide-ranging field, this text adopts a particular focus upon control, the function that directs the efforts of members towards the achievement of the objectives of the organization. Specific attention is given to audit and, here, just as with control in general, consideration is not limited to the restrictive aspects. Control can be positive, promoting enterprise and performance. Internal audit encompasses assessment of efficiency and effectiveness as well as protection against irregularities.

Despite having a focus on control, the subject matter remains broad. As a text, directed towards the CIMA Control and Audit syllabus for stage 4, it must be seen as the culmination of all earlier stages. Numerous views and approaches relevant to this subject area have been put forward and many have been successfully adopted. No single volume, as this is, could claim to provide comprehensive treatment of all the aspects included and the reader must recognize the contribution to his study of the subject offered in the literature. To this end, we have provided detailed references and further reading at the end of chapters.

Management accounting exists in practice and its application benefits substantially from practical experience. Such experience is an essential element in the development of the professional management accountant and the reader should draw on his own experience when considering the implementation of the techniques and approaches included in this book.

We would like to express our thanks to John Edwards of Aston Business School for suggestions on treatment of linear programming; to Rowan Jones of the University of Birmingham for helpful comments on public sector material; and to Gail Russell and Karen Hanson for their valuable work in the preparation of this book.

Jeff Coates
Colin Rickwood
Ray Stacey

1 Introduction

What is management accounting?

Many authors distinguish between financial and management accounting in that the former relates to the stewardship function and external reporting, while the latter relates to the provision of information to the managers of the organization for purposes of planning, controlling and decision-making. Thus, for example, Horngren and Foster, *Cost Accounting*, Sixth Edition, states that 'The accounting system ... should provide information for three broad purposes:

1 Internal reporting to managers, for use in planning and controlling routine operations.
2 Internal reporting to managers, for use in making non-routine decisions and in formulating major plans and policies.
3 External reporting to stockholders, government, and other outside parties, for use in investor decisions, income tax collections, and a variety of other purposes.'

The third purpose, commonly referred to as 'Financial Accounting' is heavily prescribed by legislation (both British and European) and accepted accounting practices (SSAPs etc). While ostensibly providing a 'true and fair' view aimed at the needs of one particular user group – the shareholders – it is commonly used by a wide variety of interested parties as one means of interpreting the performance and status of the organization; not least among these interested parties will be the managers of the organization itself.

However, it is to be hoped that the information available to the managers of most organizations will not be restricted to this limited financial view; that additional, purpose-specific information will be made available via the internal accounting system to enable managers to manage – to plan, control and make decisions. For such information, usually termed 'Management Accounting', there are no prescriptions: managers need not be constrained in any way by legislative requirements or by any 'normally accepted' accounting concepts and practices unless they want to. It is up to management to decide what assumptions, concept, techniques, presentation etc. are appropriate for a particular purpose and/or personnel at a particular point in time.

The Chartered Institute of Management Accountants, however, has more recently defined management accounting as:[1]

'The provision of information required by management for such purposes as:

1 formulation of policies,
2 planning and controlling the activities of the enterprise,
3 decision taking on alternative courses of action,
4 disclosure to those external to the entity (shareholders and others),
5 disclosure to employees,
6 safeguarding assets.

The above involves participation in management to ensure that there is effective:

(a) formulation of plans to meet objectives (long term planning),
(b) formulation of short term operation plans (budgeting/profit planning),
(c) recording of actual transactions (financial accounting and cost accounting),
(d) corrective action to bring future actual transactions into line (financial control),
(e) obtaining and controlling finance (treasurership).
(f) reviewing and reporting on systems and operations (internal audit, management audit).'

Figure 1.1 illustrates these aspects.

The reader will note that this definition is considerably wider than that propounded earlier. It may be seen by some as a continuation of the evolution of management accounting from CIMA's earlier and more specific definition[2] of management accounting as 'The application of professional knowledge and skill in the preparation and presentation of accounting information in such a way as to assist management in the formulation of policies and in the planning and control of the operations of the undertaking'.

In this text attention is directed towards those aspects of management accounting which provide management with information for control – to assess and report on management performance; monitor efficiency, effectiveness and value for money; and evaluate the efficiency and effectiveness of information systems. This therefore encompasses the complete control mechanism: (i) the setting of appropriate, relevant plans, (ii) the establishment and operation of information systems to

Introduction 3

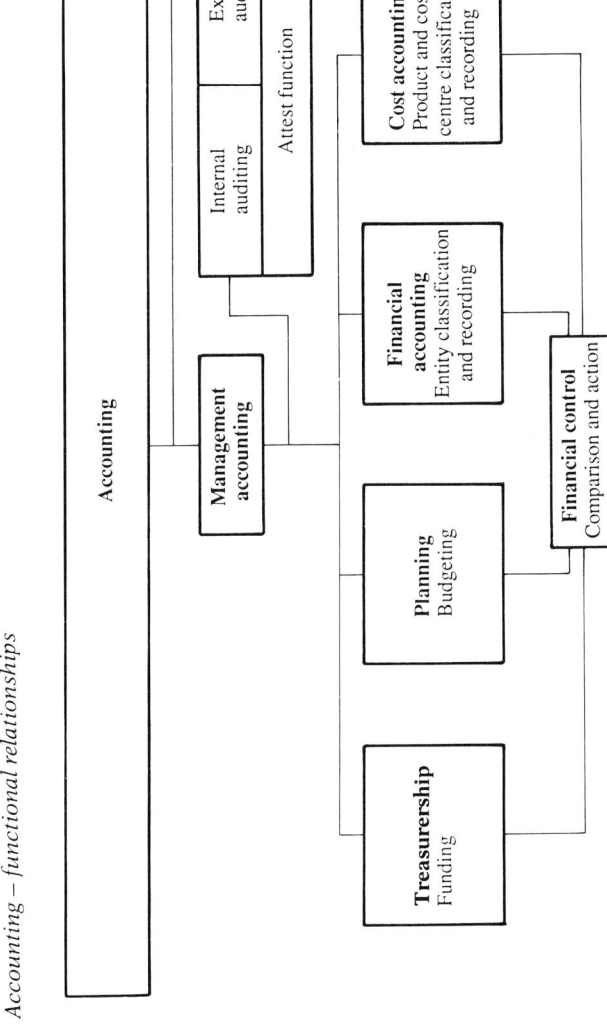

Figure 1.1 Accounting – functional relationships

provide meaningful, understandable and timely feedback, (iii) the presentation of feedback, (iv) the monitoring of events, (v) the making of resultant decisions, and (vi) the review and audit of plans, controls and decisions.

This is not a process to which a single framework can be applied; it is not possible to apply ready-made formulae which will provide ready-made solutions. Rather it requires the application of appropriate and relevant systems, processes and techniques, adapted as necessary to the specifics of the particular, i.e. the 'uniqueness' of the circumstances – the organizations, its industry, its management, its problems and resources, its *needs*. It is the multi-variety of uses and applications of management accounting to planning and control which makes it so complex, stimulating and challenging. It can be applied to any organization, whether public or private sector, whatever their size, nature, objectives, resources or location. It is universally applicable but should be uniquely applied.

Origins and development of management accounting

The analysis of management accounting, in its most basic form at least, can be traced back to at least the eighteenth century,[3] and perhaps even as far as the sixteenth century.[4] However, most historians attribute the origins of the development of modern management accounting to the latter half of the nineteenth century and the growth of large organizations and industries – textile mills, railways, coalmining and similar industries.[5,6] The size and complexity of these organizations resulted in a demand for cost and financial information for internal planning and control. These developments tended to be ad-hoc reactions by the management of these organizations to the problems they perceived, as little written literature on the subject was available. Indeed much of that which was published related the practices of those businesses which had developed some form of cost or management information systems. However, in the US and Europe, particularly during the last two decades of the nineteenth century, a number of writers on management accounting, and costing in particular, explained their 'new ideas', or, as Solomons[7] suggests, rediscovered 'ideas that were becoming of great practical importance for the first time but which could certainly have been found, though perhaps in an undeveloped state, in earlier works'.

It would be wrong to suggest that costing or management accounting systems were other than the exception, although many companies had some rudimentary knowledge of their costs if for no other reason than as an aid to pricing decisions. However, it was in this period and the early part of the twentieth century that the foundation of most modern costing and management accounting techniques were laid – cost analysis, marginal costing, absorption costing, machine hour rates, integrated cost accounts, cost allocation, departmental cost analyses, standard costing, management by exception, uniform costing, budgets. 'Virtually all of the practices employed by firms today and explicated in leading cost accounting textbooks had been developed by 1925. These practices were devised by engineers and industrialists, working in actual organizations, rather than by academic researchers. This probably explains the rapid adoption of these innovative practices by other organizations'.[8] Developments since then have been more that of refinements rather than of any new major innovation, with the exception perhaps of discounted cash flow, residual income, risk analysis and inflation accounting techniques.

Little is (apparently) new under the management accounting sun. The skill of the management accountant today is perhaps not in finding new solutions to new problems but in *adapting* old ideas to new situations;[9] perceiving and being prepared to accept the need for different measurement, planning, control and audit systems; and designing adapted or new approaches, selling them to fellow managers and ensuring that they are understood and used appropriately.

Planning, control and audit

The three levels of planning

It is helpful to distinguish between the three levels of planning and control – strategic, management and operational planning.

Strategic planning
This is the process of setting/updating/revising organizational objectives; conducting a SWOT (strength, weaknesses, opportunities and threats) analysis; and identifying alternative strategies which are capable of achieving objectives by using resources within the anticipated environmental circumstances, evaluating these alternatives and deciding upon one set of strategies to be followed over the next few years by the organization. The emphasis is on long-term planning by the senior management of an organization (or some sub-part of it). Information used is likely to be uncertain, a 'best guess', but, as errors in this planning can be expensive, even disastrous, information should be as 'considered' as possible. There is rarely the need for haste.

Budgetary or management planning
The responsibility of top and line managers, this converts necessarily broad-brush strategies into more specific action plans. It puts the flesh on the bone of the framework provided by the long-term plans in order to ensure their achievement. It is more than just a read-off of the first year of the long-term plan. It should ensure that detailed plans are

created, responsibilities and resources are allocated, and actions are taken not only to achieve the shorter annual objectives but also subsequent years' objectives. In contrast to strategic planning, as it has to some extent shorter horizons, information used may be more detailed and 'certain', and there are some time pressures. It is perhaps both less difficult and less critical than strategic planning, but vital and important all the same – after all, it is through management planning that long-term plans are implemented.

Operational planning
This is the means by which management plans are implemented. Operational planning produces nitty-gritty, short-term plans – monthly, weekly, daily or, as one practising manager put it, 'every time the phone rings'. They usually require relatively quick decisions, made by operational and line managers on the basis of relatively firm information on matters which, if errors are made, are rarely that costly or important in the long term.

Strategic and management planning inevitably 'compete' for the time and attention of senior managers in the same way as management and operational planning compete for the time and attention of middle and line managers. As shorter-term plans often appear the most urgent and addressable, there is always the danger that organizations will be managed by a series of such plans and the achievement of any specified long-term objectives may fail to occur. There is a need for managers to find an appropriate balance in their planning horizons: appropriate attention should be given to both longer- and shorter-term plans, so that neither dominates at the expense of the other and that short-term decisions with long-term implications receive the care and attention they deserve.

The recognition by managers of the types of planning they are responsible for and, in particular, have at present under consideration can be of vital importance to the organization; the refusal to make a quick decision when it is needed can be as damaging as making a critical but non-urgent decision too quickly and with too little forethought. Further, operational decisions can sometimes have long-term implications, e.g. the decision by a production foreman not to stop a long run of one product to accommodate the short-term demands of a customer for another might lead to the loss of goodwill and the customer finding alternative suppliers. Decisions with strategic or long-term implications should not be made by junior/operational managers. On the other hand, decisions of long-term strategic importance must sometimes be taken quickly, e.g. when a customer, supplier or competitor becomes 'available' for acquisition or is the subject of a takeover bid by another organization; a bad decision here may be very damaging to the organization, but only a quick decision can be made, perhaps on relatively sketchy and superficial information.

Plans and controls

The attentive reader will have noticed that the foregoing quickly moved from a planning to a decision-making mode. After all, decisions are simply the practical implementation of the planning process. The sequence 'Planning – Plans – Decisions' is, or ought to be, behind all decision-making.

A distinction, however, should be made between plans and controls; they are in fact very different processes, though they should be directed towards the same end. Plans should be the result of considering alternative means of achieving objectives in the light of uncertainty: controls should identify when these plans are failing to achieve those objectives set or are deviating in detail in their achievement. What was a good plan at the time it was set may not be so good in the circumstances of its execution, and controls should recognize this. Some plans simply do not permit control to the exercised over them in any detailed manner; outcomes may simply be unmeasurable in cost or benefit terms or too costly to supervise specifically. Besides, while plans should desirably consider all relevant facets, whether quantifiable or unquantifiable, measurable or unmeasurable, objective or subjective, controls can usually only measure the quantifiable, measurable and objective aspects. They are different aspects of management – important, interrelated, but not always completely compatible. Indeed in some situations the existence of one vitiates the other. For example, the expectation that control will be exercised in relation to a plan may encourage the planner to reduce the level of planned expectations lest they be seen to fail, the application of control by 'stick or carrot' can inhibit planners in the same way, the limited ability of control systems to measure only part of the outcomes of a plan can encourage planners to concentrate on only that facet to the exclusion of perhaps equally important but unmeasurable aspects, and the desire not to exceed budgets may dissuade a manager from desirable expenditures or to manipulate expenditures from one budget heading to another.

The control mechanism

In a management context, control is the whole process by which management attempts to direct the efforts of the organization in a complementary manner towards the achievement of common goals. It may operate to ensure that actual outcomes match or even improve upon planned objectives or outcomes. Control cannot be exercised without (i) feedback of information concerning 'actual' events, and (ii) a plan or desired state with which to compare it. The former requires an information system, which will be discussed more fully in the next chapter, although it will be assumed that readers already have some reasonably detailed knowledge of this subject. Similarly, while planning has been discussed in the preceding paragraphs and will be expanded upon in

Chapter 3, readers will be assumed to be aware of basic planning processes and the basis of budgeting in particular.

Control typically takes the form of the process of

1 Comparing feedback with prior expectations.
2 Identifying divergences from the plan (particularly those which are 'undesirable').
3 Identifying means of bringing outcomes back to or nearer those planned.
4 Establishing which actions are to be implemented.
5 Making and communicating the decision.
6 Ensuring its implementation.

The essence of control is the willingness and ability to act. Identifying divergences from expectations and deciding on possible means of correction are simply necessary precursors for control. Similarly action by itself, without prior feedback and an evaluation of the possible effects of alternative decisions/actions, is not control.

Control and human behaviour

The process of management control has much in common with mechanical control devices such as a thermostat, i.e. feedback (by measuring actual temperatures), comparison with the preset requirements, the decision alternatives (turn off or turn on), and action (turning on or off). In management control there is, however, an extra dimension – human behaviour. Thus the potentially irrational behaviour of the decision-maker, of those implementing actions and of those affected by them must necessarily be considered as part of the managerial control mechanism. For this reason therefore the following chapters will include consideration of relevant behavioural implications.

Why audit?

Audit is a vital ingredient in controlling controls. It is the means of discovering whether the established control systems are (i) being operated as necessary and intended and (ii) are adequate for the organization at present and for the future. Audit is not a control in itself, as most audit functions, whether external, internal, operational or management audits, are not required to make recommendations as to alternative courses of action, let alone make a decision on actions to be taken. However, in many organizations, particularly the larger ones, the 'influence' of the internal audit is such that managers at all levels would find it difficult to ignore criticism of their control system and refuse to change it. For this reason perhaps CIMA has defined internal audit as 'An independent appraisal activity established within an organization as a service to it. It is a control which functions by examining and evaluating the adequacy and effectiveness of other controls'.

While audit will be examined in some detail in Chapters 10–13, the reader should bear in mind at all stages of this text that control and audit go very much hand in hand. They complement and are dependent upon each other in the total process of management control.

References

1 CIMA, 'Management Accounting: Official Terminology', 1986.
2 CIMA, 'Terminology of Management and Financial Accountancy', 1974.
3 Solomons, D. 'The Historical Development of Costing', in Solomons, D. (ed.), *Studies in Cost Analysis*, Sweet & Maxwell, 1952.
4 De Roover, F. Edler, 'Cost Accounting in the Sixteenth Century', in Solomons, D. (ed.), *Studies in Cost Analysis*, Sweet & Maxwell, 1978.
5 Johnson, H.T. 'Toward a New Understanding of Nineteenth Century Cost Accounting', *The Accounting Review*, July 1981; and 'Early Cost Accounting for Internal Management Control: Lyman Mills in the 1850s', *Business History Review*, Winter 1972.
6 Chandler, A.D., *Strategy and Structure: Chapters on the History of the Industrial Enterprise*, MIT Press, 1962.
7 Solomons, *op. cit.*
8 Kaplan, R.S. 'The Evolution of Management Accounting', *The Accounting Review*, July 1984.
9 Coates, J.B., Rickwood C.P. and Stacey, R.J., 'Managed Costs and the Capture of Information', *Accounting and Business Research*, No. 68, Autumn 1987.

2 Control theory and MIS

The previous chapter has drawn attention to the scope of this book, and the principal areas of planning, control and audit have been identified. The range of the application of these functions to organizations is considerable, taking in businesses in which the structure is relatively centralized to those having highly dispersed forms. Concentration is not restricted to the business sector but extends to public sector and not-for-profit organizations. Attention is given to the special situations of service activities and of the systems in which computers play a part.

The increased use and availability of computers has had a significant impact on the recent development of planning, control and audit activities. This is an example of the impact of environment on management accounting.

Most readers will be familiar with the basic techniques of management accounting, which are designed to carry out the planning control and audit functions. In this book there is recognition of the factors which impact on their application. This chapter identifies three factors that may be regarded as providing the breadth of consideration for control. These are systems theory, organizational structure and behavioural considerations.

The systems view

A common and often successful approach to problem-solving is to carry out an analysis, breaking down the problem into manageable parts. Complementary to this is to consider how the parts relate to each other. It is this concern which lies behind a systems approach.

Russell Ackoff[1] has defined a system as 'a set of interrelated elements', and the interrelationship between the elements is one of interdependence. The position of the elements relative to others is important, so that the system view directs attention to their arrangement and not simply their aggregation. Although this may appear complex, it can be illustrated simply in a very familiar way. For example, Stafford Beer[2] introduces a pair of scissors as an interesting illustration of a system. A pair of scissors comprises three elements – two blades and a rivet. However, its performance, although dependent on the properties of those elements, can only be properly understood in the way the elements relate to each other; unless the rivet holds the blades in such a way that they can be readily squeezed together to cut, the scissors do not function.

The systems view will have substantial interest only in those systems which persist, since only then would there be any recognizable structure to be identified. The maintenance of this stability is achieved through some form of control. Control here is not seen merely in its negative sense; too often control is regarded as being a subset of authority, whereas in the systems context the reverse is true – authority is just one means of effecting control. A system's existence is dependent upon control in a much broader sense. It is the coordinating mechanism which links the elements which make up the system and it is successful to the extent that it maintains the system's existence.

Management is concerned with control of this nature too. The control objective of management should not be seen within the narrow limits of preventing actions or activities and of reactive response. Far from this, the manager as an entrepreneur has responsibility to create, develop and advance. His role is proactive, and this is entirely compatible with his need to provide control. Business organizations can be viewed as systems. Their ability to remain stable and continue to exist in the face of change is indicative of the effectiveness of their control systems.

Features of systems

The systems literature has developed certain descriptions and classifications which facilitate their study.

System specifications

There is an obvious need to be able to define the existence of a system and to separate it from the environment in which it exists. *The systems boundary* must be identified and expressed in terms of the limits which delineate it and the field in which it exists. The boundaries may be natural or constructed for convenience or other reasons.

Having identified the boundaries, one needs to consider the internal composition. Within each system there are elements, each of which can be viewed as a *sub*system distinguishable from but an element of the system. Study of the system will include examination of the part to part and part to whole interrelationships of subsystems. In turn each subsystem may be analysed so that it can be viewed in terms of sub-subsystems forming a *hierarchy of systems*. This approach to describing

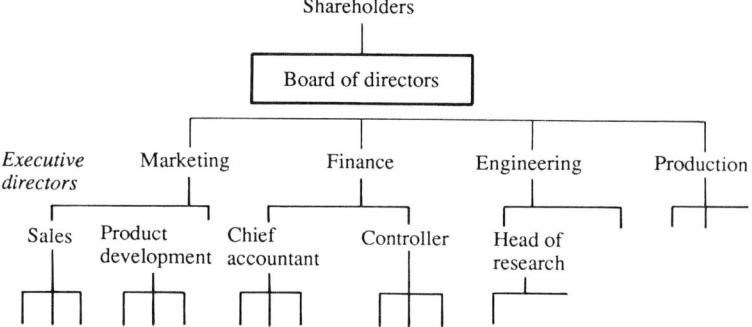

Figure 2.1 *Organization chart*

an organization is readily illustrated by the traditional organization chart (see Figure 2.1).

When human systems are the focus of attention the systems are viewed in terms of what they aim to achieve. Part of the identification of a purposive system is its system objectives.

Open and closed systems

An important basis for classifying systems is provided by the distinction between closed and open systems. A *closed system* is one with no environment or one isolated from its environment so that it has no exchange with it. There is neither impact by the system on the environment nor by the environment on the system.

An *open system* by contrast is one which exchanges matter, energy or information with the environment. It is interesting to note the inclusion of information as an important form of exchange, since this represents a major feature of many business systems. Observation of supply and customer markets would be just one of the informational intakes a business is likely to depend upon.

The concept of an open system recognizes transfers across the boundaries between the environment and the system. In this way each system can be seen as just one part of the total hierarchy, the environment comprising supersystems at higher hierarchical levels. Systems may be viewed as closed or open, depending on the approach being adopted. If interactions with an external environment are ignored, the system is being treated as closed even if reactions do occur. This approach may be adopted to simplify consideration. However, it must be recognized that this can only be a partial view.

Cybernetics and systems

Since cybernetics is the study of the regulation, evolution and adaptation of systems, it provides a framework for the development of control

Control theory and MIS 13

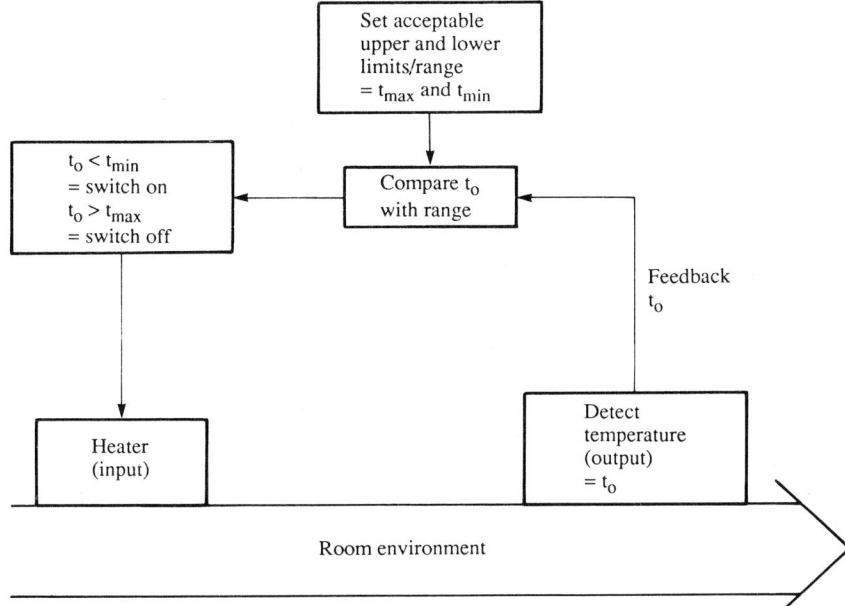

Figure 2.2 *Thermostatic control system as a general model*

processes which may be applied to the business organization. The word 'cybernetics' is derived from a Greek word meaning steersman or helmsman. The links with control follow from this. An organization cannot exist without control, since uncoordinated activities only represent disorganization. In turn management information systems must support the control activities of a business.

The cybernetic approach is generally taken to mean the adoption of model-building techniques to the analysis of control, drawing on analogies with organic systems and the understanding of systems through analysis of the interrelationships of the component subsystems. The general model of control is described in terms of the following major stages:

1 Identification of objectives.
2 Measurement of achievement.
3 Comparison of achievement with objectives.
4 Identification of corrective action to bring achievement into line with objectives.
5 Implementation of corrective action.

The process of control is carried out by successive repetitions of these five major stages. A thermostatic control system provides a simple illustration of the process (see Figure 2.2). The objectives are set in terms of the desired range of room temperatures and the thermostat's response to temperature requires measurement of achieved room temperatures. The control follows through the selection of switches to turn on or off heating or air-conditioning systems which act to bring room conditions in line with the chosen settings. The thermostatic control is shown as a closed system, the *feedback loop* operating only within its own internal boundaries.

Business control may be represented by a system in which budgets or plans are set as objectives. Management accounting may then be seen to perform its part by measuring results and presenting an exception report identifying significant variances from the budget. Management would be required to complete the process by selecting and implementing appropriate corrective policies and actions.

If these cybernetic models of control are to function, a number of conditions, each related to the major stages, must be met. These are:

1. Objectives can be defined.
2. Output can be measured.
3. Reasons for failure to achieve objectives can be identified.
4. Predictions of the impact on achievement of possible strategies can be made.
5. A strategy which permits achievement of objective can be determined and implemented.

A range of circumstances are necessary in meeting these conditions. Instability in the external environment of the firm will have a significant impact on objectives. Business budgets appropriate at the time of planning can become inappropriate if economic, legal or social conditions change. Internal change may not only affect desired outputs but also the outcomes of corrective strategies. Predictability is vital, not only in identifying the results of possible corrective actions but also in attempting to identify why outcomes fail to match up with plans.

In assessing the potential performance of a business control system, one can identify the important elements by considering again the analogy of the thermostatic control (Figure 2.2). That system was made up from an arrangement of the following: a setting giving the required objective in terms of the acceptable range; a temperature detector or sensor; a comparator capable of identifying if the measured state (t_o) is within the acceptable range ($t_{min} < t_o < t_{max}$) or is out of control – in this case identifying the direction of unacceptability (too high or too low); a decision process selecting the appropriate action (switch on or off); and the capacity to perform the resulting action (the heater and switch).

In an organization attention must be given to the same elements. Objectives are set in the form of targets or budgets. The sensors are used internally to assess results and identify needs and problems, e.g. output measurement, cost collection, reporting of stock levels, machine utilisation, order levels, etc. External sensors detect market changes, new technologies, etc. Comparisons are facilitated by management reports, exception reporting concentrating on cases where differences from targets are significant and likely to indicate an out of control situation. Critical in restoring control is the ability to select and implement decisions which provide the direction consistent with the objectives.

Two other important factors give the control system form. These are the structure of the control system and the feedback which links the various active elements.

CIMA[3] defines feedback as 'modification or control of a processor system by its results or effects by measuring differences between desired and actual results. Feedback is an element in a feedback system and forms the link between planning and control'. The word feedback indicates that it operates by *returning* information relating to the output of a system to the control mechanism to produce corrective action on *subsequent* inputs. Of course the cause of the deviation can change, owing to external influences. If the control systems takes too long to react or feed back, the reaction may have become inappropriate. The error will also continue possibly leading to further costs. Control delay detracts from control effectiveness.

In a feedback loop the system reacts to deviations in the measured output from the planned level. In the case of the thermostat the direction of the response generated is opposite to that of the deviation. If the room is too cold, it reacts to provide heat; if too hot, heating ceases. The system is designed to direct output back towards the plan. This is known as *negative feedback*. In business a production stock system may be used to illustrate a negative feedback loop. Upper and lower control levels can be set. When stock levels are below the control level, the deviation is negative and a positive response is generated by starting or increasing production. Stock is added until the upper limit is reached, when production will be stopped or reduced. The system aims to produce stability.

By contrast a positive feedback loop is designed to maintain or increase deviations. In many cases this would not produce control but would amplify any deviation, leading to instability. It is not usually appropriate in encouraging a steady state but may be useful in promoting growth. If sales of product X exceed budget, this may be taken as a sign of a growing market. In taking advantage of the opportunity this may present, the response would be to increase production and marketing effort on this product. The result should be larger deviations but possibly more profit.

A key determinant of the structure of a control system is its interrelationship with other systems. The stock control system which increased deliveries to stock when levels fell might sound suitable for stability but could lead to violent fluctuations in business activity. If customer orders for company J are very sensitive to delivery time in an industry with a small number of competitors, increases in orders may begin to stretch production capacity. Stock will fall, generating the response to increase deliveries to stock, which can only be achieved by diverting production from delivery to customers. The delivery time lengthens, and orders decline. Stocks can then build up. Customers may begin to observe that delivery times shorten and increasingly direct their custom to company J. The cycle recommences. The larger the response to stock reductions, the more violent the fluctuations. System design should consider the reaction between the company's own activity and that of its customers.

One way in which control system design may be made more manageable is to produce structures that minimize interdependence. The process is known as decoupling. Buffer stocks usually exist as a decoupling device, permitting decisions to use a stock component to be made without having to fully coordinate it with the rate of successful production. However, the production unit's ability to detect or sense an increase in demand will permit the smooth running of both producer and user with limited stocks.

If the demands could be fully anticipated in advance, even smoother relationships would be possible. It is here that *feedforward* offers an opportunity. In a feedforward system response to past deviations is replaced by a process of anticipation. Forecasting becomes the source of information, and the quality of forecasts will be a major determinant of the system's performance.

Many aspects of control are considered in this book. Systems theory offers a framework for control design which helps in analysing the elements of the mechanisms, and the importance of interrelationships and system position. However, each application will need to be considered. Interactions with other systems, uncertainty and the impact of change in a dynamic environment will combine with the difficulties of managing a system operated by people of different behavioural types to make system design a matter of skill as well as technique.

The preceding description of the control system may imply that all control decisions must be regarded in terms of predetermined responses to anticipated changes in order to restore progress to a plan. Decisions of this nature are classed as *programmed* decisions. The programmed approach is of value in increasing managerial capacity through delegation. Managers can then leave subordinates to make decisions which carry out management policy in a predictable manner by following prescribed procedures.

While it may be useful to set up systems that adopt a programmed approach, in many situations the nature of change and the appropriate response cannot be anticipated; there may be no reliable relation between response and outcome. There is no choice in these non-programmable situations but to make decisions on the basis of judgement, giving the decision-maker flexibility.

Most situations for which management control systems are to be provided are not clearly programmable or non-programmable. It is necessary to assess whether the losses or benefits of delegated predictability outweigh the advantages and risks of allowing on the spot judgement to dictate policy, taking into account the cost of operating either system.

Organizational theory and structure

The management accountant may make use of an understanding of systems theory in the procedures he or she may set down and operate in the management of organizations. Note here the context – the organization. If the environment has a material impact on a system, then system design must recognize this. Management accounting systems cannot ignore the organization which forms their environment.

Organizations are viewed by many authors as systems themselves. Barnard[4] described an organization as a 'system of consciously coordinated personal activities or forces'. Presthus' definition is 'a system of structural interpersonal relations'.[5] Both definitions emphasize people. A later section of this chapter will consider people and motivation. Other aspects given specific attention are organizational goals and structure and administration. The need for structure and coordination may be largely attributed to size. Usually organizations are considered to be of such size that relations and coordination cannot be readily maintained through casual contact between people but require some structure. The persistence of structure is a prerequisite for the organization's existence, even though the form of structure may change. Organizations do not need to hold rigidly to one form to retain integrity and continue. A rock maintains its integrity in the face of a stream's current with a rigid structure, but a river weed's bending response is not terminal. By contrast, a pile of sand lacks the interconnections which would permit it to exist in the face of a hostile current.

Organizational goals

A further attribute associated with organizations is purpose. Parsons[6] amplifies structure to indicate that organizations are structured so as to attain 'a particular type of goal'. Scott[7] considers the organization to have three objectives – growth, stability and interaction. The last can refer to interaction with the environment or among individuals within the organization. Scott's view may be consistent with no more than survival but, although a more positive view may be taken, this is not universally accepted. Cyert and March[8] state: 'Individuals have objectives; collectivities of individuals do not'.

In a free society organizations receive voluntary support from individuals as a means of satisfying their own desires. Business organizations' central purpose is identified in economic terms, which may be seen as a collective transformation of individual economic objectives. Even charities and other not-for-profit organizations have objectives, and their achievement is at least in part dependent upon economic performance.

From an economic perspective, the success of organization is a function of its relative advantage. Alchian and Demsetz[9] make a valuable contribution to this approach, identifying the advantages of teamwork. Teams permit groups of people to achieve more than the sum of achievements the individuals in the team could produce. By way of example, one man might struggle all day to carry a heavy item (say a piano) upstairs. A team of four, taking a corner each, may need to put in much less than a quarter of the exertion of one man to complete the task. The relative advantage can be shared among team members.

The teamwork advantages result from coordinated effort. Although such cooperation is beneficial, if individuals pull in different directions, the result is counter-productive. As team size grows, the coordination problems increase, and Alchian and Demsetz highlight the role of the manager in this task. A major element of his contribution to the organization is through the control of its members. He/she needs to compensate in some way for the possible impact of a 'free-rider' effect, in which an individual can shirk but benefit from the productivity of the team. In addition coordination and structure must be provided.

A further problem which the management function must fulfil is heightened by aspects of another feature of organizations – specialization. This refers to the grouping of activities assigned to a particular person based on capacity of workload and expertise or skill. The limited scope of activity of any one specialist makes him dependent upon another specialist. There is a demand for internal communication. Coordination and communication are particularly difficult for those operating automated machinery, as the continuous nature of such operations prevent such operators from leaving the machinery to communicate with others.

Management's role can be seen as generating the performance of the organization. In turn this requires management to assess the contribution to performance made by other individuals, this being an element in overcoming the free-rider effect. Performance measurement is important in managing an organization and accounting must carry this out. Although output measures, showing what is achieved, are preferable, the team effect may make it difficult to identify whose effort produced what and input measures (e.g. hours worked) may have to be used.

Theories of organization

The importance taken on by structure as organizations increase in size has already been mentioned. The management and administration of organizational structure has been the subject of considerable attention by theorists. The insights they provide are of value to the management accountant. Theoretical approaches can be classified in a number of ways,[10] largely dependent on the emphasis given to each of three views: prescriptive structure, systems analysis and behavioural approaches based on empirical observation. The analysis of theories does not produce clear distinctions, but Otley[11] has suggested that a distinction into two types can be made, one type of theory viewing organizations as a designed artefact, the other as a natural phenomenon. The former attempts to put forward views of how an organization should be designed to give best performance in achieving its goals; the latter sets out to explain observed organizational behaviour, treating managers as one of many influential elements.

The approach here will be to begin with the designed artefact view, bringing in the alternative as a part of a consideration of motivational aspects. Although writers throughout history have given attention to the subject of organizational structure, an early milestone in this as a distinct subject was made by F.W. Taylor[12] in 1913. He suggested all labour's tasks should be analysed and, on the basis of work measurement, payment schemes should be constructed to reward output and provide incentive. It treats man as a machine employed to complete specified tasks.

Later views suggest that while one may wish to 'hire a hand' to do a job, an employee must be considered as the whole person. However, 'much management accounting practice is based on the assumption that budgets and standards for human organizational performance can be set in a more or less objective and scientifically verifiable manner. To some extent this may be true for well understood tasks'.[13] The non-programmable tasks of senior management may be inappropriate for this approach.

Administrative theories of organization concentrate on three aspects: division of labour, structure and span of control. Division of labour takes up the theme of specialization and designing jobs to fit the capacity of one person. Structure considers the line and staff responsibilities linkages; the hierarchical arrangements set out in the traditional organization chart embody the 'one man – one boss' and 'responsibility must equal authority' principles. Span of control questions follow from the formal hierarchical structure. The theories suggest that the solutions in particular cases depend upon the means of communication available, the nature of the tasks and managerial styles. More recent work acknowledges the existence of an informal structure having its own processes for recognition of status, appointment of leaders and communication.

An interesting facet of structure is provided by considering decentralization. In the traditional hierarchical structure tasks are delegated on the basis of one person capacity. The extent to which subordinates have autonomy to make decisions without getting specific authority is a measure of the degree of decentralization, which will depend upon the relative advantages of coordination offered by centralization and the advantages of local knowledge and local response achieved with decentralization.

A particular type of decentralization which has become widespread is divisionalization. In this structure the organization is divided into quasi-independent units which usually contain a full range of functions, e.g. purchasing, production, administration, sales. It is most effective when, on the basis of product range or other factor, the division is able to operate with a minimum of dependence on the rest of the organization. It aims to take full advantage of decentralization and advantages from any incentives arising from the setting up of local groups and local autonomous positions. Chapter 7 specifically considers performance measures in divisions.

In the Hawthorne studies[14] attention was drawn to the behaviour of people in groups. In one case, an attempt to study the effect of a change of lighting on performance, it was found that the selection and identification of a group for study had more impact than the brightness of the lights. The explanation offered was that the interest taken in the workers and their recognition that they were a group improved their performance. Human behaviour has taken on increasing significance, and it is to this that attention is now turned.

Behavioural considerations and motivation

Many theories of motivation have been developed since the Hawthorne studies. For the purposes of this text only a limited treatment can be given to what is a subject of considerable size and complexity. The basic approaches that will be given attention had all been articulated by 1960, but they are chosen for good reason. They have provided the main foundations for later work, are more specific in setting out the external factors which lead to motivation, and have clearer relationships with management accounting areas discussed in later chapters.

The first work to be addressed is that of Maslow.[15] In Maslow's triangle of needs he sets out a hierarchy of motivating desires (see Figure 2.3). At the bottom of the hierarchy come the basic needs of food, water and warmth; towards the top come esteem and self-actualization, familiarly referred to as 'doing your own thing'. Maslow's view is that lower needs must be satisfied before higher needs motivate, but that once a need is substantially met, it no longer motivates, i.e. food and drink may be the only incentive for a starving man, but once these needs are met, attention is turned to safety and security.

In Figure 2.3 the inner triangle is used to represent fulfilled needs. It shows physiological needs almost fully met and safety and security largely provided. The most effective motivator, according to this theory, would be at the top of this triangle – the need to belong and be accepted by one's social group.

The motivation–hygiene theory put forward by Herzberg[16] is a development of Maslow's theory. His research indicated that the factors or absence of them which made employees dissatisfied were not the same as those producing satisfaction. He labelled the first group, which included money, working conditions and the people they worked for, hygiene factors. They would be the sources of complaints. The group leading to satisfaction was associated with achievement and its recogni-

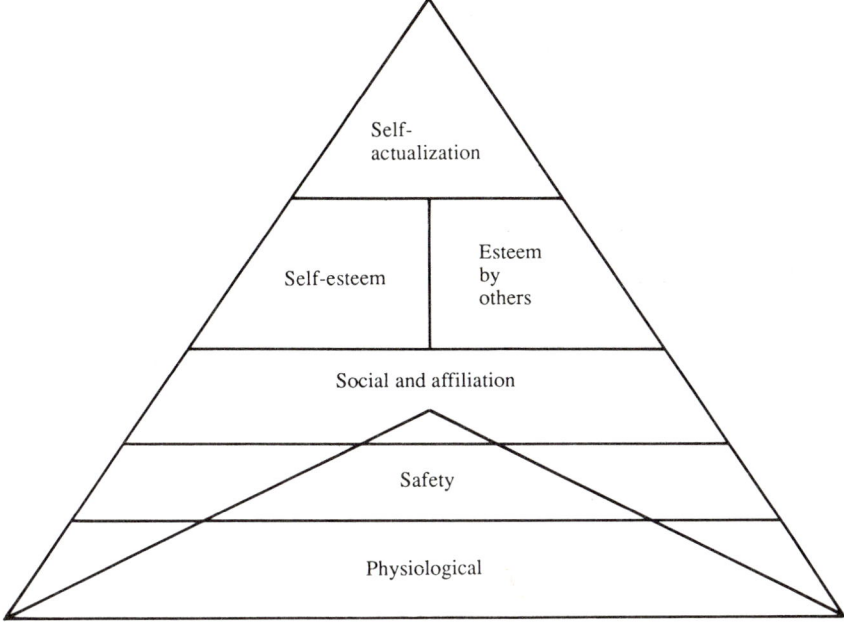

Figure 2.3 *Maslow's hierarchy of needs*

tion, responsibility and trust, plus promotion or other moves to face new and interesting challenges.

A similar perspective is adopted by McGregor.[17] He also produced a two-part framework, distinguishing between Theory X and Theory Y firms. In Theory X firms managers sought to motivate subordinates assumed to be basically lazy, lacking ambition and wishing to avoid responsibility by providing monetary rewards and paternalistic leadership. Theory Y firms attempted to make use of individuals' enthusiasm for self-achievement. Divisionalization may be one vehicle for this.

Mention should be made of work on the relation between behaviour and targets, particularly budgets. Stedry[18] reported the conclusions resulting from his clinical experiments at about the time McGregor published his Theory X and Theory Y view. Stedry's experimental methods have been the subject of criticism but it may be valuable to consider a summary of the results:

- Repeated failure to achieve targets lowers expectations and performance.
- Success increases expectations and motivates.
- Constant achievement of too easily attained goals adversely affects performance.
- Individuals work harder to achieve those expectations they have helped to set and to which they are personally committed.

The last of these introduces the idea of aspiration levels – the target which the individual sets himself and strives to achieve. Participation in budget setting is considered to bring aspiration levels closer to targets than externally imposing budgets.

Becker and Green[19] take up the theme of participation, giving some emphasis to the importance of feedback of results. They consider it imperative that a participant knows whether he should feel a failure or a success. Only then can he know if his efforts are worthwhile. Herzberg's recognition of achievement is clearly relevant here.

Conditions for targets to act as motivators can be set out as follows:

- Targets are recognized as legitimately set, by understanding the method of setting.
- Individuals must feel they can influence their own goals
- Standards should convey the 'freedom to fail' (occasional failure does not produce severe punishment so targets can remain a reasonable challenge).
- Feedback of performance is essential.

Summary

By bringing together teams of individuals, organizations enable people with limited capacity to achieve monumental tasks. The success of organizations will be dependent on their ability to respond in a coordinated and controlled manner to opportunities and threats. Structure and control systems will provide the framework for the management of organizations. Information can be seen as the vital nourishment of these systems and it is here that the management accountant can make a special contribution. In performing this function he/she must recognize that what is being sought is appropriate response from the organization's members, taking human behaviour into account. This chapter has outlined the basic considerations of control, organizational structure and motivation. Their application can now be taken up.

References

1. Ackoff, R.L., 'Towards a system of systems concepts', *Management Science*, 17,662, 1971.
2. Beer, S., *Cybernetics and Management*, E.U.P. (2nd ed.), 1971.
3. CIMA, *Management Accounting Official Terminology*, CIMA, 1986.
4. Barnard, C.I., *The Functions of the Executive*, Harvard, 1938.
5. Presthus, R.V., 'Toward a Theory of Organisational Behaviour', *Administrative Science Quarterly*, June 1988.
6. Parsons, T., 'A Sociological Approach to the Theory of Organisations', in Parsons, T., *Structure and Process in Modern Societies*, Free Press, Illinois, 1964.

7 Scott, W.G., 'Organization Theory: An Overview and an Appraisal', *Academy of Management Journal*, April 1961.
8 Cyert, R.M. and J.G. March, *A Behavioural Theory of the Firm*, Prentice-Hall, 1963.
9 Alchian, A.A. and Demsetz, H., 'Production, Information Costs and Economic Organisation', *American Economic Review*, 1972.
10 Scott, *op. cit.*; and Otley, D., 'Management Accounting and organization theory: a review of their interrelationship', in Scapens, R., Otley, D.T. and Lister, R., *Management Accounting, Organisational Theory and Capital Budgeting*, Macmillan, 1984.
11 Otley, *op. cit.*
12 Taylor, F.W., *The Principles of Scientific Management*, Harper & Row, 1947. First published 1913.
13 Emmanuel, C.R. and Otley, D.T., *Accounting for Management Control*, Van Nostrand, 1985.
14 Mayo, E., *The Human Problems of an Industrial Civilisation*, Macmillan, 1933.
15 Maslow, A.H., *Motivation and Personality*, Harper & Row, New York, 1954.
16 Herzberg, F., Mausner, B. and Synderman, B.B. *The Motivation to Work*, Wiley, 1959.
17 McGregor, D., *The Human Side of Enterprise*, McGraw-Hill, 1960.
18 Stedry, A.C., *Budget Control and Cost Behaviour*, Prentice-Hall, 1960.
19 Becker, S.W. and Green, D., Jr, 'Budgeting and Employee Behaviour', *The Journal of Business*, Vol. XXXV, October 1962.

Further reading

Hopwood, A.G., *Accounting and Human Behaviour*, Prentice-Hall, 1974.
Cyert, R.M. and March, J.G., *A Behavioural Theory of the Firm*, Prentice-Hall, 1963.
Otley, D., 'Behavioural Aspects of Budgeting', *Accountants Digest No. 49*, ICAEW, 1977.
Skousen, K.F. and Needles, B.E., *Contemporary Thought in Accounting and Organisational Control*, Dickenson, 1973.

Questions

1 You are required to examine the view that the cybernetic control model can provide valuable insights into the design and operation of management accounting information systems, but only under circumstances where an organization's environment is stable and predictable and outcomes are clearly measurable.
2 'It seems likely that what constitutes an appropriate budget system is influenced by the characteristics of individual managers, by the

type of organization in which it is implemented and by the environment in which the organization operates.' Explain and discuss.

3 (a) Examine the theories relating to the influence of participation on performance.
   (b) Evaluate the empirical evidence concerning the relationship between participation and performance.

4 According to Hopwood (1974), 'the control of complex and uncertain enterprises can never be achieved by the use of administrative controls alone.... Ultimately they must work as individual and social controls'.
   (a) Examine the nature of these three types of control and their relevance in the design of control systems.
   (b) Discuss some of the possible implications of the above quotation for the design of management accounting systems.

5 'Participative methods are best used selectively in situations where there is evidence that they will be effective, rather than as a universal philosophy. It is incorrect to assume that participative styles of management are always more effective than other styles' (Otley, 1977).

   Examine the justification for this statement and describe the circumstances which may influence whether participation affects performance.

6 'The level of costs for which a person will strive (aspired costs) will be conceived by the individual in relation to past experience, confidence in his potential skills, expectation of future difficulties and his feelings about the budget costs. Aspired and budget costs do not necessarily coincide' (Irvine, 1970).

   Discuss the relevance of this statement for budgeting activities, introducing any empirical work supporting the views expressed.

7 'To manage is to forecast and plan, to organize, to command, to co-ordinate and to control' (Henri Fayol, *General and Industrial Management*).

   Discuss the above view.

3 Budgets and planning

'There is always the danger of analysis of operating activities developing into a battle of wits between observers and observed.'[1]

Planning – budgets and standards

The application of budgetary and standard techniques to managers and segments of an organization is of considerable importance to the success of the process as a whole, particularly if budgets are created in a 'bottom-up' or participatory manner. This chapter examines the budget centre selection process, the participation of management in budget preparation in relation to alternative aspiration levels, the intended use of the budgets as a basis for planning and/or control, the recognition of resource constraints and the setting of standards. Finally the revision of budget and standards in response to such factors as changing activity levels, external economic change, inflation, or changes within an organization will be considered.

Budget centre selection

The term 'budget centre' is defined by the CIMA[2] as 'a section of an organization for which separate budgets can be prepared and control exercised'. In selecting budget centres the following factors need to be considered:

- What are management's objectives in treating a particular 'section' of the organization as a budget centre? These may be to measure the performance of a part of the organization or the management of it, or to motivate its management.
- Are the information systems able to distinguish the separable,

controllable and attributable performance of this centre and what would be the (perhaps additional) costs of doing so?
- Is management prepared to recognize such a 'section' as a responsibility centre, nominate an individual to be directly responsible for its performance and delegate the necessary authority for its management?
- What bases will be used to measure the performance of the centre, e.g. as a cost, profit, investment or performance centre.

In most organizations the selection of budget centres is likely to reflect the formal or informal organizational structure. How far down the structure the budget centres are carried is likely to depend upon a variety of factors – the number of management levels, complexity of the organization structure, the degree of participation in budget setting, and the factors considered above. Hofstede[3] advises top and middle management: 'If possible, see to it that budgets and standards are set separately for the responsibility area of each of your foremen, but at least for each line manager'.

The advantages of creating budget and responsibility centres as far down the organization structure as possible are likely to be the following:

1. It encourages and motivates the staff and improves goal congruence.
2. Responsibility and authority areas/levels and the organizational structure itself are reinforced by the delegation of authority and the negotiation of budget responsibilities.
3. More realistic budgets can result because of the detailed knowledge of lower levels of management.

The disadvantages, however, may be that:

1. The opportunities for building in slack, the fear of budgets and their implied threats, and the possible demotivational effects of any eventual budget imposition are increased.
2. The greater the number of budget and responsibility centres, the longer the budget preparation and disaggregation process, and the higher the costs of budgeting and subsequent monitoring feedback and control are likely to be.

There must obviously be a trade-off between the desirability of consulting managers at all levels, and the advantages this might bring, and the negative motivational, practicality and cost aspects.

The bases for the measurement of budget centres may be any of the following:

- Cost centres, where the budgeted (and actual) costs are identified, compared with a suitable measure of output and unit cost rates derived.

- Profit centres, where the attributable revenues and costs of budget centres are identified and the resultant 'profit' calculated.
- Investment centres, where the 'profit' achieved is compared to the capital invested.
- Performance centres, where the budget is expressed in quantified but not necessarily monetary terms, e.g. standard hours, units of output, scrap and yield percentages etc.

A budget centre may incorporate any or all of these approaches, i.e. budgeted cost, profit, investment or performance centres. Indeed each base may be viewed as measuring a different aspect of a responsibility centre's performance or for different purposes. It would be desirable, however, to establish which measures are to predominate, as circumstances may well arise where a particular action would improve one measure at the expense of another.

Profit centres appear to be very much more popular with senior management than cost or expense centre approaches, even when the latter are accepted by many managers within the same organization as being more logical.[4] Simon et al.[5] and Hofstede[6] concluded that both profit and cost/expense centres work and that there is usually no reason to go over to the often more complicated profit centre system. These topics will be discussed further in Chatpers 6 to 9.

Participation and negotiation in budget preparation

The arguments for and against the different managerial styles of budget preparation should be familiar to readers. In the 'top-down' approach budgets are developed centrally by senior management and delegated to middle and junior managers; and in the 'bottom-up' approach budgets are developed by the participation of middle and junior management. In recent years the weight of research and practice has been towards a more participative approach to budgeting. The reality is of course that, even in the most participative of planning processes, senior management must have a very significant input and impact upon proceedings. It is the senior managers' prerogative and duty to establish the corporate objectives and long-term strategies, and authorize the final plan and master budget, even if they play no part in its detailed preparation. Most organizations, however, are likely to adopt a mixed approach, where budgets are negotiated between managers at different levels in the hierarchy, thereby allowing management at all levels to participate in the budget process, and have their particular role in the budget plan.

Participation

Research by Stedry,[7] McClelland,[8] Maslow,[9] Herzberg,[10] Becker and Green,[11] Schiff and Lewin[12] and Argyris,[13] amongst others suggests that allowing individual managers to participate in the creation of that part of the budget which relates to their personal responsibilities is likely to bring significant advantages:

- Their self-esteem and the esteem of their peer group and subordinates are likely to be enhanced.
- They are more likely to internalize corporate objectives and the achievement of them as their own, and feel committed towards achieving them.

It is argued that the resultant added motivation and positive attitudes towards the company and its senior management will more than offset the potential disadvantages of:

- The inclusion of 'slack' in the budget by managers to reduce the chances of their failing to meet the budget.
- The cost of the management time in a process allowing participation and negotiation.

Argyris[14] and others have indicated that if the participation is not genuine (pseudo-participation), individuals will not accept budgets (even if they say they will), with negative motivational results. In such a situation the practice of requiring responsibility centre managers to 'sign' to indicate that they accept their budget is unlikely to have any favourable results from a corporate viewpoint.

The evidence indicates that for participation to have positive results it must be real, in that participators can and do affect the ultimately agreed plans and budgets. The implications for management are reaching farther than might appear at first reading. If participation and budget negotiation are to be adopted, management would need to begin the planning process early enough to allow the negotiation to be completed before the start of the period to which the budget relates. The authors are aware of a number of large organizations where, because the negotiation process is not complete before the next financial year is due to commence, budgets are imposed upon the individual managers of the company. This surely is the worst of all worlds. Not only is it pure 'pseudo-participation', but, worse, individuals are likely to feel more demotivated than if they had not taken part in the process at all.

Personal aspiration levels

Although the research of Stedry[9] is considered to be flawed methodologically, it is taken to indicate quite strongly that (i) managers who set their own 'targets' are likely to achieve higher performances than those who do not, and (ii) budgets with low aspiration levels are likely to yield poorer results than those with medium to high aspiration levels. It would seem therefore that senior management would be well advised to push to negotiated budget aspiration levels as high as is reasonable, as long as (a) 'pseudo-participation' is avoided and (b) it is recognized that too tight budgets are likely to be counter-productive. On the basis of this evidence there appears to be no point in setting 'loose' budgets containing substantial elements of 'slack'.

The aspiration levels of individuals, however, are likely to be very different in any given situation. Some individuals may be optimistic by nature, pleased at having and being seen to have high budget aspiration levels, and will not be too crestfallen if they fail (providing the margin of failure is not too large). Others may be more sensitive and pessimistic, being demotivated by any budget they consider at all difficult to attain, fearing to be seen to fail. Ideally these personal characteristics should be catered for in the budget negotiation process, the agreed aspiration/budget levels being tailor-made to the managers concerned. Management might facilitate this by easing the negotiation pressure exerted or by 'averaging' the optimistic and pessimistic budgets of different managers in relation to total expected outcomes.

Of course management must always remember that it may not be possible to optimise planning on the one hand and performance on the other.

Budget aspiration levels

It is pertinent to ask the following question. Is a budget intended to be (a) what is expected will happen, or (b) a target that is achievable but set at higher aspiration levels than (a)?

Ask a group of managers within an organization and the responses are likely to be quite diverse. Some will argue that a budget is a target, a motivational technique to encourage managers to improve their performances year on year. Others will argue that a budget is management's attempt to anticipate the actual events, resource needs and results of the coming year. Perhaps, too, some will argue that it is somewhere in between – a bit of both.

The potential adverse consequences for an organization where such a dichotomy of views is held are potentially very damaging. Consider this scenario.

The sales director believes a budget is a motivational target. He believes in pushing his salesmen and himself harder each year, to improve sales penetration and market share. He therefore targets his budget at a volume 10 per cent above what he might reasonably expect his salesmen to achieve and asks for marketing expenditure to support it. The production director, something of a realist, believes that a budget is what he is meant to achieve. He has been asked to obtain the output budgeted by the sales director, which includes capital expenditure for machinery to manufacture the sales increase, expenditures to recruit and train operatives, etc., etc. The net effect of this is that expenditure is generally budgeted at a level 10 per cent higher than it need be, much of which might well be committed in anticipation of increased sales. Of course it would be nice to think that in practice these mismatches do not occur, that a budget coordinator would remove these anomalies, but the potential for mismatch is rife. Accountants and managers should ask themselves: 'Is the budget aspiration level in the organization made clear to all participants and is my view the same as that of my colleagues?' Add the problems of managing personal aspiration levels and a significant problem for the budget coordinator exists.

Planning and control budgets

Budgets are usually assumed by writers and organizations to be for planning purposes, i.e. to enable management to anticipate and prepare for the period ahead, to make resources available, coordinate activities, take opportunities, and avoid pitfalls. For this purpose an 'expected actual' aspiration level would be required.

Usually, however, these same budgets are used as the basis for control, for which purpose a budget comprising some element of 'target' might have more positive motivational benefits for the organization.

The duality of purposes for which budgets are used needs to be addressed by organizations. These conflicts might be resolved by:

1. Basing budgets on an expected actual basis for planning purposes, but using alternative means for control, e.g. MBO to provide the 'target'/motivation element.
2. Budgeting on a 'target' basis for purposes of control, but introducing budgeted adverse planning variances to convert the 'target' into an expected actual.
3. Budgeting on a target/control basis but, in the expectation that not all targets will be met, keeping a very close rein on resource and expenditure levels in anticipation of, but as yet unachieved, income targets.
4. Preparing separate planning and control budgets, using the control budget for operational control, and planning budgets for top management reporting.

As will be apparent, options 2, 3 and 4 are probably riskier approaches than option 1, as there is always a danger that resources and expenditures will be committed at the target level before target level incomes are known to be achieved or being achieved. Additionally there is the possibility that:

(a) Budget-holders will soon realize that they are not really expected to achieve their targets and so will reduce their efforts, motivations and aspiration levels.
(b) Management, budget and accounting information may be brought into disrepute if it is seen/believed that two sets of books are being maintained.

However, a control budget is surely the one most likely to achieve the full benefits of participation and the motivation of individuals. The offset of the potential gains against the potential losses must be considered carefully.

Role of budget coordinator

The need for a budget coordinator has already been mentioned. Some organizations employ a budget officer and others appoint a budget committee, but in many organizations this role is automatically assumed to be that of the accountant.

The work of Argyris[15] and others indicates that budget co-ordinators have a poor reputation within their organizations. It is alleged that they:

- Think of themselves as watchdogs.
- Think budgets are a legitimate means of applying pressure.
- Are inflexible and never satisfied, always trying to increase budget levels.
- Force budgets to an unrealistically high level, leaving little chance for management to succeed.
- Do not see the other person's point of view.
- Believe other managers and workers are lazy and that pressure is needed to obtain/raise production.
- Believe they are superior to others.

With this heritage, it places a considerable burden upon the budget coordinator, whatever his background, to fulfil his role.

Argyris[11] recommended that finance staff should have training to equip them for their role as budget coordinator. This training should:

1. Help coordinators perceive the human implications of the budget system.
2. Demonstrate the effects of pressure on people and understand the advantages and disadvantages of applying such pressure.
3. Include discussions concerning the effects of success and failure.
4. Help coordinators perceive their difficult position, namely that of placing others in a position to fail.
5. Include practical techniques which can be used to get along better with managers and employees in difficult functions and at varying levels of the organization.
6. Help them to understand parochial departmental attitudes and the possible lack of group/organizational objectives.
7. Include knowledge of human relations studies.

The basic role of the coordinator is routine and administrative. He/she has to advise senior management; recommend and implement planning procedures, time-tables, forms and schedules; provide past performance data; translate corporate goals and aims to managers at all levels; collect and collate data; prepare final summaries; and disseminate approved budgets to budget-holders.

To be effective, however, the coordinator needs more than simply routine capabilities. It is necessary to 'sell' corporate goals to managers in the hope that such goals will either be adopted or internalized by them or that the goals they do adopt are not discordant with those of the organization as a whole. In addition, the coordinator must obtain true participation and encourage high aspiration levels, and ensure that budget aspiration levels are consistent across budget centres.

Constraints on resources

An essential element of strategic and budgetary planning is the identification of and planning within the limited resources available to the organization. From a planning viewpoint, the 'optimum' utilization of limited resources can be approached via techniques such as linear programming, which is usually the basis for computer modelling packages. The application of linear programming techniques to the optimization of a budget is shown in Appendix A. A number of important resource-related aspects will be considered.

Identifying resource constraints

Many explanations and schematics representing the budgetary process give little attention to resource availability. The strengths and weaknesses analysis of long-term planning should provide this vital information for the preparation of budgetary plans. Its importance lies in the recognition of those resources which are likely to constrain the organization's shorter- and longer-term tactics and strategies. It would probably be wasteful, for example, for the sales forecast to be predicted upon higher finished goods stock levels if a likely constraint in, say, finance had been recognized. Some would disagree of course, and argue that it is management's task to remove constraints or find alternative ways of obtaining the same end result – the servicing of such sales volumes as can be reasonably achieved by the sales/marketing function. This sounds very neat, but a few moments' thought will indicate to the reader the likely impracticality of such an approach.

Whichever approach is adopted, there is a need to match sales forecasts with resources, particularly those of operations/manufacture, before embarking on detailed budget preparation, in which, in turn, detailed resource implications will be identified, probably the last of these being finance availability.

Time-scale of constraints

Limiting factors are not necessarily permanent features. Some constraints may be relatively short-lived, while others may be a long-term feature of operations. A shortage of labour skills may be removed by training or recruitment, whereas a shortage of research and development knowhow or a bad reputation may take years to remedy. The likely period and degree to which a resource will be constrained is a vital element in planning decisions. Plans predicted upon a particular limiting factor are necessarily sub-optimal as compared to a situation where that resource is not limited or has lower limitations. It should be expected that any plan will attempt, as far as possible and within the long-term plan, to minimize the impact of limitations. In addition, plans will or should have been instituted to improve the supply of that resource and/or find alternatives. Energies needlessly focused on these aspects will obviously be wasteful and are likely to reduce resultant performances.

Resource interchangeability

One of the main reasons for the relatively short period for which some limiting factors are relevant is the interchangeability of resources. This can take on a wide variety of forms: the use of capital resources to acquire plant and machinery; the conversion of one type of equipment to perform a different task; the sale of surplus machinery to provide finance to buy other assets, e.g. stocks; stock-reducing programmes, such as the sale of slow moving and surplus stocks to provide the finance to buy new machinery; or the sale of a subsidiary or operating unit to permit the expansion of another.

To repeat the point made earlier, resource constraints are not necessarily long-term features. Most limitations can be removed or reduced, given time and relevant actions.

Balance of resources

An almost inevitable corollary of the existence of limiting factors is a surplus of some (other) resources. Decisions regarding the use or disposal of such spare resources should be made. Strategically, decisions are likely to be centred around the anticipated long-term need for these resources, the alternative uses they may be put to and their realizable value. Tactics should obviously be dictated by the strategic view, but assuming the surplus is short-lived, the choice is likely to be between alternative uses/opportunities available in that short term.

Setting standards

A standard is defined by CIMA[16] as 'a predetermined measurable quantity set in defined conditions against which actual performance can be compared, usually for an element of work, operation or activity'. The Institute then goes on to add that 'while standards may be based on unquestioned and immutable natural laws or facts, they are finally set by human judgement and consequently are subject to the same fallibility which attends all human activity. Thus a standard for 100 per cent machine output can be fixed by its geared input/output speeds, but the effective realisable output standard is one of judgement'.

The variety of bases for setting standards, including historical and engineered standards, is dealt with in this chapter.

Historical standards

One approach to the preparation of management's view of expected future performance can be via the consideration of past actual performances. At its simplest past performances could be averaged. The main shortcoming of this approach is obviously that historical performance will necessarily include all its efficiencies and inefficiencies and the circumstances pertaining when those performances occurred. Additionally, if the standard performance is expressed in monetary rather than physical form, an allowance must be made for future costs being higher or lower than in the past.

This is obviously a 'minimum' approach, available to any organization which cannot afford or believe it would not be worthwhile to adopt more sophisticated techniques, or is in a situation where such techniques would not be feasible. It is of course possible to 'sophisticate' this minimum approach: Management may use its subjective opinion and knowledge to adapt the historical performance to reflect those conditions and efficiencies anticipated. This approach is very common in, for example, smaller jobbing/manufacturing organizations.

Engineered standards

The inadequacies of historic standards as comparators, in situations of the sometimes high volumes of similar operations or units of output in many manufacturing industries, have led to the popularity of engineered standards, standard costs and standard costing. The term 'engineered standards' implies a scientific approach to the estimation of the necessary physical resource inputs to produce a detailed product/service specification. Such a standard would comprise the examination of alternative material, labour and other inputs with which the product could be made and the specification of the most suitable materials, grades of labour etc., bearing in mind product operation, methods of manufacture and cost, the application of ergonomics, method, work, and time and motion study to manual and mechanized operations, including the identification of required machinery and tooling.

The fact is, however, that even engineered standards require a significant input of managerial estimation. In time study, for example, a number of technical/managerial estimates are needed: the time-study engineer will watch and time an operative performing the actions necessary for a particular task and then consider whether or not the operative is typical, or working faster or slower than an average operative, bearing in mind that the times are recorded on a Friday afternoon when the operative is tired and looking forward to the weekend activities, etc., etc? Then further allowances might need to be made, for example, to allow for legitimate employee down-time and for learning curve related effects.

Managerial estimates

In situations where engineered standards would be unwarranted or unsuitable and yet a comparison with historic standards would be considered inadequate, some form of technical or managerial estimate is often possible. It is frequently suggested, for example, that standard costing is not suitable for service industries, jobbing and contract-based organizations or situations where there is relatively little repetition in operations. The likelihood is, however, that these organizations will have prepared, for each and every job they have, some form of cost estimate in order to assist sales management in quoting for the business. These estimates could be used as a quasi-standard, however 'rough and ready' these estimates might be. At the very least a comparison with such an estimate would give some feedback as to the adequacy or otherwise of the estimation/quotation approach they have adopted. In many jobbing and contracting organizations there is likely to be some reasonable data available – perhaps an estimate of the quantities of various materials and components required, or of labour or machine hours, or analysis of cost between labour, materials, expenses, overhead recovery and profit. Whatever their origin, they are vital information sources from the viewpoint of the organization's profitability.

In any event a wide range of methods and estimating procedures adopted within organizations may not fulfil the full 'sophistication' of engineered standards. Nevertheless they can be usefully applied as a basis for comparison of organizational and product/service performance.

Standard expectations

The levels of performance built into standards is perhaps the most critical element to their acceptance and use. The 'choice' of ideal, normal, target or expected actual levels of performance and efficiency has potentially significant effects both upon those to whom those standards are applied and on those who use those standards for decision-making.

Management might prefer an expected actual level if standards are to be easily incorporated into the budgetary process, but perhaps a target if used as the basis for employee incentive payment. In the latter case of course it is quite common for standards used as a basis for incentives to be 'negotiated' between management and employee representatives, in which case the resultant standard may bear little resemblance to any 'choice' of performance level. Miles and Vergin[17] suggest that the standards for management control systems could reflect just such a process, i.e. 'be established in such a way that they are recognized as legitimate ... that the method of deriving standards must be understood by those affected ... that 'employees' should feel that (they have) some voice or influence in the establishment of (their) own performance goals'. However, Lupton[18] implies that if standards are used as the basis for payment systems, such are likely to degenerate and be distorted fairly rapidly.

Indeed while it may be tempting to establish a standard of physical performance which can remain unchanged over time (even if the monetary standard 'inflates'), in practice standards can be expected to change. Standards after all are based upon assumptions of conditions and circumstances prevailing in a future period which may never result or may not persist for more than short periods of time. Thus such standards might need to be updated to reflect, for example, the learning curve phenomenon, operations outside the previously assumed relevant range, changes in operational methods and experience of actual performances.

Thus standards cannot be considered as being fixed for all time. Management must weigh up the desirability and cost of updating standards in the light of the purposes to which the standards are put.

Revision of budgets and standards

Budgets are considered by many organizations to be unchangeable and unviolable. The reasons for this are probably twofold. Firstly, there must be a danger that budgets will fall into disrepute if management is prepared to alter them. How seriously would managers take the budget preparation process if they realized that senior management accepted that budgets would need to be changed before the end of the budget period? Secondly, the comparison of the original master budget with actual revenues and costs is a valuable one, even if the latter operated under very different conditions from that originally anticipated: The resultant variances should be examined to establish (i) how far actual results diverged from those budgeted, which after all represented (or ought to have) the first stage of the organization's long-term plan, and (ii) why the organization's management failed to anticipate the actual situation and identify how such failures might be reduced in future planning, plans and budgets.

However, there are situations where management may consider that the original master budget is insufficient as a prediction of future outcomes and/or as a control yardstick, and where alternative measures may be desirable.

Flexible budgets

The term flexible budgets has a very specific meaning in accounting usages, even though some managers and accountants attribute other interpretations to it. CIMA[19] defines a flexible budget as 'A budget which, by the difference in behaviour between fixed and variable costs in relation to fluctuations in output, turnover, or other variable factors such as numbers of employees is designed to change appropriately with such fluctuations'.

Essentially, flexible budgets are adaptions of the original master budget which reflect a change in the level of activity from that planned, all other assumptions being considered constant. The value of such flexed budgets is that (i) in the budget preparation phase management can identify likely outcomes should their output be higher or lower than that planned, i.e. sensitivity analysis, (ii) as a control mechanism managers can be made aware of what their revenue, expenditure and efficiencies should be if activity levels are proving to be different from that planned, and (iii) management can exercise control by comparing actual performance against the flexed budget, which variance will not be clouded by any differences caused by the differences between actual and budgeted activity levels. In principle the flexing of budgets relies upon two factors, (i) knowledge of cost behaviour (the fixity and variability of costs with changes in activity levels), and (ii) identification of a suitable activity measure.

While a knowledge of an organization's cost behaviour might be considered a desirable prerequisite to good managerial decision-making, many managements have not obtained such information, and even if they have, the problem of the relevant range over which each cost is fixed or variable may be very different one from another. These factors need not, however, eliminate the possibility of applying flexed budgets within an organization. If, when managers are preparing the budgets for their responsibilities, they were required to state and justify at what levels of activity they would expect to need, say, extra supervisory assistance, or to reduce the same, these could be used as a surrogate for a full cost behaviour analysis, be able to reflect the variability of semi-variable costs and approximate the relevant ranges of fixed costs. While this approach would not be so practicable as using a top-down budgetary approach, and might be considered too time-consuming, it is applied successfully in many organizations.

The identification of a suitable activity measure is very difficult in many organizations, as units of output is unlikely to be adequate in a multi-product/service organization. Standard hours is perhaps the most likely activity measure, but that presupposes that this information is available within an organization. 'Tons of output', for example, is apparently popular as a measure of output within the foundry industry, but has inherent anomalies regarding product mix, i.e. the work done and time consumed on a small complicated item may be larger than that on a large, heavy but simple item. It is right that different industries and business adopt those activity measures which they feel most suitable to their circumstances.

Rolling or continuous budgets

Some organizations adopt what are usually termed 'rolling' on 'continuous' budgets. CIMA, for example, defines these as 'The continuous updating of a short term budget by adding, say, a further month or quarter and deducting the earliest month or quarter so that the budget can reflect current conditions'.

It is argued that 'Such procedures are beneficial where future costs and/or activities cannot be forecast with any degree of accuracy,' in CIMA official terminology. However, this argument is surely illogical. If it is difficult to forecast ahead accurately (Isn't it always!) when, once a year perhaps, management devotes considerable time and attention to it, how likely is it that managers can do the same forecast more accurately every month or quarter? The danger is that the rolling budget will become the last period 'plus or minus a bit', and be representative of absolutely nothing by way of policy, and meaningless for prediction or control purposes.

If, however, management expects the rolling forecast to be 'updated' both by adding another period and by updating the intermediate periods to changed circumstances, it could be argued that management should obtain a more realistic forecast of the coming months than it would if no updating or rolling of budgets was required. In such circumstances management must necessarily ask how valuable such revised forecasts are likely to be in relation to the cost of the time spent by managers updating their forecasts.

Forecast revisions

If management wishes to identify what the (annual?) budget periods' actual results are likely to be, an alternative to rolling budgets is to require managers to re-forecast each period/month/quarter the expected actual figures at the end of the total budget period/year. This would enable management to identify the extent to which their managers' anticipated outcomes will vary from their last forecast and thus to 'keep in touch with' and understand the problems being encountered by managers, month by month and quarter by quarter.

Actuals could then be compared with both the original budget and the revised forecast of, say, the last quarter. While this should create a better managerial awareness of current and future operating conditions and expectations, the benefits from a control viewpoint are less easily identifiable.

Revision variances

An alternative approach to updating which has the virtue (if that it be) of retaining awareness of the original budget is the adoption of revision variances. Under this approach updating of the original budget to revised circumstances and expectations is achieved by adding an allowance for expected variances (plus or minus) to the original budget to reflect the deviation expected from it. Control may then be maintained by analysing the total actual variance from the original budget and comparing this with the revision variance, this difference reflecting changes from that more recently anticipated.

External economic change

The environmental assumptions upon which strategic and budgetary planning are based may well prove to be very different from those conditions encountered during the budgetary period. In these circumstances the master budget may be considered less than ideal, even inappropriate for either planning/resource allocation or control purposes.

The alternatives available to the organization are (i) to continue with the original budget, making allowances as necessary, (ii) to adapt the original budget to reflect the changed circumstances, (iii) to adopt a rolling budget or forecast revision approach, or (iv) to rebudget from scratch. The decision is likely to depend partly upon the degree of variation from the budgeted assumptions and partly upon the uses management makes of the budget, e.g. as authority to spend or limits on spending.

If environmental conditions are not significantly different from those budgeted for, it may be sensible to retain the original budget and expect middle and junior managers to adapt to the changed circumstances within the framework of the original budget. This would retain the integrity of the budgetary planning procedures and probably be a practicable and economic approach.

If the different conditions revolve around only one or two assumptions made, it *might* be sensible and practicable to adapt the master budget to the new situation, particularly if the budgetary data are held in a sophisticated computer financial model. However, this presupposes that the changed circumstances do not require a complete rethink of the budgetary plan and that information is held in a suitable fashion for it to be updated. As the revised budget would be based on the original budget, it is more likely to be 'accepted' by managers, who would appreciate the need to reflect the new conditions. Additionally, such changes are unlikely to be expensive.

Rolling budgets and forecast revisions are more likely to be practised as a matter of routine managerial philosophy rather than as a response to a particular or unexpected situation. Such an experience, however, may well be the trigger for the routine adoption of such information processes.

The larger the divergence of actual conditions from those budgeted, the more logical would be the decision to recognize the inappropriateness of the original budget and the need to rebudget. Failure to do so might permit managers to waste limited resources or use them inappropriately to the new circumstances either because they are unaware of the changes, or because they believe they are still expected to try to attain the original budget despite the changes in circumstances. Thus, for example, operational management might continue to recruit and train new employees for the budgeted expansion which senior marketing personnel now realize is unlikely to occur; or middle and junior selling and marketing managers might pursue a price increase oriented campaign in spite of increased competition and price cutting by competitors, because they believed such was still senior management's strategy or tactics, or because their own performance measures required it.

The cost of rebudgeting must be recognized and offset against the advantages of doing so. If circumstances are significantly different, the continued use of a budget that managers perceive as being inappropriate may not only lead to bad decisions but create low morale. Even in this situation, management would do well to remind managers at all levels that the original budget is not totally forgotten, and be prepared at some stage to ensure that all managers remember the 'lessons' from the failure to anticipate actual conditions and apply them to future planning situations.

It is essential that managers at all levels adapt to new environmental circumstances, and that strategies and tactics are changed if necessary. The failure to do so could be catastrophic. If that means sacrificing the 'sacred cow' of the master budget, then so be it.

Internal changes

In contrast, a reluctance to change shorter-term budgets and standards because of internal changes may well be justified. Such budgets are less likely to impact seriously upon the organization's survival, market position and long-term prosperity.

However, the impact of internal changes upon an organization can be very significant, even within a budgetary period of, say, a year, and may make the agreed budget, certainly in its detailed form, completely inappropriate to the situation. Consider, for example, such changes as:

- An organizational restructuring, say, from a functional to a divisional structure.
- A modification of objectives, financial or otherwise, particularly if this causes changes in the product/market portfolio of the business.
- The merging of acquired businesses within the existing organizational framework.
- Mechanization/automation resulting perhaps in significant learning curve effects.
- The earlier than expected completion of R & D, resulting in either new production technology or new product/markets.

The state of flux in such situations may of course be such that it would be impracticable to budget for it, and would in any event waste managerial time and energies better spent ensuring the changes are made efficiently and effectively. The danger, however, must be that, where no budgetary control exists, cost control is neglected in the drive for completion of change, and that effectiveness is achieved at the expense of efficiency. Obviously in managerial situations much must depend upon the specific case in point, the degree of change, the quality of the managers and the availability of control measures other than that of the budget.

Impact of inflation

The impact of inflation upon revenues and costs has been incorporated into the budgetary planning of most organizations for many years. This did not derive from a sudden rise in inflation or the inflation/current cost accounting/SSAP 21 debate of the 1970s but from an earlier, perhaps instinctive, recognition of the need to reflect estimated actual revenues and costs in planning data if realistic budgetary plans and controls were to be obtained.

Although the high levels of inflation in the UK of the 1970s will, it is to be hoped, not be repeated, inflation is a possibility, and one certainly difficult to forecast. Management may reflect inflation in its budgets by (i) requiring managers to budget today's levels of costs and revenues, and incorporating inflation as a separate element, (ii) budgeting under inflation rates assumed by senior management, or (iii) budgeting under inflation rates assumed by local/middle management.

The advantage of the former two approaches is that, as the budget for inflation is known or easily calculable, (a) plans can be revised to reflect different levels of inflation and (b) control by means of variance analysis can differentiate between the effects of inflation and that of other causes. The other side of the coin is that individual budget-holders may have a much better appreciation of the likely effects of inflation in their industry, types of cost and locality than would more senior management. However, there must always be the danger that the delegation of the decision on inflation levels to each budget-holder encourages pessimism, the building in of 'slack' and the creation of unrepresentative budgets.

With the advent of computer modelling in budgetary and indeed strategic planning, the desirability of the separate identification of inflationary effects would appear to be overwhelming. The 'revision' of budgets to reflect inflation should perhaps be seen in a very different light to the revisions due to external and internal changes discussed above. Such adaptations can surely be viewed similarly to flexible budgeting, i.e. as part of variance analysis. In the same manner that flexible budgets reflect variations of the original master budget due to changes in volume of activity, so inflationary budgets reflect changes in levels of revenues, costs and profits due to changes in inflation from that anticipated. Flexed inflationary budgets, can then be seen to reflect variances caused by factors other than volume or inflation, remove an excuse for managers to hide behind, and concentrate attention upon the real cause of any variances.

The exception to these considerations, however, may be when the impact of inflation upon a business is significantly different between revenues and costs, one type of cost and another or one unit or another. Consider, for example, a situation where costs are increasing faster than sales price for some products or services. In such circumstances management may need to rethink its whole product/market strategy/tactics. Thus, if labour costs are increasing at a faster rate than, say, capital equipment, it may be best to switch to labour-saving manufacturing/operational processes. In larger companies, with operating units in different countries, relative changes in the rates of inflation on operating costs may result in the switching of work from one unit to another, perhaps necessitating a significant revision of short- and long-term plans.

References

1. Amey, L.R. and Eggington, D.A., *Management Accounting: A Conceptual Approach*, Longman, 1973, p. 448.
2. CIMA, 'Management Accounting Official Terminology', 1986.
3. Hofstede, G.H., *The Game of Budget Control*. Tavistock, 1968, p. 295.
4. Coates, J.B., Rickwood, C.P. and Stacey, R.J., 'Examination of the Differences Between Academic Concepts and Actual Management Management Accounting Practices', Report to ESRC, British Library Document Supply Centre, August 1987 and Hofstede, G.H. *The Game of Budget Control*, Tavistock, 1968, p. 295.
5. Simon, H.A., Guetzkow, H., Kozmetsky, G. and Tyndall, G., *Centralisation vs. Decentralisation in Organising the Controller's Dept.*, New York Controllership Foundation, 1954.
6. Hofstede, *op. cit.*
7. Stedry, A.C., *Budget Control and Cost Behaviour*, Prentice-Hall, 1960.
8. McClelland, Atkinson, J.W., Clark, R.A. and Lowell, E.L., *The Achievement Motive*, Appleton-Century-Crofts, Inc., New York, 1953.
9. Maslow, A.H., *Motivation and Personality*, Harper & Row, New York, 1954.
10. Herzberg, F., Mausner, B. and Synderman, B.B., *The Motivation to Work*, Wiley, New York, 1959.
11. Becker, S.W. and Green, D., Jr, 'Budgeting and Employee Behaviour', *The Journal of Business*, Vol. XXXV, October 1962.
12. Schiff, M. and Lewin, A.Y., 'The Impact of People on Budgets', *The Accounting Review*, Vol. XLV, No 2, April 1970.
13. Argyris, C., *op. cit.*
14. Argyris, C., *op. cit.*
15. Argyris, C., 'Human Problems with Budgets', *op. cit.*; and 'The Impact of Budgets on People'.
16. CIMA, *op. cit.*
17. Miles, R.E. and Vergin, R.C., 'Behavioural Properties of Variance Controls', *California Management Review*, Vol. VIII, No 3, Spring 1966.

18 Lupton, T., *Payment Systems*, Penguin 1972.
19 CIMA, *op. cit.*

Questions

1 (a) In high technology small batch manufacture accountants sometimes take the view that standard costing cannot be applied. The move into high technology is generally accompanied by a shift away from labour-dominated to capital-intensive processes.
    You are required to appraise the application of standard costing in the circumstances described above.
   (b) In order to secure and direct employee motivation towards the achievement of a firm's goals, it may be considered that budget centres should be created at the lowest defined management level.
    You are required to discuss the advantages and disadvantages of creating budget centres at such a level.
2 Magna plc has a practical operating capacity of 100 Magna-widgets. Historical trends show increasing demand and output which has reached 90 Magna-widgets this year.
   A young and enthusiastic marketing/sales director, recently appointed, is optimistic about the future prospects of the company's products. While he estimates that sales of 100 units are likely to be achieved in the coming year, he believes in setting himself and his staff hard though achievable targets, to encourage and extend performance achievement. His budget for the coming year is therefore based on 110 units.
   The production director is hard-bitten man with long experience in the organization, having started as an apprentice in 1950 and become production director 3 years ago. In recent years he has experienced an increasing demand on his production capacity which, while resulting in high plant utilization and overtime/shiftworking, has strained resources from time to time, for which his department has been criticized. He dislikes the pressures placed upon him and resents the high regard in which the new sales director is held. He has been told that the sales budget is for 110 units. With the increasing trend in output demands over the past few years, the criticism of actual output in the past, and recognizing that his current practical capacity is only 100 units, he decides to organize his department with resources (machinery, staff, etc.) for a production output of 120 units.
   Examine and comment fully on this situation.
3 The Fuels Department of Bionic Engineering Inc. is a semi-autonomous unit manufacturing and selling a product known as Krypton. The management of the department is responsible for purchasing raw materials, setting production levels and selecting the

method of production to be used. Bionic Engineering also run an independent department of Economic Forecasting, which supplies information to central and departmental management.

Two formulae are available to the Fuels department, producing Krypton X and Krypton Y respectively. Each method of production requires all the inputs for a particular batch to be introduced into huge chemical vats at the start of the process; processing takes 1 month to complete. However, before the processing of each batch, it is necessary to carry out extensive cleaning and calibrating work, which takes 2 months. The nature of this work is such that there are very large savings from combining cleaning and calibration. Once started, it is impossible to change the calibration, and calibration settings must be adapted specifically to the batch volume and formula to be used.

Planning in the Fuels department is made easier by the existence of a contract with Titanic Distributors requiring all output to be sold to them at a price given by the following:

Price in pence per 100 litres = $4{,}400 - 0.04q$

where q is the quantity sold in units of 100 litres.

Titanic makes payments for the output immediately processing is completed. The following production data is available:

Materials	Krypton X (per 100 litres)	Krypton Y (per 100 litres)
DNX	50 litres	–
DNY	–	8 kgs
Biobase	12 kgs	12 kgs

Conversion costs
Variable cost (in pence) $900 + .1q$ $900 + .1q$
where q is the quantity of Krypton produced (in 100 litres).

Fixed costs are £8,000 per month during processing and £6,000 per month during cleaning and calibrating. Under a long-term contract Biobase is bought at £0.50 per kg. All materials are ordered 1 month before processing begins and paid for 2 months later, at which time conversion costs are met. DNX and DNY are received 2 days before processing begins; any of these materials left unused must be discarded.

Central management uses a system of budgetary control to assess the performance of departments. On 1 March 2001, based on the forecasted prices for DNX of £0.28 per litre and of DNY of £1.70 per kg, central management budget for Fuels to produce a profit of £22,350 in the quarter ending 30 June 2001.

On 31 March the forecasts predict prices for DNX of £0.34 per litre and DNY of £2.05 per kg. On this basis Fuels management calculates the optimal quantity of output and formula. By 1 May the prices to be paid are known, DNX being £0.30 per litre and DNY £2.00 per kg, and a profit of £10,150 is forecast, given that the departmental plan must now be carried out. This latest forecast is duly achieved.

Central management is concerned that the profit achieved is less than half the budgeted figure and a variance analysis is carried out as follows:

	£	£	
Actual profit			10,150
Selling price variance		1,800 F	
Cost variances			
DNY		10,800 U	
Conversion		4,500 F	
Rate variances		4,500 U	
Volume variances		7,700 U	
Total variances			12,200 U
Budgeted profit			22,350

A meeting is called to review the results. It is suggested on behalf of the department that their action was entirely caused by the revision of forecasts and the economic forecasting department is to blame for the volume variance. The forecasting department considers its forecasts to have helped and argues that, if the original plan had been adopted, things might have been worse. The head of chemical research offers another point of view: 'I have carried out a few calculations and consider the most serious mistake was making Krypton Y in the first place. It would have been cheaper to have made Krypton X this month. A profit of £15,000 could have been achieved'.

You are required
 (i) To present statements showing the budget, departmental plan, actual results and the suggestion of the head of chemical research.
 (ii) Critically compare all three approaches to variance analysis, using the calculations carried out above.
4 In what circumstances would standard costs not based on engineered standards be appropriate for an organization.
5 'Participatory budgets are a waste of time when eventually the plans of senior management will be those which are to be implemented.' Discuss.
6 What do you consider as being the prerequisite for the successful implementation of a participatory budgetary approach?
7 In what circumstances might it be appropriate to change the annual budgets before the end of the accounting year and what might be the repercussions of doing so?
8 'Rolling budgets are essential if an organization is undergoing rapid

change.' Is this really true, and what are the arguments for and against such a budgetary approach.

9. Bob Lord, the new managing director of the Abco Group, has engaged Ray Consultants to advise him on the operation of the group's budgetary planning and control. Bob Lord's previous experience has been within companies where there has been little or no participation in the budget preparation process other than that of senior management.

The Abco Group has a highly participative budgetary process. All managers with budget responsibilities play a part in the preparation of their contributions to the overall budget and these are used as a significant part of the annual performance appraisal and thereby can lead to financial and other rewards.

Bob Lord has asked Ray Consultants to write a report for him, explaining and summarizing as clearly as possible the believed *practical and theoretical* pros and cons of a participative budget approach, the problems such an approach is likely to encounter and how these can be best ameliorated, in order to obtain as balanced a view as possible to aid him in his consideration of the existing system within Abco.

What should such a report contain?

4 Budgets and control

Introduction

In this chapter aspects of the collection and presentation of budget information for control purposes are considered, followed by a discussion of the ways variance investigations may be triggered.

Control of an enterprise is the principal responsibility of management, and this responsibility includes all aspects of budgetary planning and control: strategic and tactical, long-term and short-term. These activities are a part of management's objective to develop a successful business. The focus of this chapter, however, is on control in the narrower but perhaps more usually understood meaning of exercising regular control over current budget plans by comparing planned with actual results. The emphasis of such comparisons is corrective in the short term, though the process of establishing how and why differences have arisen contributes not only to bringing activities back into line immediately, but also to the identification of fundamental changes in the conditions on which plans have been founded and hence to amendments and revisions of longer-term plans.

It is conventional to regard these comparisons as being a part of the scheme of management by exception in which, if there are no significant departures from plans, then all is deemed to be under control and proceeding as anticipated. Managerial time, effort and cost are only to be expended where the differences according to certain criteria are judged to warrant it. It would be overly simplistic to proceed this way at all times though: for example, plans which are regularly full realized may themselves need investigation on the grounds they are too unambitious.

The fundamentals of budgetary planning and control and standard costing systems have long been established and there is a substantial history surrounding their usage. Solomons[1] traces the development of cost ascertainment methods, including standard costing, budgets and budgetary control, and variance analysis back to significant periods in their emergence as separate entitites, finally coming together in the early part of this century in systems which would be readily recognized today. Towards the end of his paper he remarks: 'If there is one conclusion to be drawn from the foregoing study, it is that there is remarkably little in modern costing which our fathers did not know about. What can be fairly claimed for the period 1910–1950 however, is that great strides were made in converting ideas into widely adopted practices'.

Since then there have of course been many notable further advances in the practice of budgetary planning and control. Important among them has been the recognition of the cost of information, a subject which has received much attention from the late 1960s onwards. Previously, by implication, information was treated as costless, being available as and when required.[2,3] One of the principal points which emerges from the debate on information economics is the pervasive presence of uncertainty as the background to all management decision problems. This in turn affects both the cost of acquiring information and the benefits expected from it. A satisfactory balance in the cost–benefit trade-off needs to be achieved, if possible.

Additional significant issues which have been debated over a roughly similar period and up to the present deal with the need for an understanding of the part played by managers in the creation and capture of information, and the way information is presented to them and subsequently handled. Recognition and proper appreciation of behavioural influences are as important, from an organization's point of view, in the successful pursuance of control as are the accounting numbers which provide the immediate basis of analysis and for investigation.[4] A stereotyped picture of the way management accountants may be thought to (or actually) behave with respect to the application of these systems is described by Tait.[5]

Collection and presentation of budget information for control purposes

Many books and articles[6] discuss this activity of collection and presentation. Key among them are the definition of the sphere of managerial responsibility, the controllability (by a manager) of the variables to which budget data relate and the main purposes of the control activity. These purposes may be briefly summarized as:

- Notification of the extent of departure of actual from budget.
- Analysis and presentation of information explaining the nature and causes of such departures, to be used as a basis for pursuing corrective action, which could include major revisions to budgets.
- Provision of information for use in the assessment of the per-

formance of sections of the business: achievement of targets, improvements in productivity and efficiency.

Interest in outcomes is obviously not confined to subordinate managers and their immediate superiors but goes right through to top management, subject to filtering and amalgamation of data. It is also increasingly becoming a province of interest to internal audit departments in their role as independent observers and reporters on departmental target-setting and performance achievement.

Using actual company cases,[7,8] we now introduce three examples which serve to illustrate how certain organizations have addressed a number of the technical and behavioural issues in the creation and transmission of information for budget-control purposes.

Case 1

The report format in use by company management accountants is given in Table 4.1. It was devised following an organizational restructuring which decentralized its operations. The main purpose of the scheme was to secure as accurate an attribution as possible of direct costs to various levels of the company, from product lines to the company as a whole. This helps to ensure that both responsibility and controllability are properly matched, with apportionments of cost kept to a minimum.

Direct marketing costs are predominantly packaging, but for the

Table 4.1 Report format

	Operating company	Business centre	Individual product lines
Sales	x	x	x
Prime costs	x	x	x
Sales gross margin	x	x	x
Direct marketing	*x*	*x*	*x*
Net product margin	x	x	x
Product attributable			
Indirect Costs	*x*	*x*	*x*
Product contribution	x	x	x
Business centre			
Attributable indirect costs	*x*	*x*	
Business centre			
Contribution	x	x	
Factory general overheads	x		
General selling expenses	x		
Company administration	x		
Company marketing	*x*		
Operating company contribution	x		
Apportioned services	*x*		
Gross trading profit	*x*		

remainder the stratification of information clearly recognizes controllability and responsibility, since managers are assigned to product lines. Prime costs and direct marketing are regarded as variable, though the company is fortunate here to be able to use temporary labour to achieve variability in direct labour costs. Probably the most difficult category to define and assign is that of indirect cost into the 'product' and 'business' attributable categories. The condition used as the criteria for the division is that it must be possible to 'manage' the costs in line with changes in the level of business generated within some specified time limit. Managers' agreement is needed to an item being classified one way or the other or being split. Costs which would come in for examination would be, for example, indirect labour and supervision, power, depreciation, heat, light, maintenance, shift premiums, insurances.

The level of costs in the managed category is set by decisions preceding actual activity and hence the costs are budget totals, but not now automatically carrying labels of 'fixed' or 'variable'. Once there is a commitment to the acquisition or disposal of certain resources, it may indeed result in an essentially fixed level of expense for a certain period. Even then, if there are marked variations in activity from planned, managers are expected to avoid entering into commitment as to resources which will create difficulties in the future. Overall line managers are accepting the need to manage their resources to no more than that which the general level of business can support.

A similar set of appraisals takes place at the level of the business centre, where managers accept certain amounts of administrative and selling expense as being necessary to run their part of the business. This is not the result of a simple apportionment process, but of realistic identification of what would be needed if the business were on a stand-alone basis, though it must be tempered to some extent where appropriate by the benefits of economies of scale, e.g. in the provision of such services as accounting. The aim is to minimize the extent of arbitrary apportionment so far as possible, important in costs which account for 58 per cent of total value added in the operating company. One management accountant's view of apportionments carried out the traditional way was, 'they generate a lot of heat and not much light'.

Case 2

In this case also the emphasis is on how production and other managers are encouraged to manage costs, though here the labels of variable and fixed were being applied. Lack of precision in defining cost variability outside the ambit of a few items such as direct materials is recognized, but the aim is to obtain the 'right response' from managers having expenditure responsibility. This is considered best attained by labelling expenses 'variable' wherever there is reasonable doubt whether or to what degree a cost really is variable. The psychology of the case for approaching the problem this way is that to call a cost 'fixed' invites the response that there is little that can be done to control it in the short run.

Approaching the problem along these lines is thought to help put pressure on managers to improve efficiency in adverse conditions, though the twin dangers of finally causing managers to reach the conclusion that the variability is spurious and efficiency therefore unattainable and what to do if conditions finally improve, have to be carefully monitored. The company in question has been in a period of long-term contraction, so the latter problem has not really emerged. Little hostile reaction is reported from managers whose spending budgets have been controlled in part at least this way. The application of the idea is to most cost elements except the very evidently fixed ones such as depreciation and rates.

Case 3

Set out in Table 4.2 is the report format in use by the internal audit department of a large multinational company. The report itself is used to provide the department with all that it regards as being the necessary salient information in monitoring division and product line performance. It is not dissimilar to the Case 1 example, but each comes from a totally different industrial sector.

As in the earlier case, considerable effort is made to ensure costs are directly attributed and, as before, the main problem area lies in the division of the indirect costs. An interesting feature of this case was that the manager responsible for the product group was also primarily responsible for determining the extent to which the overhead costs – in the main, production and marketing – were to be divided between directly attributable and apportioned non-attributable. This does not

Table 4.2 Multinational's report format

		Product (budget)	Actual	Proportion of total business (%)
1	Sales (including inter-company transfers)	x	x	
2	Cost of sales	x	x	
	(*Prime costs*)	–	–	
3	Sales gross margin	x	x	
4	*Direct overhead*	x	x	
5	Contribution	x	x	
6	Indirect (apportioned) costs (including interest charged on assets)	x x	x x	
7	*Operating profit*	x	x	
8	Assets managed % return on assets managed (7 ÷ 8)	x	x	

have any effect on the overal return on assets managed measure, but it does affect the contribution figure, which is a key element in monitoring the profitability of the product group within the business as a whole.

A manager would on the face of it seem to have carte blanche to adjust the overheads figure in his favour, even to the extent of recording no controllable direct overhead. However, the internal audit department, while accepting that absolute precision cannot be achieved in valuing each category of expenditure, looks for a reasonable attitude in the acceptance of some responsibility for this type of spending by the product group manager: the actual existence of the group must mean it causes a certain proportion of the overheads to be incurred. Where a manager is trying to improve his performance by too obvious an attempt at minimizing these costs, he provokes a visit from the internal audit staff.

The Budget and Actual columns also record the standard profit and the variances of individual items of sales and costs as a percentage of that figure, showing the significance of each element in turn in the way if affects the achievement or otherwise of the standard profit. This provides managers and auditors alike with the initial information on where significant departures from plan appear to arise. Internal audit operations also have the further guide of the proportion of business accounted for by the product group. In a business with some fifteen main divisions and a very large number of product groups, this document serves as the key to highlight what are regarded as all the significant areas for the exercise of control, while leaving operational managers within a substantially decentralized environment.

Measurement and control of staff performance

Department or section output, ratio analysis of resource usage and variance analysis all contribute as measures of performance for the group of individuals working within a department. Individual contributions themselves are frequently less easy to measure, especially in service departments, where, for example, a person is producing advice based on expertise. Often much reliance is placed on the 'professionalism' of the person for assurance that his/her activities are both effective and economic. Management by Objectives (MBO) is a tool which has been in use for some time, though not apparently uniformly or with total success[9] across companies. It aims to put some substance, particularly in staff situations, into the assessment of the level and content of work which it is expected staff will perform. The programme of work is agreed with individuals concerned as to content, time allowed and scheduling, and is subsequently audited by managers.

An appropriate example is taken a company's accounting department, which is divided into six main functional areas. One of these deals solely with accounting for inventory. In the first place the objective of the function is stated, followed by a listing of the activities which

Table 4.3 Staff task plan

Objective	Control Area	Project completion date	Staff assigned	Risk factor
1 Develop and publish for approval a work in progress valuation	Inventory	10/87	J. Smith	M
2 Develop and implement a bill of material audit analysis, etc.	Manufacturing	11/87		L

come within its purview, such as control and reporting of stock positions, product cost development, finished goods administration and so on. These are the objectives the unit as a whole is expected to aim at. To do so will frequently require completion of specific tasks, to which individuals can be assigned. In this section, a plan (Table 4.3) is drawn up.

It is the section manager's job, carried out with the function head's approval, to establish this plan and assign persons to projects. The risk factor covers the competence of the person given a project to complete the task without assistance and within the period allotted. The more assistance needed from outside the function, the greater the preceived risk level. In turn this forms part of the background to the final project appraisal, where reasons for over- or under-achievement are required in exactly the same way as explaining a standard cost variance. The degree to which such projects can be accurately measured depends on the section manager's own experience and his knowledge of his staff's abilities. Such project assessments are common of course where the service is or contributes directly to a saleable product, e.g. in the development of computer programmes in software houses, or aerospace engineering projects, but is a less common planning and control feature of routine service and administration sections.

Variance analysis

The purpose of calculating a variance is to show departures from standard or budget, which may either favourable or unfavourable. The systems which incorporate the forecasts and budget plans and capture the actual data for comparison with them are often detailed and complex, requiring budget manuals in order to see they are properly executed. In contrast, there is much less formality and guidance available as to how to use the variance information thrown up by the comparisons, yet the choice to investigate a variance or not is central if not crucial to the achievement of operating control.

Some of the important elements of the problem may be considered as follows:

- The fact that a variance has been recorded (favourable or adverse) does not automatically mean anything is wrong or doing particularly well. The result may be one that has occurred simply by chance.
- To investigate a variance will cost money – the time of persons assigned to the task, those who have to be interviewed, maybe material and equipment costs in test work.
- Benefits may be even more difficult to discern and evaluate than costs: improved competitiveness, better customer goodwill may well be, for example, among the eventual outcomes of an investigation which leads to improved quality and service, but they will not be easy to quantify. On the other hand, as part of the same investigation, scrap and rework cost reduction is much more readily evaluable. The problem with benefits is compounded by the possibility that nothing is out of control, in which event no benefits arise from a study, but there will be costs.

Experience is certainly a valuable asset in the circumstances, since it contributes insights and knowledge not apparent in the figures: for example, is the recurrent nature of a result new or has it occurred in the past; if so, how was it dealt with and with what effect? Experience will also help to spot cause and effect and interlinked outcomes, again contributing to better decision-making on the choice of whether to investigate a variance or not.

Thus many factors and unknowns enter this particular decision area, to the extent that it is not possible to be prescriptive as to how to proceed. A number of choices are offered, some quite formal and systematic, others, such as experience, far more intuitive. Again they need not be regarded as exclusive alternatives to each other. The most widely discussed approaches are the following:

Reliance on experience

A partial or complete reliance on experience is likely to be widely adopted in practice. Even if more formal analysis is applied to earmark apparently important variances, it is still probable that a judgement based on experience will be the deciding factor as to whether an investigation should proceed.

Ad hoc rules

The development of ad hoc rules are used to highlight what are considered to be variances of a size which potentially require investigation. Commonly:

(a) The ratio of the variance observed to budget (standard) or actual cost. Choice of a ratio, the size of which if equalled or exceeded would make a prima facie case for investigation, is a matter for the company.

(b) Ratios ignore absolute size: very large ratios are derivable from insignificant costs. Hence the absolute size of a variance may be considered a more important indicator of the need for investigation and a value chosen accordingly.

Of course each of these two criteria may give contradictory information if used in isolation: much unproductive work may result from a reliance on a ratio criterion (10 per cent, 15 per cent of standard cost, for example) if carried out without reference to the absolute size of a variance. Similar drawbacks attach to the use of absolute size alone. However, to attempt a joint criterion based on both elements would be no better a guide than perhaps saying look at all variances. Judgement founded on good experience must be used in conjunction with chosen criteria in this case.

Statistical control methods

Statistical control methods have been advocated. Support for them has been based on the parallel between the purpose of variance accounting and statistical quality control, namely the use of process defect rates and cost variance to indicate whether the underlying processes are in or out of control or are moving in the out-of-control direction.

The statistic used to define levels of in or out of control is measured in terms of the standard deviation. A series of observations of the performance of a process are made, say in relation to the actual usage of direct material in comparison with the prescribed standard. From the values obtained, the mean variance and its standard deviation may be calculated. Conventional statistical quality control charts identify warning limits, say at a level where the chance of the observation is 1 in 40 times, and action limits, where the chance may be set at 1 in 100 times. The standard deviation is used to measure these limits, but their selection is again a judgement for the company to make. A typical chart may appear as in Figure 4.1.

The figure shows information on departures from standard plotted on a daily, weekly or monthly basis, with the situation initially apparently within the area which would be regarded as 'in control', then exhibiting a trend toward 'out of control' – firstly breaking through the warning limit (which should trigger at least preliminary investigation of the circumstances to reverse the trend) and finally going through the upper action limit (which demands that an investigation takes place, since the underlying situation is now deemed out of control). The underlying philosophy is simply that, since budgets and standards are substantially based on predictions of future conditions, it must be accepted that departures from them in the form of variances will occur more or less by chance and hence do not indicate that anything is seriously amiss. However, as the size of variance increases, the likelihood of it occurring by chance becomes progressively smaller, until at some stage (defined by managers) there is a presumption that something is going wrong

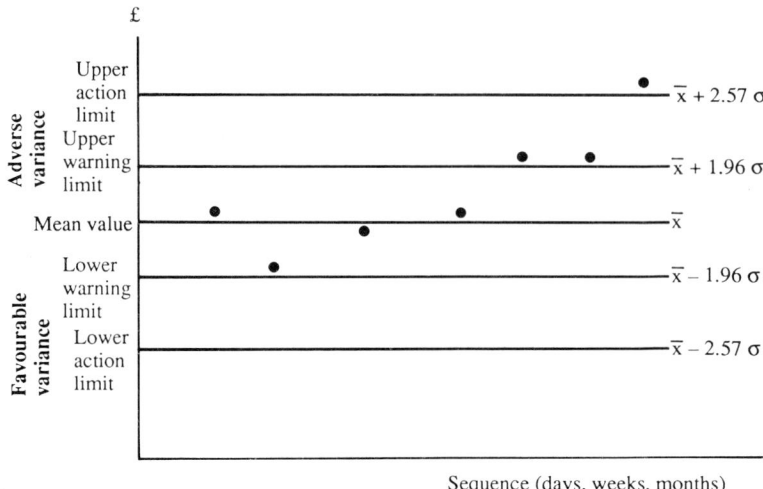

Figure 4.1 *Statistical control chart*

and ought to be investigated. Investigation of variances does not follow automatically, since costs and benefits still need to be ascertained, though they could be among the considerations in establishing the scheme at the outset.

It is an appealing idea, which in practice appears to have attracted few adherents. Statistical schemes require quite long runs of data in order to establish the ranges within which outcomes may be normally expected to vary and hence to establish reasonable warning and action limits. The data must be consistent from one period to the next. In process and high volume manufacturing conditions both the quantity and stability of data factors are likely to be present, so that for production quality control schemes the basic data requirements are met. Standard cost and budget data are usually assembled to cover broad intervals of time, so that the number of measurements taken is much smaller per period than in the volume production case, leading also to the point that before sufficient information is accumulated, the underlying parameters may well have changed and data in one period are no longer comparable with those from preceding periods.

Although there is a distinction between standard cost and statistical quality control variances, a relationship remains. For example, examination of material purchase quality against specifications would produce the same outcomes – either the material is acceptable or not – whether measured in a quality control or standard cost variance analysis. The same could be said of many other SQC applications. The preference is also to catch departures from specifications (standards) at this point rather than waiting for them to be valued in order to produce cost variances, since they provide the opportunity to conduct investiga-

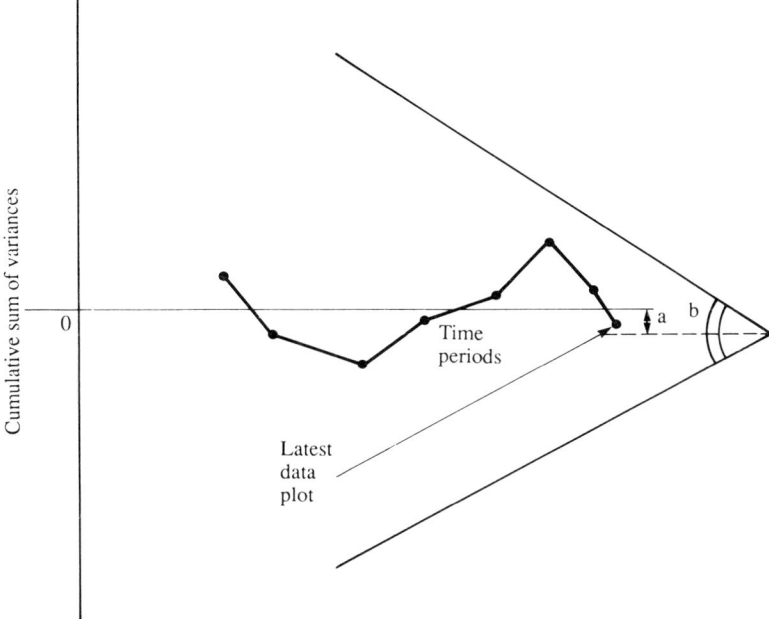

Figure 4.2 *Cusum graph*

tions at an earlier rather than a later stage, much improving the chance of determining causes and reducing the possibility of future problems.

Important contributors to the idea of the adoption of SQC (statistical quality control) schemes have been Bierman, Fouraker and Jaedicke[11] and Dopuch, Birnberg and Demski.[12] In a further contribution Kaplan[13] extends (*inter alia*) the application of conventional statistical schemes to the use of cusum graphs. Here the cumulative sum of positive and negative variances is plotted, providing a graphical presentation useful in itself, since it helps to identify the point in time when an out-of-control situation may have developed. In order to give greater precision to the actual assessment, a V-mask may be calculated and added to the graph. The angle of the V-mask determines the sensitivity of the test of whether a situation is still within or has moved out of control, and this angle in turn is set by two parameters, 'a' and 'b'. Parameter 'b' is defined as a number of periods ahead of the most recent graph plot, while 'a' controls the angle of the V-mask and depends on a determination of the size of variance that would be considered indicative of a significant shift in actual against standard/budgeted out-turns. The cusum graph is illustrated in Figure 4.2.

The figure shows an in-control case, with the angle of the V-mask equal to the ratio of a/b. When the cusum plot cuts the mask, an out-of-control case is signalled. It is a relatively simple technique to apply, though space does not allow further discussion here. Readers are referred to Lewis.[14]

Decision theory models

These deal specifically with the analysis of the costs and benefits of carrying out an investigation and hence can be used in conjunction with any of the three ways of identification of variances apparently worthy of investigation as listed above as a further evaluator serving a decision as to whether to proceed or not.

The basic model can be illustrated as a two-state model, i.e. a process is either in or out of control and the two actions possible are investigate the variance or do not investigate. In addition, information has to be obtained as to:

- The prior probabilities that a process is in or out of control (effectively given by SQC-based schemes).
- The cost of conducting an investigation and the value of likely benefits. The latter principally comprise the saving in costs otherwise incurred if control is not re-established.

This model may be shown as in Table 4.4

Table 4.4 Decision theory model

Decision	State of process	
	In control X_1	Out of control X_2
Investigate	$-C$	$B-C$
Do not investigate	0	0

where: C = cost of investigating
B = benefit of investigating

If the following data is assumed:

p	= probability the process is in control = 0.9
(1−p)	= probability the process is out of control = 0.1
C	= £800
B	= £3,000

then the immediate decision would be not to proceed with an investigation, since the cost (C) at £800 is greater than the expected value of the benefit $(1 - p)(B) = £300$.

This decision model is about the most simple available, but nonetheless contains many difficulties. How does one estimate the cost of investigation before it takes place and before, possibly, having any idea of what may be wrong? This latter difficulty extends also to the estimation of benefits. Then there is the judgement as to the prior probabilities. Again, in the absence of evidence, how is it possible to assess them with any hope of accuracy? In the example given, were the probability that an observed variance indicating the process to be out of control to change from 0.1 to 0.3, the expected value of the benefit would become £900 and the decision becomes to investigate. Beyond these issues are ones concerning the attitudes of the decision-makers towards the risk consquences of their decisions and the complexity of the decision model itself, i.e. a two-state, single period model, when several states and sequential effects may be a more accurate representation. Finally there is the question of actually taking action; waiting for all these models to be created and evaluated could well mean the passing of the most effective point in time for intervention to take place.

There is no evidence pointing to widespread use of models of this nature. Their most likely beneficial effects lie in the way they demonstrate the salient points needing to be addressed in the decision process and use as part of a management training programme. Thereafter, in the practical situation, managerial judgement takes over in actual decision-making.

Conducting variance analysis

If information on variances is to be of any value, it must have reference to two main sets of conditions:

1. The actual presentation of the information, as regards speed and timeliness, relevance and accuracy.
2. The acceptance by managers of the validity of the plans, measurements and attributed responsibilities which are the basis for the derivation and application of variance analysis.

The factors referred to in 1 above are well understood, and only their interaction requires some further comment here. For successful investigation of current situations the general rule is to obtain variance data as soon as possible and hence there is a possible trade-off between accuracy and speed, certainly between fully costed variances and their presentation in physical usage units. For example, in the latter case it may be possible to provide data on actual against standard material consumption in units of volume or weight rather more rapidly than a standard or actual cost valuation of over or under usage. For the purpose of investigating the cause of excessive consumption against the standard amount, it is decidedly preferable to know about the occurrence of the event as soon as possible. This of course adds another facet to the process of deciding when it becomes worthwhile to conduct an investigation. On the other hand, certain variances have longer-term implications, perhaps being indicative of fundamental shifts away from the bases of current plans, as may be the case, for example, in the capacity utilisation component of the volume variance. The appropriate response to such a situation is more likely to be founded on a build-up of these variances over time, which could ultimately call for a revision of the entire business plan, than one which presumes immediate correction is desirable and possible. Hence speedy action, within limits at least, is less likely to be a pressing need.

The question of the degree to which managers are able to exercise control over variances depends on how well responsibility and authority are identified in the managerial hierarchy. It is sometimes debated whether non-controllable variances should appear on the operating statements of individual managers, since they may detract from action which should be taken on those which are controllable, e.g. because of their size. On the other hand, there are likely to be some clear indirect links: it may not be possible, for instance, for a manager to control rates, depreciation charges, insurances, service charges by direct action on those costs, but organizing and maintaining a throughput of goods as efficiently as possible will contribute effectively to the maximum absorption of those costs. It is a truism to say that all costs are controllable at some level in an organization's hierarchy, and in a responsibility accounting sense that point should be clearly identified. It is equally true, though, that inability on the part of managers to exercise direct control over an expense item does not mean it is necessarily uncontrollable in so far as their actions contribute to keeping down unit costs.

Relevance and accurancy may be considered also in the context of inflationary situations. In addition, there are situations where the underlying assumptions of budgets and standards are being progressively eroded by changes such as those brought about by increases or decreases in general economic activity, changes in the market for products and changes in the technology which produces goods and services.

Periods of rapid rises in resource cost, brought about by general inflation, which were experienced in the UK in the 1970s and early 1980s, rapidly undermine the meaning and significance of fully costed variances. The reaction observed in a number of companies to this problem was:

- To revise resource prices frequently and regularly, a common interval being quarterly.
- To concentrate on resource usage reports, on the grounds that price was becoming an uncontrollable variable.

It may be noted that companies dealing in commodities such as copper and coffee tend to suffer continually from the fact that these materials are unpredictably volatile in price. The custom and practice of trades affected by this volatility tends to be that prices charged to customers, eventually at least, will reflect the supplier passing on the commodity price increases or savings pretty well automatically. Except for merchants whose trade is solely as dealers in these commodities, most processor manufacturers would not risk speculating on commodity markets, though they might take action to cover their transactions.

However, returning to the question of price changes brought about by inflation, it is clearly valid to try to ensure that the impact of the main body of controllable variances is not obscured by the less controllable – possibly dominating – impact of adverse price variances. *Less* controllable makes the point that even in these circumstances it would be wrong to ignore them altogether. Companies engaged in competitive situations, especially internationally, could well have to absorb at least some of these price effects, since they may not, perhaps because of exchange rate movements caused by differential inflation among competing countries, be able to maintain competitive market prices. Price variances are some measure of the problem faced.

Such changes may be presented as 'revisions variances' (CIMA terminology),[15] though the expression refers to the general range of resources used by an organization and to usage and volume as well as price variances. Such variances apply wherever conditions have changed sufficiently markedly from those underlying the original budget and associated standards to warrant budget reappraisal.

Over a longer period it has been observed in some companies (e.g. Crossways)[16] that standards and hence some budgets have been allowed to drift away from the reality of changing production and market scenes by clinging to concepts evolved for conditions which have ceased to exist. Most likely a series of ad hoc amendments will have been made to the original case, but without a great deal of care the lack of a fundamental review of developments leads to accounting reports being seen as irrelevant and consequently ignored. Instances of this occurring have been noted in cases where transfer to high technology manufacture with scarcely any direct labour base still leaves overhead being recovered on direct labour. Not only does this start to produce very high recovery rates, it also masks the deep change in the nature of the manufacturing process that has taken place, e.g. by apparently focusing on direct labour activity when this is really no longer significant. Attention as to the real problems has been misdirected. Similarly shifts in the market with an increasing demand for product differentiation have a possible knock-on consequences of some cost changes, shorter production runs and capacity loss. Standards based on the idea of production runs more suited to a past era of high volume mass production are again no longer relevant.

Besides the above issues, effective preparation of the groundwork for variance investigation must have reference to the possibility of interdependence between variances. This must lengthen the period required before publication to managers of various analyses. If attempts at responsibility shifting and the creation of an adversarial climate are to be kept to a minimum, then it is probably the accountants' responsibility to try to produce an objective report, incorporating reasoned explanations for the occurrence of events as far as possible. For example, at a simple level they may state that the use of a new or non-recognized supplier of materials or components, for whatever reason, may be a significant possible contribution to higher than expected material usage and lower than expected direct labour and/or machine or process efficiency. Obviously responsible managers' contributions to the explanation of given situations cannot be in any sense diminished by preliminary studies undertaken by the accountants, but management meetings to discuss variance reports can be put on a better directional basis as a result of them.

In organizations where priority has been given to the establishment of good inter-department relationships, much of the latter groundwork can be reduced; for example, in one company where departmental quality ratings are given considerable prominence, it is the practice for discussions to be arranged between representatives of departments when one believes that a fall-off in its quality standards may be in part at least due to faults coming through from a previous department. Owing to the environment created for the organization as a whole, departments see themselves as contributors to the company goals and not as independent islands, with the result that debates are conducted in a positive, amicable atmosphere, which generally results in an agreed resolution of the problem (in so far as it is within their power to achieve it) and without much direction by the management accounting department.[17] A further extension of this situation is that the realization of required standards of quality is not subject to a cost/benefit appraisal of input resources to a valuation of results, but is simply built into the product and costed at the specification level, in the expectation this will be achieved. This lessons and without any tendency to pass on sub-standard work solely for the purpose of fulfilling production quotas and getting products 'out of the door'. Variances, represented immediately by rejects and rework and in the longer term by guarantee/warranty claims and even loss of business, are kept to a minimum with little formal accounting input.

Clearly this situation links into the condition of ac hoc rules where a substantial body of literature exists on the topic of motivations and behavioural responses.

Managerial participation in budget planning and control

A superficial characterization of budget plans and a scheme of control in which variance analysis plays a significant role is that of the carrot and the stick. Accountants are sometimes accused of wielding too much stick in a rather negative fashion.

The body of literature devoted to this central aspect of management accounting is substantial indeed, far too great to even attempt to précis here. All aspects have received attention, from forecasting requirements through to setting budgets and standards, motivation, participation and reward schemes. Sometimes there is the accusation that this is just playing with buzzwords, but it is believed there is a general acceptance that the studies and analyses conducted do represent a reality which should be acknowledged in the procedures of any budgeting system. Among the many significant contributors are Cyert, March and Starbuck;[18] Hofstede in the aptly titled book, *The Game of Budget Control*;[19] Hopwood;[20] and Otley;[21] and Emmanuel and Otley[22] provide an extensive list of papers and books devoted to this subject.

The results of this research show, *inter alia*, budgets to be widely perceived as motivational devices aimed at obtaining desired levels of performance by the company through its management. Mere expressions to the effect that improvement is desired or required are considerably less successful in producing the improvement than are the use of quantified budgets as targets to aim for.

At the same time it is recognized that simply presenting a budget as a target (take it or leave it) will not of necessity do much better. The key to the issue is seen as management's perceptions of budgets and its participation in their preparation. It is commonly observed that budgets should be both 'tight' and 'fair' in order to be accepted. Both are highly subjective concepts, likely to be perceived differently by different managers, but they encapsulate central elements by which managers will judge and respond to budgets they are working to.

If it is granted that the most successful route to establishing budgets and targets is via participation, consultation and mutual agreement, there will probably need to be some give and take between departmental/section managers on the one hand and planners/accountants on the other. The result should be targets within reach, but not too easily, and a consequential judgement they are equitable. Hofstede[23] makes three major claims as to how managers' participation in the budgetary process helps to secure a better performance from them:

- By ensuring a subordinate accepts the budget, which thereby becomes a motivational target.
- The process of participation produces clearer understanding of the circumstances behind setting the budget and thus produces more realistic standards.
- Given the clearer understanding, there is less chance of information being distorted and manipulated.

Even so, participation is held to be unlikely to attain what is aimed for in all managers under all circumstances.

The level at which a budget is finally set must be such that its attainment presents a challenge and hence is likely to give some satisfaction in its attainment. If it is set too far out of reach, especially if this is combined with a poor personal appraisal of the likelihood of its achievement, efforts to achieve it are expected to be either non-existent at the outset or become steadily and progressively extinguished. The nature and psychology of the managers themselves, whether they are uncertain or confident of their abilities, is also an important contributory factor to the establishment of budgetary targets in pursuance of acceptable corporate performance. Performance measures used in conjunction with budgets require similar considerations.

Finally it is recognized that, while satisfaction may well be found in the achievement of targets, the main motivational drive is the hope, prospect or expectation of the rewards for doing so. These include improved salaries, bonuses, perks, promotions and so on.

Given a sound budgetary foundation, including the standards incorporated into many budgets, along the above lines, unless the surrounding business environment turns out markedly different from that which was envisaged, exceptional variances between actual and plan should be the exception rather than the rule. The objective, as with the quality example, is to get the plan as near right as possible in the first place, so that variances do relate to circumstances largely outside the control of the individual manager.

Conclusion

The activity of management accounting centres around the creation of planning budgets and their comparison with actual results. To achieve efficient control means close attention has to be paid to three major issues: creating a cost/benefit effective procedure to ensure plans are being followed and variances shown up by comparisons are investigated; ensuring standards and budgets are kept properly up to date to maintain their validity; and finally that the human and industrial relations aspects of the procedures are acknowledged and acted upon. After all it is the staff of the organization through whom the system is developed, maintained and progressed.

One of the benefits of new technology information systems is that information creation, capture and management should be much easier and more effective than in manual systems. There should certainly be much less excuse about timeliness, speed of arrival of information and its accuracy than there has been in the past.

References

1. Solomons, D., 'The Historical Development of Costing', in Solomons, D. (ed.), *Studies in Cost Analysis*, Sweet & Maxwell, 1952.
2. Kaplan, R., 'The Evolution of Management Accounting', *The Accounting Review*, July 1984.
3. Scapens, R.J., *Management Accounting*, Macmillan 1985, Chapter 8.
4. Emmanuel, C. and Otley, D.T., *Accounting for Management Control*, Van Nostrand Reinhold, 1985 p. 119.
5. Tait, G., 'The Truth About Standard Costing', *Management Accounting*, October 1985.
6. Horngren, C.T. and Foster, G. *Cost Accounting' – A Managerial Emphasis*, Prentice Hall, 1986, 6th ed. Part 2.

7   Coates, J.B., Rickwood, C.P. and Stacey, R.J., 'Examination of the Differences Between Academic Concepts and Actual Management Accounting Practices', Report to ESRC British Library Document Supply Centre, August 1987.
8   Ibid.
9   Coates, J.B. and Longden, S.G., 'Management Accounting in New and High Technology Growth Companies', Report to CIMA, November 1987.
10 Likert, R. *The Human Organization*, McGraw-Hill, 1967.
11 Bierman, J., Fouraker, J.C.E. and Jaedicke, R.K., 'A use of Probability and Statistics in Performance Evaluation', *The Accounting Review*, July 1961.
12 Dopuch, N., Birnberg, J.G. and Demski, J., 'An Extension of Standard Cost Variance Analysis', *The Accounting Review*, July 1967.
13 Kaplan, R., 'The Significance and Investigation of Cost Variances: Survey and Extensions', *Journal of Accounting Research*, Autumn 1975.
14 Lewis, C.D., *Industrial and Business Forecasting Methods*, Butterworths, 1982.
15 CIMA, *op cit.*
16 Horngren and Foster, *op. cit.*
17 Coates *et al. op. cit.*
18 Cyert, R.M., March, J.G. and Starbuck, W.H., 'Two experiments on risk and conflict in organizational estimation', *Management Science*, Vol. 7, 1961.
19 Hofstede, G.H., *The Game of Budget Control*, Tavistock Institute, 1968.
20 Hopwood, A.G., *Accounting and Human Behaviour*, Prentice-Hall, 1974.
21 Otley, D.T., 'Budget Use and Managerial Performance', *Journal of Accounting Research*, Vol. 16, 1978.
22 Emmanuel and Otley, *op. cit.*
23 Hofstede, *op. cit.*

Questions

1   (a) The investigation of a variance is a fundamental element in the effective exercise of control through budgetary control and standard costing systems. The systems for identifying the variances may be well defined and detailed yet the procedures adopted to determine whether to pursue the investigation of variances may well not be formalized.
   Critically examine this situation, discussing possible effective approaches to the investigation of variances.
   (b) Explain the major motivational factors which influence managers in their actions to eliminate variances from budget.

(CIMA May 1987)

2   The ABC company is a large manufacturer of domestic appliance equipment.

Internal accounting is based on a standard costing and budgetary control system introduced some 20 to 25 years ago in business conditions which could be described as a 'seller's market', with new product manufacture heavily based on a number of long-running standard lines. Since then greatly increased competition, buyers' demands for product differentiation and greatly changed manufacturing technology (some of which is installed and operating in the company) have dramatically changed the company's business and manufacturing environment.

The results of a 4-week operating period in one of the production departments making component parts, are given below:

	Budget	Actual
Output (standard hours)	4,800	4,460
Direct labour:		
production time (hours)	4,000	3,900
attendance time (hours)	5,000	4,900
Direct materials used (kgs)	20,160	20,962

The direct labour production standard incorporates a 20 per cent efficiency factor. There is a standard downtime allowance of 20 per cent.

Costs budgeted and actually incurred in the 4-week period are:

	Budget £	Actual £
Direct material	30,240	33,539
Direct labour	16,800	17,500
Indirect costs:		
indirect wages of direct workers	2,500	3,000
variable overhead	2,000	2,400
fixed overhead	25,200	28,000

Variable overhead recovery is based on production time and fixed overhead recovery on standard hours output.

You are required to:
(a) Obtain all the relevant variances from the above data.
(b) Comment on the variances in the light of the change in the business situation from one dominated by long production runs to the relatively shorter runs imposed in meeting the current demand for differentiated products;
(c) Use the situation problems of standard setting in programmed and non-programmed decision-making circumstances.

(CIMA, MCA Specimen Question Paper)

5 Budgeting in not-for-profit (NFP) organizations

Introduction

Many organizations in both the public and private sectors of the economy have primary objectives other than the pursuit of profit, the predominant motive attributed to commercial enterprises. The absence of the profit yardstick in respect of both planning and control makes it considerably more difficult to establish acceptable requirements for resources, acquire them and measure the efficiency and effectiveness of their use. This is at least in part because there is no bottom line measure which shows the activity to be producing a profit or making a loss. As a result, the whole question of what is required in the way of outputs of goods and services from NFP organizations, what may be justified, or, after the event, how well they have performed, loses a recognizable focus and tends to become diffuse, subject to wide-ranging value judgements.

There is also an additional problem in that organizations are not necessarily either wholly for profit or not for profit. A more useful way of looking at the problem may be to adopt Anthony's[1] categorization:

1 Profit-oriented. Organizations whose primary goal is the pursuit of profit.
2 Type A non-profit. Non-profit organizations whose financial resources are obtained entirely or almost entirely from the sale of goods and services.
3 Type B non-profit. Non-profit organizations which obtain a significant amount of financial resources from sources other than the sale of goods and services.

This chapter deals principally with category 3, the Type B NFP business. Type A, which in the UK context is mainly (but increasingly less accurately) represented by nationalized industry, is discussed in Chapter 9. The designation of an organization to any one of these categories is clearly 'on balance', since there may well be sectors in each which do not conform to the main objectives, or at least whose outcomes are not readily measurable in those terms. Thus there may be peripheral activities in profit-oriented organizations which may be said to contribute ultimately to the profit goal, e.g. expenditures on environmental projects, public relations and so on, but which would be difficult to quantify so far as their effect on profit is concerned. Equally, certain services within Type B organizations could be considered as commercial, e.g. building repairs and maintenance, with cost/profit comparisons for work carried out capable of being made directly with commercial profit-oriented undertakings. Altogether, clear cut, hard and fast categorization of entire organizations and their constituent activities would be difficult to maintain.

The range and economic significance of the Type B organizations is considerable. Examples given in this chapter will refer mainly to local authorities, but it is worth noting some of the other organizations that generally fall into this category. In the private sector examples would be clubs and charities. In the public sector come the local authorities, many central government funded services, such as defence, health, welfare, education, road transport and a myriad of others.

The question of budgeting, particularly in the latter type of NFP organization in the public sector, becomes an important issue because of their demands on scarce resources. These demands are not checked by a price to be paid for them directly by the consumer in a market-place transaction. It is true that central government taxes, local authority rates and poll taxes are raised to cover the major part of expenditure on such services. However, the mechanism financing their provision is not that of the competitive market place and hence it is difficult to evaluate them, to assess how much of scarce national resources they should command. It would appear in the case of the demand for health services, for example, that they will always increase to absorb any amount of resources made available to them.

It is not being suggested that budgetary planning and control, if exercised properly, is some kind of panacea to make up for the lack of a market-place valuation of services. Indeed, in principle, there is no real difference in the requirement for effective budgeting among any of the three organizational categories or in the manner in which budgets are generated. Ultimately what is of interest is to judge whether any particular methods of budgeting are likely to serve the Type B NFP case better than others, in either or both of the planning and control dimensions.

In this chapter particular attention is given to three relatively new approaches which are directly or indirectly concerned to secure improvements in the way budgeting is conducted in practice within not-for-profit organizations, though attention is paid principally to local authorities. The three are:

1 Zero-base Budgeting (ZBB).
2 Programme Planning and Budgeting Systems (PPBS).
3 Value for Money Audits (VFM).

It may be noted, however, that the first and last of these procedures are broadly applicable in any organization, though PPBS has been seen as primarily relevant to public-sector activities.

Budgeting in local authorities

A number of authors (for example, Pendlebury,[2] Pendlebury and Jones,[3] and Butt and Palmer[4]) have characterized the 'conventional' budgetary procedures in local authorities as the incremental approach – last year's allocation plus or minus a sum for the next year, depending on factors such as the expansion of services, limitations on resources, expectations of inflation. It is a practice not unique to local authorities or NFP organizations in general. It is frequently justified on the grounds that it maintains the level of service previously provided. On the other hand, this equally may be seen as one of a number of weaknesses:

1 That little or no attempt is made to see whether the bulk of the funding is justifiable: it is assumed that because a sum was spent on an activity in the past, it is *ipso facto* also a justification of future expenditure of at least broadly the same amount.
2 It is a self-perpetuating system which, while making life generally easy for all concerned, is likely to lead to complacency and must eventually extinguish any spark of a critical evaluation faculty that may once have existed.
3 The existing situation is regarded as static rather than dynamic. Priorities may change continually and maintenance of the status quo could in effect be drawing funds away from potentially more valuable budget areas.

Where it is difficult to obtain reliable and objective measures of resource consumption and the benefits produced, and where value judgement plays a significant role in determining what resources are required or are adequate, then what was apparently deemed acceptable last year, plus or minus little, clearly offers a seductively simple and seemingly reasonable point of departure for next year.

However, pressure on resources, particularly in the public sector in recent years, has brought with it a demand for a far more rigorous examination of the way local authorities and others have disposed of their resources. ZBB, PPBS and VFM are among the main concepts and ideas which have been applied to this problem, although they are not necessarily mutually exclusive of each other.

Zero-base Budgeting (ZBB)

Introduction

The Chartered Institute of Management Accountants defines[5] ZBB as:

> A method of budgeting whereby all activities are re-evaluated each time a budget is formulated.
> Each functional budgets starts with the assumption that the function does not exist and is at zero cost. Increments of cost are compared with increments of benefit, culminating in the planned maximum benefit for a given budgeted cost.

In contrast with the creeping incrementalism referred to previously, there is no longer any presumption that simply because an activity has existed in the past it should continue to do so in the future. Expenditure justification starts from the zero-base and comparisons of costs and benefits take place at sequentially defined levels of activity/service from that point. Hence its principal attraction may be seen to be the maintenance of a continuing pressure on spending departments to commit themselves to a programme of thorough reappraisal of the value of their activities. Instead of adding or subtracting a little from a previously budgeted or actual amount of expenditure, as though this in itself is an acknowledged and therefore justified point to build on for the next round of budget preparation, ZBB forces managers to address the fundamental question of whether an activity is necessary at all and even if this is conceded, at what level it should operate – in theory a complete break with what has happened in the past.

Viewed simplistically, it might seem that ZBB opens up the possibility of ad hoc budget approvals taking place without any coherent, cohesive planning framework to hold them together, especially as the process is commonly referred to as 'bottom-up' budgeting, and everything is up for reappraisal at the start of each new round. In practice, however, although budgets are indeed seen as being developed from the basic activity levels upwards, it should be a process taking place within the broader planning mechanism aimed at securing and supporting the achievement of management's overall strategic objectives for an organization, so that budget approvals are part of a well defined total plan.

ZBB is, at least so far as its formal name is concerned, a fairly recent introduction as a planning tool, credited to the United States Department of Agriculture in 1962.[6] It seems likely though that the idea has been applied earlier, though not referred to as ZBB. Indeed it is probable that this continues to be the case at present, since there is no compulsion to refer to the particular style of budgeting as ZBB.

It is likely that the ZBB approach is adopted without any questioning of the need in many situations; new business enterprises, disposals and acquisitions of existing business, expansions and contractions of business, are obvious cases where a zero-base approach to budgeting may well be taken in practice if not in name. Equally changes in the levels of economic activity, more particularly significant downturns, will in all likelihood bring about a zero-base attitude, with a thorough reappraisal and justification of all expenditure in a drive for economy.

However, recorded applications of ZBB in the UK appear to be relatively few, suggesting that the practice has not been adopted widely here in spite of its apparent value. Perhaps the differentiation between use and non-use lies in whether it is a concept fully integrated into an organization's regular budgetary cycle. In the examples cited in the previous paragraph, the events are irregular and the process thus becomes one of occasionally conducting a special exercise. By contrast, a throughgoing ZBB programme means budgeting is permanently placed on this footing. In turn the operation of such a scheme demands substantially greater administrative resources, particularly in terms of managers' and accountants' time, certainly more than traditional incremental budgeting, which possibly accounts at least in part for its failure to be adopted here on a widespread scale.

Zero-base budgeting in operation

The focus of attention of ZBB is the functions of an organization which are regarded as necessary if it is to achieve the success it aims for. Although the budgets are created from the bottom up, they are examined and filtered in accordance with organization objectives. It is the responsibility of top management to see that units are given sufficient knowledge of their objectives, and that they and senior managers understand the assumptions of the plan it is aimed to achieve. The latter should be set, of course, within the context of the organization's strategic development plans.

The mechanics of operating a scheme require a clearly recognized organizational framework, built around well defined functions. As a total entity, an organization will be composed of several functions and each of these in turn will be examined on a zero-base; it is not just individual activities which come under scrutiny, but functions as a whole will need to justify themselves.

Figure 5.1 illustrates a typical function hierarchy. The first-line 'decision packages' on which ZBB is founded are shown at the base. Assume that the function is within a large local authority and represents one with a responsibility for road construction, repairs and maintenance and road clearance. Then, following the line from the head of the function through the hierarchy:

1 Divisions could correspond to districts within the authority.
2 Departments represent various aspects of the main function, e.g. new road construction, maintenance, liaison with such other services e.g. telephones, traffic control.
3 Operating units represent individual units within the departments designated to particular aspects of the work, e.g. major/minor road construction, surveillance of major roads, flyovers and so on.

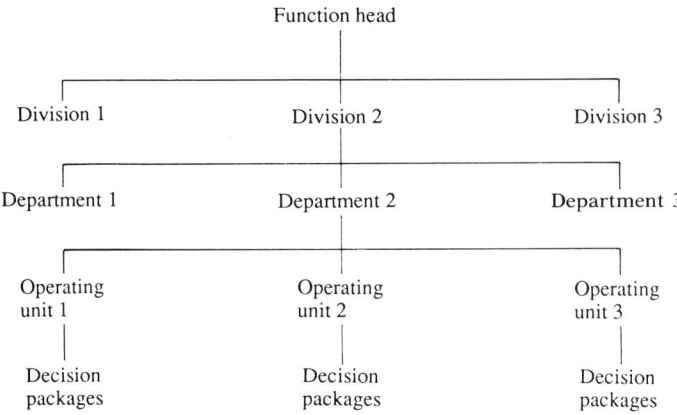

Figure 5.1 *Function hierarchy*

Each of the sections could demonstrate its operational capacities at varying levels of activity and this information would be contained in the decision packages. The departments and districts, and ultimately the function itself, are the 'decision units' whose budgets are eventually to be determined. The administration of a ZBB may thus be summarized as requiring:

(a) A statement of objectives of an organization and its functions.
(b) Identification of decision units.
(c) Identification of decision packages.
(d) A system for ranking the selection of decision packages.

Continuing the example of the local authority roads function:

1 *Function objectives* may be defined on the following lines: to ensure that (i) the provision of road capacity within the authority is sufficient to ensure a smooth, free flow of traffic; (ii) that construction of new roads is to the highest standards; and (iii) that road repairs are completed to an accepted standard, and within a specified time period of a maintenance need being reported.
2 *Decision units* are units for which the budgets are prepared. They stand above the level of operating units. In principle the selection of the levels at which decision units should be identified is on the grounds that too great a level of aggregation of activities will make it difficult to single out individual features, while too great a level of disaggregation will materially affect the cost of information preparation. In the example, the departments might well serve as the lower level of decision units. Each unit will require clear objectives to work to and will be in the charge of a responsible manager.

3   *Decision packages* are often referred to as the 'building blocks' of ZBB. Pendlebury and Jones[8] cite two types of decision package:
    (a) *Mutually exclusive*: packages which identify alternative ways of operating the unit to which they relate, including that of doing without it altogether.
    (b) *Incremental*: various levels of resource/cost input are measured against the realisation of various levels of output. Table 5.1 provides a generalized illustration of this process.
4   *Ranking decision packages.* Once the packages are completed, within each decision unit, starting at the lower levels, it will be necessary to rank the packages in priority order for selection. The process is illustrated in Table 5.1.

The 'descriptions' (Table 5.2) would refer back to those given to the specific packages within the operating unit: so, for example, four packages were identified in the case of each of the operating units listed and first priority was given to package number 2 (from the four listed) in operating unit 1. This is followed by package number 1 from unit 3 and so on. It should be noted that, provided the funds are available, higher numbered packages may be added to the list; in the above example package number 3 from operating unit 1 is ranked fourth, automatically incorporating the level of service defined in package number 2 already accorded first priority. If available funds amounted to £240,000 then this would be the level to which operating unit 1 would work. The filtering out of the decision packages would take place upwards in line with the priorities seen for the individual decision units.

If a ZBB approach were adopted within a commercial company, the rankings would probably be established more objectively than within a not-for-profit organization, since cost-benefit trade-offs can probably be quantified with a greater degree of precision and certainty. In the not-for-profit organizations, especially those in the public sector, the ranking is certain to be a more subjective process, with political value judgements likely to play a major role in determining priorities.

Conclusion

ZBB is a very formal system. It differs from the normal budgetary process in that detailed budgets are prepared at the lowest defined level of activity in a way which shows several levels of outcome starting from the zero-base, rather than from a point attained in an immediately preceding period. Instead of targets and budgets being pushed downward through the management hierarchy, here they are built upwards within a framework of known organizational objectives, with successive levels of management receiving increasing quantities of information, leading to the agreement of a conventional master budget. The link to the master budget also shows ZBB to be part of the short-term tactical planning process.

The clear merit of ZBB is to force a detailed re-evaluation of what a

Table 5.1 Incremental decision packages

	Package nos			
	1	2	3	4
Definition of level of output/activity	Minimum required to maintain a presence	Poor standard of service	Current service level	Improved standard of service
Incremental cost (£)	30,000	20,000	20,000	15,000
Cumulative total cost (£)	30,000	50,000	70,000	85,000
Comment	No more than keeps service together. Emergency cover only.	Emergency cover provided. Only 40% coverage of other demand within specified time period. Long backlog develops.	Emergency cover provided. Other demands met to 75% within time limits. Backlog of demand exists.	As with 3, but 100% of normal demand within specified time limits.

Table 5.2 Decision package ranking

Rank	Description	Package number	Incremental Cost (£)	Cumulative Total cost (£)
1	OU1	2 of 4	50,000	50,000
2	OU3	1 of 4	80,000	130,000
3	OU2	2 of 4	90,000	220,000
4	OU1	3 of 4	20,000	240,000
5	OU4	1 of 4	30,000	270,000
6	OU2	4 of 4	10,000	278,000
etc.				

function is able to achieve in order of preference in line with its objectives. Its main disadvantage is probably its own administrative cost. In theory it should be a permanent part of the budgeting cycle. Treated as a once-off blitz procedure to haul organizations back to an acceptable level of performance from a previously unacceptable one runs the obvious risk of a drift back to inefficiency once the pressure is relaxed.

Planning, programming and budgeting systems (PPBS)

Introduction

Anthony and Young[9] suggest PPBS contains three central ideas: 'first, it is a formal programming system; second, it uses a program budget as contrasted with a line by line item budget; and third, it emphasises benefit/cost analysis'.

PPBS represents one of the first moves in the public sector away from incremental budgeting towards a more formal approach both in programme structure and analysis. In contrast to incremental budgeting (and also to zero base budgeting), it is a centralized, top-down process which seeks to define clearly the objectives and sub-objectives of the various activities for which an organization may be responsible and set their achievement on to a longer-term basis. In this way it has the appeal of a rational–logical planning procedure. However, it is commonly thought[10] that the day of PPB systems has come and gone, indeed that few, if any, examples really exist that it ever had a true application. It is possible that there may be a subconscious impact on the planning systems operated within organizations induced by the exposure to the idea of PPB, but this would be difficult to prove. It is an attempt to change the way budgetary planning is done within the public sector which is thought to have failed. However, since the *concept* has the appeal of rationality, it is probably one worth keeping alive.

Background to PPBS

The 1960s was the period during which, especially within the US federal government, efforts to introduce PPB systems were actively pursued. By the early 1970s these efforts were waning, and indeed by the mid-1970s the officially inaugurated programme of the US government and experimentation with the ideas at state and local levels both within the US and UK appear to have ceased. Against the attraction of the ideas constituting PPB it is of more than academic historical interest to try to appreciate why it did not have greater success.

The PPBS framework

The contrast between PPB and the traditional incremental budgeting already referred to is best summarized as the difference between a clearly stated, planned set of long-term objectives whose resource implications have been carefully evaluated, to the case where the future is seen as more short-term, largely dependent on the extrapolation of past developments, with relatively hazy objectives, especially in the long-term, both within individual activities and activities relative to each other.

Establishing PPBS

This requires the identification and evaluation of:

1. The goals of each of the main spending programmes within an authority.
2. Each of the sub-goals whose individual achievements are an integral part of the successful accomplishment of one of the main goals. These are generally referred to as the *programme categories*.
3. The activities which in turn constitute the means by which each of the sub-goals is to be realized. These are referred to as the *programme elements*.

The starting point of determining a budget for any spending programme is agreement on what it is intended it should accomplish, not simply over the annual budget cycle period but with respect to the time properly needed to realize the goals. Not only does this give clarity of purpose, it should also provide greater stability during the period of its execution, with less susceptibility to short-term pressures for changes of direction of the kind likely to be brought about by the ever-changing political complexion of authorities (though here is also the most likely key to the failure of the idea to gain adherence).

A simple example of a PPBS structure is given in Pendlebury and Jones[11] and is reproduced here with permission. It deals with land drainage, in the context of water reorganization in England and Wales. The objective of land drainage is 'to ensure that the vital contribution of land drainage and flood protection to both urban and agricultural areas alike is maintained, and where appropriate expanded'.

Pendlebury and Jones[12] then proceed to describe and illustrate the goals, programmes, programme categories and elements along the lines of a PPB system:

> The beneficial impacts of a land drainage programme relate to the avoidance of the loss of agricultural production caused by flooding, and also the avoidance of damage to property. Providing the areas at risk can be adequately estimated it ought to be possible to express the benefits of land drainage in monetary amounts. The benefits would therefore be measured in terms of the economic consequences of avoiding crop spoilage, or livestock losses, or domestic and commercial property damage. Ideally, of course, measures reflecting the benefits of protecting human beings from death or injury, or benefits concerned with the 'quality of life' or 'peace of mind' should also be included. However, the more easily measurable economic benefits offer a starting point.
>
> The land drainage activities of water authorities are usually administered for the major catchment areas or land drainage districts of the authority and the *programmes* might include the following:
>
> Main river flood protection
> Water course flood protection
> Sea defences
> Pumping
> Flood warning
>
> Under each of the basic programmes there will be a variety of programme categories. For example, the *programme categories* for the 'sea defences' programme might include:
>
> Hard sea defences – concrete and steel defences
> Soft sea defences – earthbanks, groynes, dunes, etc.
> Dredging of estuaries
> Tidal barriers
>
> The *programme elements* and the related costs and benefits for the 'soft sea defences' programme category could then be expressed as in Table 5.3.

Each programme element would be similarly treated and evaluated; these are added to give the total costs and benefits of each programme category, leading on to the total for the category (here, land drainage) as a whole. The evaluation should be based on costs and benefits in financial terms as far as possible. In the example certain items such as loss of crops, livestock, damage to property could be given a financial value, but others such as 'peace of mind' for residents living in areas threatened by flooding would be much more difficult to appraise. Indirect measures, such as anticipated improvements to property values, may be used as surrogates for direct measures.

Table 5.3 Example of programme elements presentation showing the costs and related benefits of each programme element

Programme category 'Soft sea defences' Programme elements	Cost/benefits Monetary measures (in Year 0 prices) represented by X. Physical measures represented by Y. Year 0 = current year						
	−1	0	1	2	3	4	5
1 Existing soft sea defences							
1.9 Estimated costs	X	X	X	X	X	X	X
Estimated benefits:							
1.1 Agricultural area offered protection	Y	Y	Y	Y	Y	Y	Y
1.2 Financial benefits of 1.1	X	X	X	X	X	X	X
1.3 Urban area offered protection	Y	Y	Y	Y	Y	Y	Y
1.4 Urban population offered protection	Y	Y	Y	Y	Y	Y	Y
1.5 Financial benefits of 1.3 and 1.4	X	X	X	X	X	X	X
1.0 Total financial benefits	X	X	X	X	X	X	X
2 Extensions to soft sea defences							
2.9 Estimated costs							
Estimated benefits:	X	X	X	X	X	X	X
2.1 Agricultural area offered by protection	Y	Y	Y	Y	Y	Y	Y
2.2 Financial benefits of 2.1	X	X	X	X	X	X	X
2.3 Urban area offered protection	Y	Y	Y	Y	Y	Y	Y
2.4 Urban population offered protection	Y	Y	Y	Y	Y	Y	Y
2.5 Financial benefits of 2.3 and 2.4	X	X	X	X	X	X	X
2.0 Total financial benefits	X	X	X	X	X	X	X

Source: Pendlebury, M. and Jones, R., *Public Sector Accounting*, Pitman, 1984

In the final analysis certain items may not be amenable to direct or indirect measures, but could be judged significant or not, depending on the extent to which schemes can be appraised on land data alone.

This type of cost–benefit evaluation is the same as for ZBB in principle. The key difference between the two systems appears to be the reorganization likely to be required for PPBS in order to realize clear, specific long-term objectives for an activity. The aims, objectives, evaluation procedures and criteria for programme elements follow, being transmitted downward through the organization. In contrast, the conditions for ZBB to operate do not demand such organizational change, and the planning framework may be correspondingly less specific. Nonetheless it would seem possible for a PPB system to incorporate a ZBB approach.

Advantages of PPBS

Given the apparent unpopularity of the concept in application, 'advantages' may be thought to be limited. Looked at objectively, however, there would seem to be some substantial potential gains:

(a) It focuses on the provision of clear long-term policy aims and objectives.
(b) Activities to be linked in achieving a programme are identified and brought together.
(c) Waste is reduced by removing duplication of activities.
(d) It promotes the evaluation of resources allocation through the use of cost–benefit appraisals.

Altogether it offers a coherence to the planning process, particularly in central and local government, which could improve the level of service enjoyed from a given level of resource input by having a distinct long-run objective and avoiding the waste caused by continually chopping and changing programmes and duplicating effort.

Conclusions on PPBS

Since there is no reason to doubt the ability of personnel to develop and administer a programme, even if it is granted that some measurements of benefits may be difficult to determine, its lack of success has probably to be seen in terms of the unwillingness of persons concerned with the direction of programmes to accept such a definitive, centralized, long-term planning procedure. Party politics obviously intrudes into these areas and, with the differing emphases placed on the various aspects related to programmes which stem from differing political views, it is hardly surprising that politicians at least would prefer a looser and hence more flexible framework to work within. In addition, the need to rationalize departmental activities into matching programme areas not only affects traditional empires but it is also not necessarily easy to split joint costs in cases where more than one programme may be served by a department, e.g. the provision of schools' facilities for community leisure activities, which would entail a cost split between the education programme and say community welfare and leisure.

PPBS could well be considered a once fashionable idea that has had its day, seemingly because of human unwillingness to implement it properly. There are analogous organization problems in private sector industry where firms are divisionalized along product group or market area lines. These too must be given as much separate identification by way of objectives and criteria for judging success as possible, and are also for the most part long-term arrangements. At least at first glance they do not differ all that much from the PPBS suggestion for the public sector, yet they are made to work in practice.

It could be that in time, newly emerging, 'green-field' public sector activities could be placed at the outset on a PPBS footing. Altogether it seems to be a planning concept whose principles should continue to be borne in mind rather than written off as a failure.

Value for money (VFM) audit

Introduction

'Value for money' is virtually a generic phrase, widely used in everyday conversation, when it has little more than a subjective meaning. Increasingly it has also been taken up, especially in the public sector, to refer to schemes to reduce extravagance and waste in government departments by improving their efficiency and economy in the acquisition and use of resources. It can equally well be applied as a concept in private industry. The point is the phrase itself has little substance: it refers to no formal methodology or formulae, and its 'embodiment' is the unique detail of the programmes designed to achieve it and measure its actual accomplishment. These programmes and measures will not always readily find expression in tangible monetary valuations; resort has to be made to expressions such as 'quality of life' and other intangible attributes. Although economy and efficiency are basic ingredients in a VFM scheme, a third element, that of effectiveness, has also been added to most VFM studies, to cover the dimension of the degree to which objectives have been attained. It is a concept in many ways rather more difficult to comprehend and measure than the other two.[13]

Although a part of public sector audit practice for some time, it is probably only since the 1970s that the promotion of value for money to a specific goal has taken place in government. In 1973 the issue of an Audit Code of Practice, aimed at local authority auditors, required them to ensure that accounts being audited did not contain any significant loss arising from waste, extravagance, inefficient financial administration, poor value for money, mistake or other cause. This rather general exhortation has since been strengthened considerably, *inter alia*, by the Local Government Finance Act of 1982 and the National Audit Act of 1983.

VFM is usually referred to in the context of a VFM *audit*, so it may seem out of place in a chapter on budgetary planning. However, the nature of this kind of audit means that the reports emanating from the Audit Commission, district and local auditors are directed toward improvements which by definition will be made in the future and hence incorporated in budgets at that stage. The other side of the planning coin, control, comes through in the same reports and is given further consideration in Chapter 9.

A requirement of the 1982 Finance Act was that the local government auditor should ensure that not only are accounts properly prepared by authorities, but also that they have made *proper arrangements for securing economy, efficiency and effectiveness in the use of their resources*. It was a requirement made against the background from the mid-1970s of increasingly constrained resources available for public sector activities, the application of cash limits and demands for greater disclosure and accountability by local authorities. The move does not seem to have been a direct response to the failure of internal budgetary control systems much as ZBB and PPBS to make much impact within local authorities, though ultimately, if successful, it should result in such an improvement taking place.

The Local Government Act of 1972, stated that local authorities could choose to appoint private accounting firms instead of the district auditors to audit their accounts, but although auditing remained principally a verification process concerning legality, amounts spent and procedures followed, matters such as wasteful spending were to be investigated. Following the 1982 Finance Act, the Audit Commission was set up in 1983 as a single independent body not only to oversee auditing within local authorities but also with the wider role of improving management within authorities. Central to the latter is the value for money audit.

Once again a precursor to the application of an idea within the UK can be found in the USA, where 1972 saw the publication of the Standards for Audit of Governmental Organizations, Programs, Activities and Functions. These were revised in 1981. All US government audits are covered by the standards, and they contain reviews of economy, efficiency and effectiveness among the objectives of such audits. Pendlebury and Jones[14] point to the US example as a clear influence on developments in the UK.

Economy, efficiency and effectiveness

These qualities are defined by Glynn[15] as follows:

1   Economy: acquiring appropriate resources for the minimum cost.
2   Efficiency: seeking to ensure that the maximum output is obtained from the resources devoted to the department (or programme), or, alternatively, ensuring that only the minimum level of resources are devoted to a given level of output.
3   Effectiveness: ensuring that the output from any given activity is achieving the desired results.

Goals/objectives have to be established in order that effectiveness may be evaluated, which could be quite a difficult task in some cases. Economy and efficiency measures have to be developed in line with programme objectives: quality and cost factors are of major importance in the study of economy while efficiency – in essence a concept relating output of goods and services to a quantity of resource inputs on a standard and actual basis – requires careful attention to the development of measures of standards of performance, which in turn is not always likely to be a straightforward task.

As a brief example, consider the provision of residential care for the elderly.

To operate *economically*, the quality of resources needed to provide a defined and acceptable standard of care has to be assessed. The auditor then has to ensure that these resources have been acquired at minimum cost. This cannot be done to any absolute standard, since it must take into account local conditions, e.g. shortages of particular grades of staff, which may arise for a variety of reasons in different parts of the country.

To operate *efficiently*, authorities would need standards they could aim to achieve, subject to special local conditions. In the example the principal measure of efficiency would be the number of people given accommodation (the output) compared to the resource costs (inputs). Achieving efficiency against a standard obviously depends on examining the number of residents and the level of costs.

To operate *effectively*, the objectives of the exercise have to be defined, a problem which could be particularly difficult to resolve in the case of the present example, probably centred on the 'quality of life' provided for the residents.

The Audit Commission

This Commission came into being in 1983, bringing local authority auditing under the control of a single independent body, and having the additional responsibility of looking at the management of local government. It is a self-financing body, with most of its fees arising from its audit work in local authorities. Figure 5.2 from an Audit Commission publication,[16] shows how it is organized.

Achieving value for money

Volume 2 of the Audit Commission *Handbook*[17] quotes the level of expenditure by local authorities in the period 1984–5 as over £30 billion per annum and over £1,600 per household – substantial sums with the prospect of realizing substantial savings through the application of the 'three Es' concept. By way of further emphasizing the importance of securing proper value for money from local authorities, the *Handbook* also points out that most councils are very large organizations where even a small district employs over 500 people, putting them in terms of number of employees among the 1,000 largest industrial concerns in the UK.

The Commission recommends some 40–50 per cent of local authority auditors' time should be spent on reviewing the arrangements for securing VFM within authorities and to undertaking specific VFM projects focusing on particular services or costs. Guidance for auditors is avail-

Figure 5.2 Organizational structure of the Audit Commission

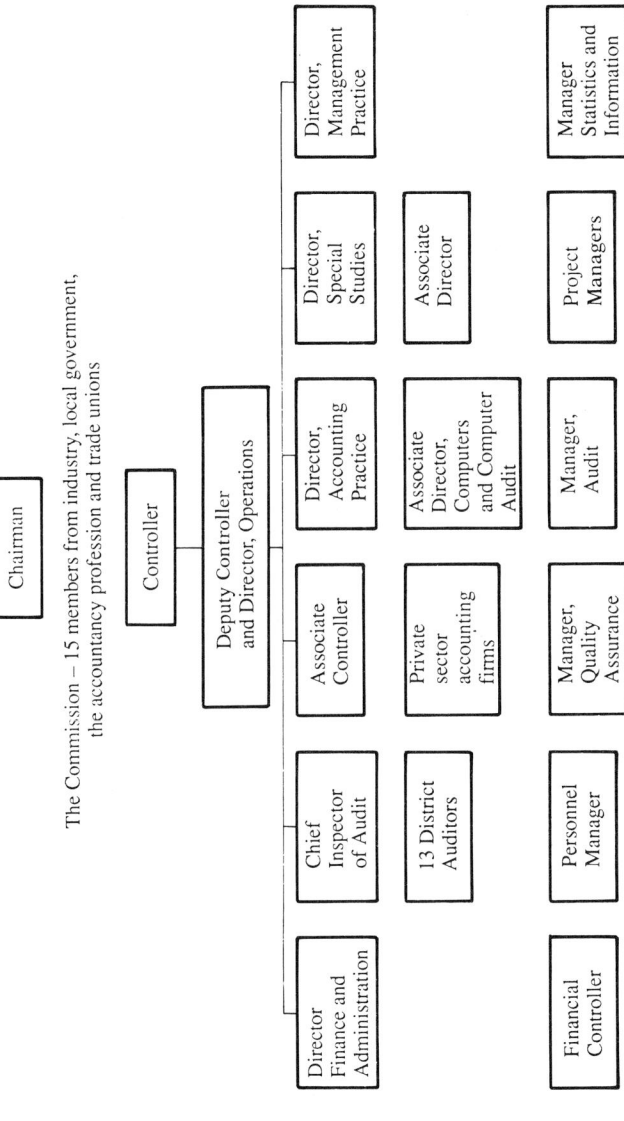

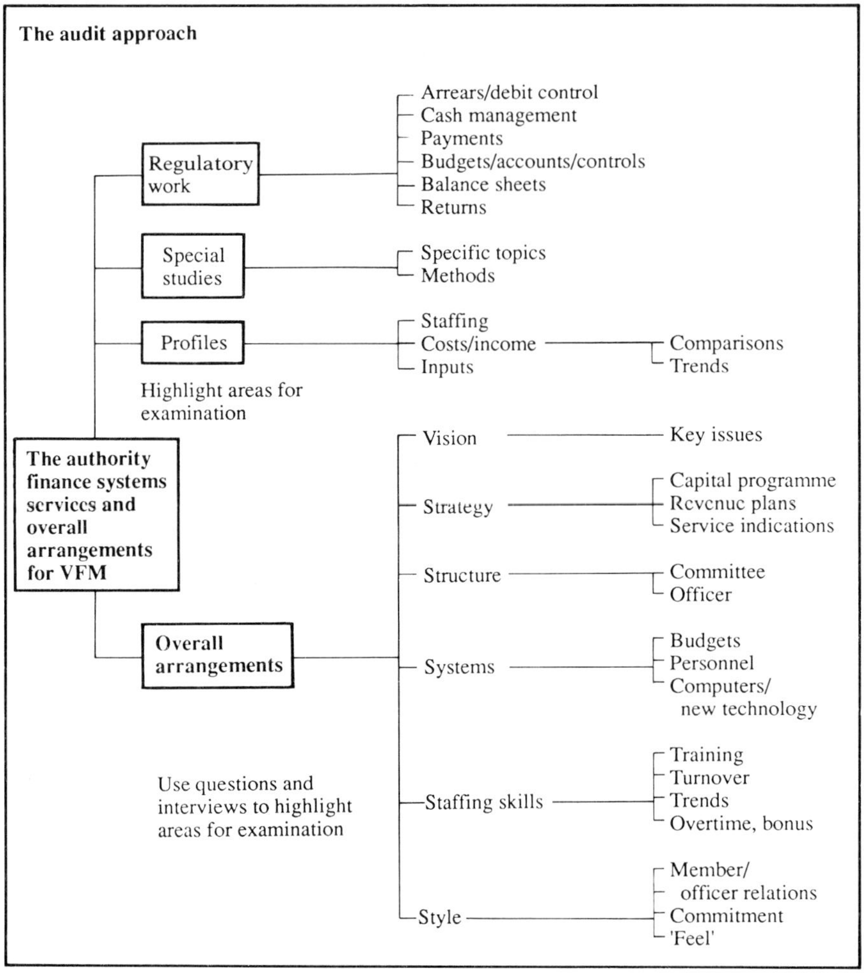

84 Control and Audit in Management Accounting

Figure 5.3 *Arrangements for securing economy, efficiency and effectiveness*

able in the form of statistical 'profiles' of different authorities, designed to help both the authority and the auditor to identify those elements of costs or those services on which attention should be concentrated. In addition, there are Audit Commission Special Studies as well as audit reports from district auditors and auditor firms.

Figure 5.3 illustrates the Audit Approach, a systematic breakdown of the approach to VFM work, showing how the various aspects are identified and relate to each other. VFM is probably most closely identified with the special studies branch, because of the publicity these receive, but the figure clearly shows a broad approach to securing improvement in local authority management.

The Audit Commission[18] also provides a working framework which

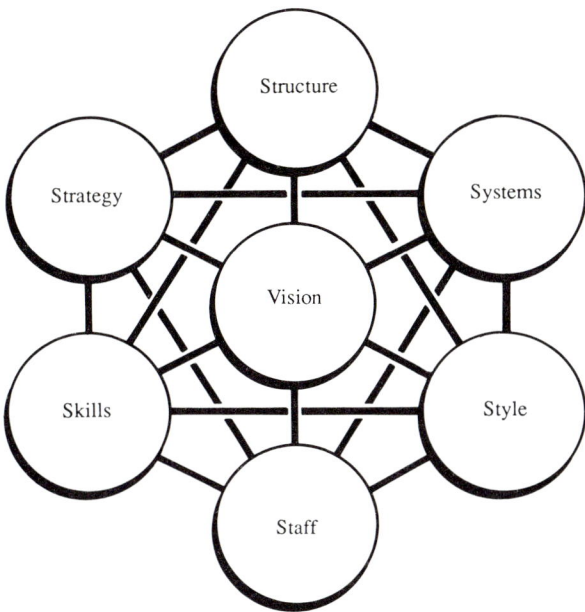

Figure 5.4 *An overall view of organization*

identifies the interrelated elements within an organization whose achievement will add up to the realization of value for money measured against objectives to be attained (Figure 5.4).

(a) *Vision*: what an authority aims to become or achieve.
(b) *Strategy*: the means by which the 'vision' is to be realized.
(c) *Structure*: how the authority, its members and staff, are organized to implement the strategy.
(d) *Systems*: the way in which the people in the organization plan, decide, control and monitor day to day actions as well as longer-term progress.
(e) *Staffing and skills*: the way in which the critical resource in every authority – people – is acquired, trained, deployed, motivated and rewarded.
(f) *Style*: the 'way we do things' and the way members, officers and employees relate to each other and to those they are to serve.

Reference will have to be made to outside political influences as well, but the above list of points serves as a starter guide on issues to be covered in a VFM audit. As an example, Figure 5.5 illustrates how this guide was used in a special study by the Commission of a central transport organization.[19]

More direct expression of guidance to auditors may be on the following lines:

86 *Control and Audit in Management Accounting*

Vision	Provide a central transport organization that will provide service departments with vehicles 20 per cent cheaper than if obtained on contract hire

Strategy	Structure	Style	Systems	Skills/staffing

• Offer a 'contract hire with maintenance' service to the users
 	
• Use available scale to negotiate better purchasing discounts on new vehicles and spare parts. Spread overheads over the whole fleet
 	
• Check internal hire rates against private firms. Users free to go outside if consistently cheaper to do so
 	
• Pool all reserve vehicles (except police and fire)
 	
• Maintain vehicles owned by police and fire (in counties)
 	
• Seek arrangements with neighbouring authorities for maintenance of out-stationed vehicles and pooling reserve specialist vehicles
 	
• Contract-out for vehicles and maintenance where more economic to do so (e.g. for specialist maintenance work, vehicles with irregular demand)
	• Central control of all transport provision and maintenance.
	
	• Maintenance treated as a separate cost centre with transport
	
	• Use outside garages for maintenance where appropriate
	
	• In countries, locate workshops close to the main users' depots
		• Run like a commercial hire firm. Non-bureaucratic approach
		
		• Treat user department as 'customers'
		
		• Liaise with neighbouring authorities
		
		• Market services to neighbouring authorities and health authorities
		
		• Council Committee agrees budget and main programme but avoids involvement in details
			• Computerized management information system
			  – utilization
			  – fuel consumption
			  – maintenance
			
			• Individual vehicle costing on a whole life basis
			
			• Easily administered bonus scheme, based on vehicle availability
			
			• Regular checking of internal charges and costs against
			  – contract hire
			  – spot hire
			  – private garages
			
			• Workshop manning levels based on support man hours
				• Lean, professional staffing (two or three central staff in a district, no more than ten in a county). Assign the following responsibilities*:
				  – procurement and disposal of vehicles
				  – customer liaison/sales manager
				  – utilization officer to co-ordinate spot hiring and secure utilization of 1,500 hours/year
				  – information officer
				  – maintenance manager, with a target of £700 per weighted vehicle
				
				• – Transport manager 'buys-in' central services (e.g. financial and legal) from Treasurer etc.
				
				* Usually, not full-time posts

Figure 5.5 *Overview of a successful transport organization*

1. Identify the central objectives of policy.
2. Examine organization structures with particular reference to (a) above.
3. Examine how well subordinate managers understand and implement policies laid down for them to follow by top management.

4 Examine information and information sources to see how well managers are served in making appropriate decisions.
5 Examine performance indicators as to their validity for measurement in given policies, programmes, departments.
6 Examine the results of the application of performance measures.

The translation of these guides into the conduct of a VFM audit takes the auditor beyond the traditional financial audit. Some of the methods and techniques which could be employed are quite technical; at all events, they may be more generally thought of as part of a much wider toolkit of business analysis. A few ideas are listed below:

- Input-based review, where the emphasis is on costs attributable to specific activities and on making cost comparisons with, *inter alia*, other areas functions, previous years and the private sector, to try to keep costs at the most economical level and make managers more cost-accountable. (There are a number of bodies from which data for this kind of comparison study may be obtained, such as The Chartered Institute of Public Finance and Accountancy (CIPFA), Local Authorities Management Services and Computer Committee (LAMSAC) and The Centre for Inter-firm Comparisons (CIFC).
- Systems-based review, where the emphasis is on the process (of the service or function) and the way in which it is organized, to try to establish the most efficient arrangements and to ensure that the system is relevant to current requirements and is being operated correctly.
- Output-based review, where the emphasis is on the outputs produced by the entity and on defining them, measuring them and comparing them with the objectives of the organization, in order to establish the most effective arrangements. Determination of acceptable performance measures must be a part of this review in the light of the difficulty likely to be experienced in measuring achievements.
- The application of particular techniques such as:

    (a) Terotechnology (or life-cycle costing), which makes a comprehensive study of projects (a well known example being the GLC island building) from design through to ultimate monitoring and control.
    (b) Value analysis and cost reduction programmes, comprising the detailed analysis of, for example, product specifications, to see whether designs may be simplified to reduce material requirements or whether specifications are simply beyond those needed for products to function to a required standard.

Audit Commission special studies

Each year a number of activities are selected for detailed examination. In the period 1984–5 four major studies were conducted, representing some £6 of expenditure; it was estimated that around £400 a year savings could be made on the operation of these services at prices then ruling without any reduction in the standard of services.

Targets and performance indicators

This section is related to the 'Local Authorities' section of Chapter 9, p. 181.

Development of target and performance indicators represents the central objective of the special studies work; these indicators are standards by which authorities may judge their success or otherwise with respect to meeting the 3Es criteria. There are no absolute values, since the circumstances of individual authorities will vary on different issues, e.g. the age structure of the population resident within a district or the degree of industrialization. Following studies conducted over a number of authorities, the Audit Commission publishes details of the approaches it considers may lead to the adoption of sound management practices.

In conjunction with the management scheme for a central transport organization illustrated in Figure 5.5, a list of indicators which may be used in measuring performance in one area of transport management, vehicle maintenance, was devised and is reproduced in Table 5.4.

The two columns of Table 5.4 labelled 'Practice' and 'Unsatisfactory practice' are yardsticks by which authorities can judge their own efficiency: the former of course represents what may be regarded as a sound performance level, while the latter, if recorded, would indicate poor performance and inefficiency in resource utilization. The concept of a 'weighted vehicle' illustrates the way in which comparative standards may be derived. Each type of vehicle operated by authorities in general is given a weight, which reflects the 'typical' extent of maintenance work it requires; and from this information it is possible to assess the total number of maintenance hours which would be required to support a vehicle fleet's operation. The accompanying report also points out the need to record reasons for poor labour utilization, such as ineffective working, undeclared lost time and so on, in order to effect proper control.

A further illustration is taken from the Commission's special study of energy management within authorities.[20] Energy costs were noted to be large, with wide variations in authorities' performance in energy management. Opportunities for saving £135 million p.a. were considered to exist, given that necessary investment and management action was undertaken.

Energy costs are of course very much related to the type and standard of buildings managed by authorities, and these vary considerably across individual authorities. In order to produce standards and comparisons, it was necessary therefore to devise a uniform indicator by which energy consumption could be measured and which allowed for factors

Table 5.4 Proposed indicators of vehicle maintenance performance 1984–5

Indicator	Practice	Unsatisfactory practice
Days off-the-road per annum		
– cars and light vans	6	12
– medium vans	10	15
– heavy goods vehicles up to 7.5T GVW	15	25
– heavy goods vehicles over 7.5T GVW	20	30
– refuse collection vehicles	25	35
Annual maintenance cost per weighted vehicle	£700	£850
(Parts cost included in above Maintenance cost)	£250	
Weighted vehicles per workshop employee (all grades)	30	
Weighted vehicles per fitter	40	
Booked hours per weighted vehicle p.a.	41	
Weighted vehicles per bay	35	
Bay utilization	70%–80%	
% Maintenance contracted out (counties)	15%	
Safety check intervals (normal mileage, excl. Special HGV)	12 weeks	

outside the immediate control of the authority, e.g. the number of hours of use, the degree of exposure of the building to the elements, the prevailing weather conditions in the locality and the floor area of the building.

The resulting measure, termed a Normalized Performance Indicator, expresses energy consumption as KWL (kilo-watt hour) per square metre of floorspace per annum, adjusted to average hours of use, normal exposure and average weather. Figure 5.6 and Table 5.5 show the range (defined as .68 of a standard deviation on either side of the mean value) in NPIs for a set of buildings commonly found within local authorities (Figure 5.6) and against a measure of standard hours of use per annum, a yardstick of efficiency and an indicator of poor efficiency (Table 5.5).

Dorset CC was used as an example to illustrate the potential benefits of an energy-saving programme, which showed a reduction of 23 per cent in energy used over a 5-year period and cumulative savings always exceeding cumulative investment, making the programme self-financing throughout. It is through studies such as these, as well as direct audit work, that information is fed back into authorities in a way which shows the potential for improvement in particular areas where it arises. Budgets can then be drawn up around targets aiming to realize these benefits in the future. However, one must still recognize the difficulties.

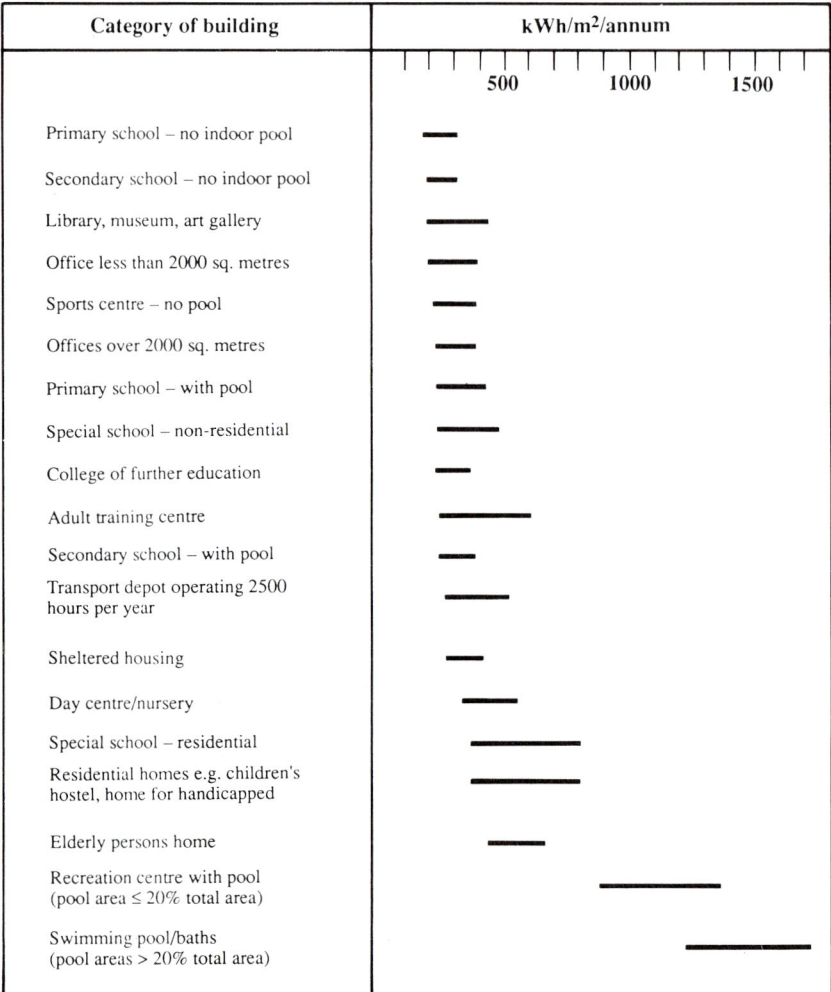

Figure 5.6 *Range in normalized performance indicators for different categories of building (normalized performance indicator kWh/m²/annum)*

Problems of VFM auditing

These are numerous, as will have become clear to readers already. They arise in the main from the immense range of applications and in particular from the difficulties in arriving at objective evaluations of concepts such as 'output'. Some aspects are described as follows:

- Outputs may be hard to define and measure. With hospitals, residential homes, and educational establishments it is easy to

Table 5.5 Normalized performance indicators

Category of building	Standard hours of use per annum	Yardstick of efficiency kWh/m²/annum	Indicator of poor efficiency
Primary school, no indoor pool	1,480	180	320
Primary school with indoor pool	1,480	230	440
Secondary school, no indoor pool	1,660	190	300
Secondary school with indoor pool	2,000	250	390
Special school, non-residential	1,570	230	490
College of further education	2,530	230	370
Special school, residential	8,760	380	820
Adult training centre	2,150	250	620
Elderly persons' home	8,760	450	680
Day centre/day nursery	2,200	330	590
Residential home (e.g. children's home, hostel, home for handicapped)	8,760	380	820
Sports centre, no pool	4,700	220	410
Leisure/recreation centre with pool*	4,800	900	1,400
Swimming pool/baths**	4,000	1,250	1,750
Library/museum/art gallery	2,540	200	440
Offices over 2,000m²	2,600	230	390
Offices less than 2,000m²	2,400	200	400
Transport depot, operating approx. 2500 hours per annum	2,500	270	520
Sheltered housing	8,760	270	430

* Pool area less than 20% of total area.
** Pool area more than 20% of total area.

Source: Consumption data on about 3,200 buildings from thirty authorities analysed in the special study.

measure the number of people processed and produce a cost per person (e.g. £150 per person per week) to measure efficiency. But people are not identical. In a hospital a patient for heart surgery is more expensive than one having tonsils removed. Young children and incontinent geriatrics are more expensive to keep in homes that fit retired people. Medical students cost more than history students.

- Emphasis on unit costs suggests that throughput should be increased to keep unit costs down. This can usually be done by sacrificing quality. Graduates can be produced very cheaply if there is very little tuition or examining. A social worker could easily deal with two or three times as many clients, but the value of a 5-minute visit by a social worker once a month may be negligible. An

apparently efficient organization, with low unit costs, may be lowering the quality of its output and failing to achieve its (especially longer-term) objectives.
- Effectiveness is much more difficult to define and measure. Often objectives are not clear, and may be conflicting. A police force could be thought more effective if it succeeded at crime prevention than if it prosecuted large numbers of offenders and vice versa. The objectives of an education system may not be adequately assessed in terms of numbers of examination successes. In seeking a measure for effectiveness these measurable achievements may be given undue emphasis at the expense of less measurable achievements. The danger is that the only things that count are the things that can be counted.
- As costs are easier to define and measure than outputs or objectives, VFM auditors may tend to concentrate on costs. Emphasis on costs in practice may lead to undue stress on the organization's own revenue expenditure, to short-term decisions rather than long-term implications, to too little regard being given to capital expenditure, the best use of assets and to costs to society. A unit in one area (a hospital ward, or a home) may be closed down, but this could result in greater costs being incurred elsewhere. Further social work visits could result in more children being taken into care or more people returning to crime and prison. It is much more difficult to assess these longer-term costs to society.
- Even efficiency is not a clinically neutral concept. If any job is very narrowly defined, it is usually possible to find a cheaper way of doing it, by employing lower grade staff, for example. But most jobs contain more than narrow definitions might imply (hospital cleaners for example tend to talk to patients, pass important information to nursing staff and do other odd jobs). Most jobs require flexibility in changing circumstances. Relatively untrained staff who are perfectly capable of fulfilling the minimum requirements of a job, for example, may be quite inadequate in changed circumstances, which may lead to disaster in an emergency.
- In commenting on effectiveness the auditor is in danger of concerning himself with policy issues. It may appear legitimate to comment on the effectiveness, for example, of regional aid policies, but even here policy questions are raised. It may be sensible to subsidize motor manufacturers moving to unemployment blackspots in Scotland or elsewhere, but the use of equivalent incentives for construction related to North Sea oil (which cannot go elsewhere) may not be a very effective policy or an efficient use of resources.
- VFM auditors are inevitably dependent on those who work within an organization to supply them with the information they need to prepare their reports. Internal management may be reluctant to supply them with information likely to lead to critical reports. Many management accountants are well practised in supplying suitably partial explanations which satisfy external auditors who have little

real knowledge of the organization they are examining, or of the extent and limitations of information produced.

VFM conclusion

Preparing the groundwork for value for money audits is not a task that can be carried out overnight; comprehensive coverage of all local authority activities will take time. In many respects it is early days to assess the impact of the approach on the management of local authorities. There have been warnings that authorities have not been moving very quickly to secure the improvements on locally agreed VFM projects and that auditors have not been properly reporting on unsatisfactory progress.[21] The Audit Commission has produced a framework for studying authorities' management arrangements and given them guidance on how to make improvements, but it has no direct power to enforce the necessary actions.

This section has concentrated on local authorities because the implementation of VFM appraisal appears to have been put on to a more routine basis with them than other public sectors. However, central government has conducted similar enquiries through the Rayner reports and the National Audit Office: the 1983 National Audit Act required the Comptroller and Auditor General to review the 3Es in central government departments, while the Monopolies and Mergers Commission has done the same for nationalised industries.

Finally, however, commitment to secure the improvements must come from within the public sector organizations themselves.

The Cambridgeshire Experiment

All secondary schools in Cambridgeshire from mid-1987 were given responsibility for managing their own finances, within given cash limits.[22] The local authority gave the opportunity to schools to manage their financial affairs, thereby relieving itself of much detailed financial planning, and by monitoring schools directly in this activity hopes to achieve a more effective distribution of funds granted. Before the full scheme was initiated, a pilot scheme lasting 4 years was undertaken in seven schools. Their experience proved that this would be a generally beneficial scheme, hence the extension to all schools.

The financial management and budgeting responsibility being devolved to schools covers the major proportion of their expenditures, including teaching staff, some non-teaching staff and an extensive list of other items, ranging from rent and rates, fuel and light to office expenses, library books, educational visits – virtually all the normally identified expenditure headings. In the pilot scheme schools were permitted to change amounts spent under different headings, and over and under spends have been permitted to be carried forward from year to year. Schools are provided with information monthly on expenditure against budget to assist the management process.

Initial results, as stated, were encouraging, showing that decentralization had resulted in more effective management of funds, with schools able to create and keep within their budgets as well as being able to generate earnings and be able to spend more on books, materials, and so on. Effectiveness in achieving targets was displayed, as was efficiency in the conversion of resource inputs to outputs. In principle other social services could be treated the same way, and of course, other councils will be encouraged to adopt the same process.

A recent Audit Commission report[23] provides considerable support for the wide extension of this approach within education authorities.

General conclusions

Budgeting in NFP organizations is a far from straightforward task. It would be unwise to be dogmatic about how it should be carried out. Under the circumstances it is more than probable that useful ideas on budgetary planning, using the term in a comprehensive sense, can be gained from each of the approaches outlined in the chapter. Outright rejections of one approach in favour of another suggest a singularity of circumstance which is altogether at variance with the complexities of reality. In principle at least there seems no reason why within limits an integration of the various courses of action should not be attempted.

Finally, let us remind ourselves that the NFP budgetary problem is not confined to the purely NFP area alone, but is present, perhaps increasingly so, among the activities of normal commercial organisations.

References

1. Anthony, R.N., *Financial Accounting in Non-business Organisations*, Financial Accounting Standards Board, Connecticut, 1978.
2. Pendlebury, M., *Management Accounting in Local Government*, Chartered Institute of Management Accountants, 1985.
3. Pendlebury, M. and Jones, R. *Public Sector Accounting*, Pitman, 1984.
4. Butt, H. and Palmer R., *Value for Money in the Public Sector. The Decision Maker's Guide*, Blackwell, 1985.
5. *Management Accounting. Official Terminology*, Chartered Institute Management Accountants, 1986.
6. Pendlebury and Jones, *op. cit.*, p. 88.
7. Lyden, F.J. and Miller, E.M., *Public Budgeting, Program Planning and Implementation*, 4th edition, Prentice-Hall 1982, Chapters 11 and 17.
8. Pendlebury and Jones, *op. cit.*

9 Anthony, R.N. and Young, G.W., *Management Control in Non Profit Organisations*, Irwin, 1984.
10 Pendlebury and Jones, *op. cit*; Lyden and Miller, *op. cit.*
11 Pendlebury and Jones, *op. cit.*
12 *Ibid.*
13 Tomkins, C., *Achieving Economy, Efficiency and Effectivness*, Institute of Chartered Accountants of Scotland, 1987.
14 Pendlebury and Jones, *op. cit.*, p. 288.
15 Glynn, J.J., *Value for Money Auditing in the Public Sector*, Institute of Chartered Accountants of England and Wales, 1985.
16 Audit Commission for Local Authorities in England and Wales, *Auditing Local Government. A Guide to the World of the Audit Commission*, 1984.
17 *Audit Commission Handbook*, Vol. II, *Improving Economy, Efficiency and Effectiveness in Local Government in England and Wales*, December 1984.
18 *Ibid.*
19 *Ibid.*
20 Audit Commission, *Saving Energy on Local Government Buildings*, November 1985.
21 Barker, Kate, 'Commission Puts Onus on Auditors', *Accountancy Age*, 16 January 1987.
22 Burgess, T., 'Cambridgeshire's Financial Management Initiative for Schools', *Public Money*, Vol. 6, No. 1, June 1986.
23 Audit Commission, *Delegation of Management Authority to Schools*, HMSO, June 1988.

Questions

1 (a) In the 1982 Local Government Act in the United Kingdom a specific duty was laid on local authority auditors to promote 'value for money'. You are required to explain the scope and significance of the introduction of this requirement in the context of accounting for local authority expenditure.

(b) Using the information on Dorsetcc obtained by the Audit Commission through the appraisal of certain local authority expenditures (page 89 et seq.) you are required to present a report analysing how the information could be applied in improving 'value for money' within an authority.

Note: A Normalized Performance Indicator (NPI) is the annual energy consumption expressed as $kW/h/m^2$ (kilowatts per hour per square metre) of floor space, adjusted to average hours of use, normal exposure and average weather.

(CIMA, November 1987 (adapted))

6 Assessing performance in businesses

Introduction

This and the following three chapters will consider the application of performance measurement to various aspects of business operations and in particular the role of accounting measures in performance evaluation. These considerations should be related to the preceding chapters on budgets and budgetary control.

Objectives, rewards, measurement and motivation

One of the most complex aspects of business operations in recent years has been the attempt by senior management to motivate employees at all levels of the organization towards the achievement of (senior management's) corporate organizational goals. Such approaches usually centre around the creation of reward/penalty systems, thus requiring the development of suitable feedback and formal performance evaluation systems and criteria.

Figure 6.1 attempts to illustrate the complex interrelationships between goals, reward systems, performance evaluation systems and aspects of behaviour within and without organizations.

The distinctions between corporate goals and those of stakeholders in a business, particularly those of shareholders, senior management and other managers and employees should be familiar to the reader. Naturally, as corporate goals are established by senior management, a greater congruence is likely to exist between corporate goals and these managers' individual personal goals than with the goals of other stakeholders in the business. That is not to say, however, that corporate goals simply represent the agreed common personal goals of senior managers, for it is likely that senior management's perception of other stakeholders'

Assessing performance is businesses 97

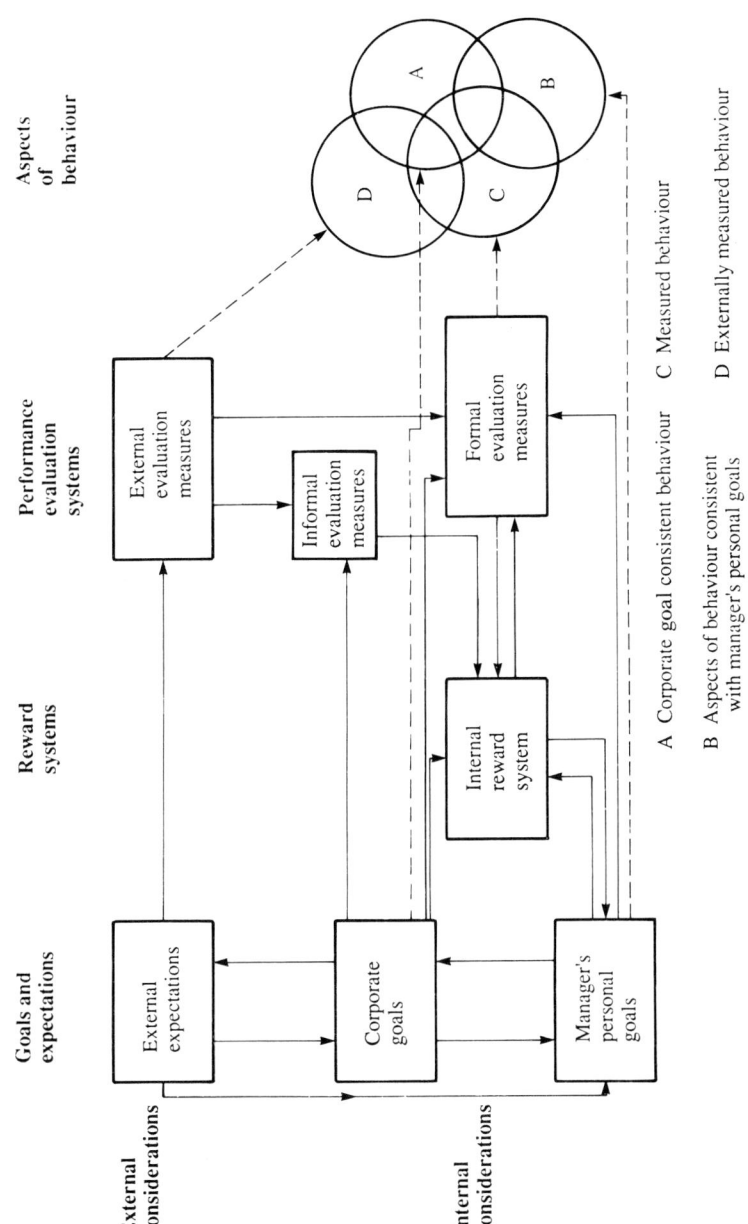

Figure 6.1 *Goal, reward, evaluation and behaviour relationships (Adapted from Hopwood, A., Accounting and Human Behaviour)*

expectations and the expectations of those external to the business, such as financiers and the stock exchange, will be considered and incorporated.

The linking of personal rewards of employees and managers (including senior management) to their achievement of some or all parts of the corporate objectives of an organization is today a most popular approach to the motivation of managers at all levels. The establishment of such reward systems must necessarily be dependent upon the establishment of suitable and relevant information systems and evaluation measures.

While formal evaluation measures might be expected to reflect the quantification of corporate goals, they frequently also incorporate elements of both an individual manager's personal goals and those goals assumed as necessary to meet external expectations. The reliance upon financial or accounting measures as the basis for most evaluation criteria probably stems from the nature of corporate objectives on the one hand, and the difficulty in quantifying non-financial objectives, on the other. This places a significant responsibility upon financial management to identify criteria which (i) have a congruence or positive correlation with corporate objectives, (ii) strike a balance between cost, profitability, liquidity and quantitative measures, (iii) reflect both long- and short-term aspects of goal achievements, (iv) are measurable consistently and fairly over time, and (v) have a minimum of interdependency on the actions and results of other segments and individuals of the organization.

In this respect some basic questions needs to be addressed. Should the yardsticks adopted, whatever they might be, reflect (i) internal considerations alone or those of external comparators such as other organizations; (ii) behavioural considerations and employee morale, e.g. be established with or without participation; and (iii) short- or longer-term achievements and objectives?

Curiously perhaps, in many organizations the formal performance evaluation methods to which a manager is subject frequently contain measures of greater variety than those adopted as the basis of the (financial) internal reward system. Further, the reward system criteria adopted are frequently those of short-term measures and not those of the long term. While it may be pointed out that quick rewards reinforce behaviour more effectively than those which are remote from specific actions, there should be concern that such an approach encourages suboptimization, e.g. the maximization of short-term performance at the expense of the long term.

The behavioural implications of the foregoing are not insignificant. Obviously the greater the congruence between the corporate goals and those of individual managers, the more likely that those goals will be achieved. The feedback of the performance evaluation and reward systems is likely to further enhance this likelihood. The corollary, however, is that goals whose performance is not reported upon are less likely to be striven for by managers, and are therefore less likely to be achieved, unless of course they coincide with individual managers' own personal goals. Management might therefore be tempted to adopt a number of performance and reward measures that reflect the totality of corporate goals, a course which in practice would probably be both impracticable and counter-productive. Management therefore faces a dilemma – the desire for a comprehensive, multifaceted measure on the one hand and an easily understood, attention directing measure on the other – a choice of some significance to the success of an organization.

This and the following chapters consider a variety of performance measures and their applicability to particular situations and in relation to the problems raised in the foregoing paragraph. In particular this chapter will consider the application of inter-firm comparisons as a basis for performance measurement both of one's own business and of others in which one may be interested.

Inter-firm comparisons

Businesses, whether independent limited companies or public limited companies, divisions, subsidiaries or operating units, find it both necessary and beneficial to compare themselves with similar organizations, particularly those with whom they directly compete.

The purposes of such comparisons are likely to be:

- With a view to improving business performance, and to identify those areas of their business which are comparatively/relatively weak and with scope for improvement.
- To examine the business as others would, to understand more clearly:

    (i) The likely prospects, potential and costs of raising equity and/or loan finance.
    (ii) The organization's relative attractiveness (or otherwise) and the potential 'threats' of takeover bids, disposal or closure.
    (iii) How customers, suppliers, trade unions, employees and others might view the status of the business in respect of their interest in it.

- As an aid to strategic and managerial planning, to identify the relative strengths and weaknesses of the business, particularly in relation to those of competitors both present and prospective. Further, to relate these to perceived opportunities and threats in the formulation and selection of strategic and tactical alternatives.

Inter-firm comparisons tend to concentrate, in the first instance, on financial data through the analysis of published reports and accounts, using ratio analysis and industry/governmental statistics. While this aspect of comparison will be considered first in this chapter, in prac-

100   Control and Audit in Management Accounting

tice other less publicized sources of information may be just as important.

Financial ratio analysis

Financial ratio analysis is usually illustrated in texts via skeletal analysis concentrating upon:

1   Operating performances, in the areas of profitability, cost control and asset utilization, using a pyramidic analysis of the ROCE ratio.[1]
2   Financing and liquidity ratios, concentrating on equity and medium and short-term borrowed capital sourcing and gearings.
3   Investment return ratios.[2]

These ratios may then be compared with alternative yardsticks of:

(a)   Past periods, in order to demonstrate trends.
(b)   Data of other companies.
(c)   Industry or governmental indices.
(d)   Budgets for the same period (which are only likely to be available to the managers within a business and not to outsiders).

The art of financial analysis lies in the selection of sufficient suitable and comparable ratios and yardsticks, and the interpretation of these measures *as a whole* – a process which has been likened to the examination of a patient by a doctor, i.e. selecting relevant questions, taking measurements (temperature, pulse, etc.), identifying symptoms and making a diagnosis. It should be remembered, however, that, as in the medical analogy, (a) good diagnoses can usually only be made from a variety of corroborating evidence, (b) relevant experience of similar situations in the past is an invaluable aid, and (c) symptoms usually lead to probable diagnoses at best, certainty being a rare commodity in most instances.

Limitations of ratio analysis

The usefulness of financial ratios may be limited by:

- The differences in accounting policies adopted by companies in areas such as fixed asset depreciation and revaluation, stock valuation, bad debt provisions, R & D and goodwill write-offs, and profit recognition.
- Differences and changes in asset ownership, renting and leasing practices.
- Difficulties in consistent interpretation of ratios over time and between organizations.
- Changes in the value of money over time.
- Differences in the trading environments over the periods being compared.

- Window dressing of financial statements to hide short-term fluctuations.
- Difficulties in deciding on a suitable yardstick and the direction of change, i.e. while a higher ROI or EPS can generally be considered good, a higher acid test ratio is more difficult to interpret.
- Historic performance only being of relevance if it can reasonably be considered as relevant to future activity.

These factors will be examined in more detail in the following chapter.

Internal or external comparisons

The yardsticks relating to external business are limited, the amount, content and format of data businesses are required to divulge to others being partly stipulated by law, partly influenced by accounting standards and partly by the quotation requirements of stock exchanges. Additionally, of course information is given 'confidentially' to government and trade organizations, aggregated with that of other organizations and made available in statistical or general terms only. While information gleaned from reports and accounts tends to be mainly financial, that available from trade and governmental statistics often includes both financial and quantitative data, often statistically analysed into, for example, quartiles, deciles, means, etc. Such quantitative data, otherwise held confidentially within a business, may then be usefully compared with these statistics as a further and perhaps very different perspective on the performance of an organization. The accuracy of source data, its comparability with that of other businesses and the delay before such statistics are available are considered by many to reduce any value such data may have as comparators, but this is probably an overly negative view.

The value of physical and quantitative information, even if limited to that within an organization, e.g. trends over time and against budget, is considered by many to be a useful, even vital explanatory and indicative adjunct to the financial comparisons and ratios available within the organization and in relation to external entities.

Adjuncts to ratio analysis data

No ratio analysis of an organization's financial statements would be complete without an attempt to refine the diagnosis reached by the search for additional and/or corroborative evidence from other 'public' sources. These are likely to include:

- The *report* that comes with the accounts and in particular the directors' report (and the chairman's report if given). This in any event contains the minimum data prescribed by the Companies Acts as well as other gratuitous data. Copies of the report and accounts may be obtained from Companies House when registered, but earlier

copies may be obtained for public companies by the purchase of shares in that business.
- **Share ownership**, which entitles the shareholder to attend the AGM and question the directors and auditors regarding the conduct of the business and the content of the annual accounts.
- **Prospectuses**, prepared either in the raising of new finance or in compliance with stock-exchange flotations contain information which may not be available elsewhere.
- **The Press** – financial, national, trade and local.
- **Bankers, brokers and investment advisors** have sources of data not available to others and are in the business of analysing this data in order to advise their clients and customers.
- **Audit rating organizations** such as Dunn & Bradstreets.
- **Statistical and market research of trade associations** (although these may only be available to contributors).
- **The PR and marketing literature** of organizations; their products current, new and deletions; and the price lists, including perhaps discount structures, etc.

The reader may well add other items to the list, particularly those related to businesses in particular industry or market sectors. The point must be made that sources of data which can corroborate or refute analyses of financial statements are an important and integral aspect of meaningful ratio analysis. It is as vital that an organization is as aware as possible of these sources. A business is not judged solely by its financial statements: it is the 'package' of information available to the outside world which influences the judgement made of the business.

Assessing competition

As indicated earlier, one of the prime uses of inter-firm comparisons by businesses is, as part of long-term planning, the need to identify their own strengths and weaknesses in relation to that of their competitors.

The foregoing inter-firm comparisons can provide some useful insights into a competitor's business. However, there is likely to be a real barrier to a meaningful analysis of many competitors, which are likely to be operating units, subsidiaries or divisions of a group, their operations, finances, assets and profitabilities being aggregated with those of other parts of the group. In those circumstances, while some segmental information is required to be given in the annual report, e.g. sales and profitability by the main sectors of a group's business, such information tends to be of minimal value in the investigation of a competitor.

However, it could also be argued that where a competitor is part of a group of companies, it is the group as a whole which provides at least some of the strengths (or weaknesses) of the competitor. For example, whatever the 'paper' finances of a competitor, in practice it is the ability and willingness of the group as a whole to raise finance efficiently that is the real strength or otherwise of that business. Thus

Assessing performance in business

it might prove harder to win a war of attrition against a competitor which is part of a large group than against one which is not – one reason why many analysts argue that in the aero engines market Rolls-Royce operates at a significant disadvantage against its main American competitors, which are part of very large conglomerates, such as General Electric Co.

It is quite conceivable, however, that such strength could be quite illusory in some situations. Would a group support a cash-hungry business if its forecast profitability over the next few years was poor? Might this not depend upon the alternative demands for resources from other parts of a group? Is a competitor which is but a small part of a large group's portfolio of companies more vulnerable to cash constraints, closure or disposal than if it were independent, larger or part of a smaller group?

On the other hand, large groups, and particularly conglomerates, frequently demonstrate a reluctance to support operating units or divisions which are either cash-hungry or have low short- or medium-term profitability prospects, particularly if, or as a result, they do not fit into the group's long-term product strategies.

The investigation of a competitor tends to be a complex task. Moreover, it could be argued that any such financially based analysis is likely to be of less relevance to the design of business tactics and strategies than that of a competitor's operational capabilities and plans.

In an increasingly complex business world, confidentiality and secrecy are scarce commodities. Diligent investigators have a variety of means of gaining information about their competitors' capabilities and activities – 'tapping the information grapevine'. These information sources are likely to include:

1 Broker, banker, credit agency and inter-firm comparison reports, bearing in mind that each may well receive information not directly available to others.
2 The press, bearing in mind newspapers and periodicals appear able to attract disclosures of confidential information from disaffected, injudicious, publicity-seeking or simply greedy employees.
3 Trade association and chamber of commerce meetings, exhibitions and promotional material.
4 Equipment and material suppliers, advertising media and agencies and customers.
5 Market research, including perhaps observation of a competitor's operating units. One business before a takeover bid employed investigators to sit outside its victim's premises, logging comings and goings and interviewing employees when entering or leaving.
6 'Visiting' the competitor's operations. While simply walking in to a competitor's premises is less easy in this security-conscious world than it used to be, many organizations are prepared to show visitors around. This might apply to the general public, students, customers, suppliers, outside maintenance staff, etc.

7 Buying in expertise, i.e. the employees of competitors or their business advisers.
8 Nefarious activities such as bribery, bugging and industrial espionage in general.

All illustration of a competitor assessment is provided by the Stapylton, company,[3] of which the following is a resumé:

> S, a wholly owned subsidiary of a very large international group, was a manufacturer of hygiene and cleaning materials sold directly to retailers, principally supermarket chains. One major quality product with a good market share was sold with distinctive packaging at a premium price in competition with own label and other named brands. Competition arose from a major competitor whose major product had been losing market share.
> S collected competitive awareness information by a variety of means: weekly surveys by sales staff of retailers, the collection of competitors' and retailers' advertising material, monthly market survey reports undertaken by an agency, examination of press reports, brokers' reports, regular contacts with suppliers both of equipment and raw materials and various financial reports. This information was used in a routine way in regular management meetings, where consideration of competitors was a recurrent agenda item.
> A small Scottish retail chain had been threatening not to stock the L brand. In order not to lose the customer, L gave the retailer advance information about its product repackaging and reduced selling prices. This information was then used by the retailer to attempt to lever lower prices from S.
> S already had a good idea of L's operational capabilities, gleaned over time from equipment suppliers and certain customers during 'own-label' negotiations. L's production methodology, although different to that of S's main product, was very similar to that used by S for 'own label' production. This enabled S to forecast reasonably accurately the cost and revenue structure of the L product. Although L was part of a small group, the data could be crosschecked against the annual report and accounts, as L's product range was dominated by the product of interest. Additionally, indicators of capital investment plans and labour changes were usually outlined in the group's directors' report. This data was further crosschecked against the investment analyst reports of specialist stockbrokers.
> In order to judge their response, S needed to establish:
>
> (i) Whether L's operating capabilities had changed. Discussions with processing and packaging-equipment manufacturers indicated no change in these areas. This was confirmed by the sales literature given to the Scottish retailer, and enabled S to estimate L's product's variable and prime costs.
> (ii) What costs L was expending on operating charges and, in particular, in advertising costs. The latter was indicated partly by L's own literature, and partly by advertising agencies hoping to persuade S to match L's expenditures.
>
> This additional information, together with that already obtained, effectively enabled S to produce a 'financial model' of the L operation and

deduce from this its management's thinking, the volumes and market shares needed to justify its strategic change, etc., etc.

S was now in a significantly better position to consider and evaluate its response. Alternative tactics and strategies were considered and their likely impacts upon both S and L evaluated both as a means of maintaining a competitive advantage and to better anticipate any further reaction from L to S's responses.

The authors have become increasingly aware over recent years that corporate assessments are an increasing part of the industrial and commercial scene. For example, competitive assessment is used in strategic and tactical planning, and managerial, valuation and profitability assessments in takeover and divestment situations.

As the Stapylton example indicates, however, it is necessary to obtain confirmatory evidence whenever possible, as most sources of information will not be completely reliable. The greater the confirmatory evidence, the greater the certainty and the more confidently the data can be used. When important decisions are at hand, businesses cannot afford too many guesses.

Finally, while businesses are obviously concerned with investigating those other businesses they are interested in, they should not forget that the reverse may be true – they are being investigated and evaluated, too!

References

1 CIMA, *Official Terminology*, 1986, Figure 8.2, p. 101.
2 *Ibid.*, Figure 8.1, p. 94.
3 For the Stapylton company, see Coates, J.B., Rickwood, C.P. and Stacey, R.J., 'Examination of the Differences Between Academic Concepts and Actual Management Accounting Practices', Report to ESRC, British Library Document Supply Centre, August 1987; and Rickwood, C.P., Coates, J.B. and Stacey, R.J., 'Managed Costs and the Capture of Information', *Accounting and Business Research*, Vol. 17, No. 68, Autumn 1987.

Questions

1 Why are inter-company comparisons of doubtful value today as bases for comparison?
2 Why are governmental statistics of little value as a basis for performance appraisal of any one company?
3 (a) List and explain the means by which you would investigate the affairs of a potential takeover target.
   (b) What role in the appraisal should the financial team play and why?

106 Control and Audit in Management Accounting

4 What routine information would you expect to gather on your competitors if you were:

   (a) a large retailer
   (b) a large manufacturer of consumer products, or
   (c) a small manufacturer of industrial products?

5 *Celle Engineering Co. Ltd – financial measurement*

The balance sheet of Celle Engineering Co. Ltd for the last 3 years is as follows:

	Year 1 £		Year 2 £		Year 3 £	
Fixed assets						
Plant original cost	270,000		500,000		708,000	
Less depreciation	70,000	200,000	108,000	392,000	158,000	550,000
Current Assets						
Stocks	200,000		300,000		500,000	
Debtors	200,000		220,000		250,000	
Cash	40,000		20,000		–	
	440,000		540,000		750,000	
Current liabilities	240,000		284,000		250,000	
Net current assets		200,000		256,000		500,000
Total assets less liabilities		400,000		648,000		1,050,000
Creditors over 1 year (loans)		–		220,000		572,000
Net assets		400,000		428,000		478,000
Capital and reserves						
Ordinary share of £1		300,000		300,000		300,000
Profit and loss account		100,000		128,000		178,000
Shareholders' funds		400,000		428,000		478,000

Turnover and profits in the 3 years were as follows:

	Year 1	Year 2	Year 3
Turnover	£1,000,000	£1,200,000	£1,500,000
Net profit (before loan interest)	£80,000	£128,000	£210,000
Net profit (before tax)	£80,000	£108,000	£150,000
Net profit (after tax)	£52,000	£70,000	£97,500
Net profit (after tax and dividends)	£14,000	£28,000	£50,000

By ratio analysis (a) indicate changes in the financial affairs of the company over the 3 years, and (b) suggest how (i) shareholders and (ii) bankers would view its management's performance and financial situation.

6 **BF (Engineering) Ltd**
   Financial measurement balance sheets as at 31 December

		Year 1 £000		Year 2 £000		Year 3 £000	
Fixed assets:							
Land and buildings	– Cost		185		185		185
Plant	– Cost	800		900		900	
	– Dep'n	400	400	470	430	540	360
			585		615		545
Current assets:							
Stock		150		255		343	
Debtors		150		255		294	
Cash/Liquid Assets		15		–		–	
		315		510		637	
Current liabilities:							
Creditors		150		128		123	
Overdraft		–		164		253	
		150		292		376	
Net Current Assets			165		218		261
Total Assets less current liabilities			750		833		806
Creditors over 1 year			150		250		250
Net assets			600		583		556
Capital and reserves							
Ordinary share capital (£1)			400		400		400
Reserves (retained profit)			200		183		156
Shareholders' funds			600		583		556
PROFIT AND LOSS STATEMENT FOR YEAR							
Turnover (sales)			900		1,020		1,176
Less costs:	Depreciation	60		70		70	
	Overdraft int.	–		12		46	
	Other costs	732	792	867	949	990	1,106
Operating profit			108		71		70
Less: loan interest			18		36		45
Profit before tax			90		35		25
Tax			45		12		12
Profit after tax			45		23		13
Dividends			40		40		40
RETAINED PROFITS			5		(17)		(27)

BF (ENGINEERING) LIMITED
RATIO ANALYSIS

		Year 1	Year 2	Year 3
1	Op. profit: sales	12%	7%	6%
2	Sales: capital employed	1.2	1.22	1.46
3	Op. profit: capital employed	14.4%	8.5%	8.7%
4	Sales: plant	2.25	2.37	3.27
5	Sales: stock	6 (2 months)	4 (3 months)	3.4 ($3\frac{1}{2}$ months)
6	Sales: debtors	6 (2 months)	4 (3 months)	4 (4 months)
7	Current ratio (CA:CL)	2.1	1.75	1.69
8	Acid test (CA-Stock:CL)	1.1	0.8	0.78
9	Gearing (loans:CE)	20%	30%	31%
10	Interest cover (Op. profit: Loan interest)	6 times	2 times	1.5 times
11	Earnings per share (Profit after tax / No. of shares)	11.25p	5.75p	3.25p

Op. profit before O/D int:sales $\quad \frac{108}{900} = 12\%\quad\quad \frac{83}{1{,}020} = 8\%\quad\quad \frac{116}{1{,}176} = 10\%$

:CE $\quad\quad\quad\quad\quad\quad\quad\quad\quad \frac{108}{750} = 14.4\%\quad\quad \frac{83}{833} = 10\%\quad\quad \frac{116}{806} = 14.4\%$

	Year 1	Year 2	Year 3
Profit before tax:share funds	15%	6%	4.5%
Dividend cover (profit after tax: Div.)	1.1	.57	0.33
Sales: creditors	6	8	9.6
Interest Cover (Profit before interest : All Int.)	$\frac{108}{18+0} = 6$	$\frac{83}{36+12} = 1.7\%$	$\frac{116}{45+46} = 1.3$

Evaluate **BF** (Engineering) Ltd from the perspectives of (a) a shareholder and (b) the company's bankers.

7 Assessing segmental performance

Centralization and decentralization

Centralization describes situations where relatively few managers within an organization have the authority to make decisions. Such a situation may exist within small businesses with functional organizational structures (see Figure 7.1) where major decisions of a particular specialist nature are made by the appropriate functional head.

Decentralization exists where the authority to make decisions is delegated to lower levels of the organization. This usually is necessary where an organization's growth and complexity reach the point at which centralized decision-making is no longer practicable, either economically or logistically.

The degree of decentralization adopted will depend upon the balance senior management makes between the perceived advantages and disadvantages in their particular circumstances.

Advantages of decentralization

Specialization
A manager may be responsible for a smaller and less diverse part of the organization than a manager in a centralized firm, and is likely therefore to have more detailed and specialized knowledge. This should improve the quality of decision-making.

Timeliness
The spreading of decision-making more thinly between managers should result in quicker and perhaps better results. Further senior managers' time is released for more important strategic decision-making.

Motivation
The delegation of authority is likely to have positive motivational impacts. The 'freedom' to make decisions which affect managers' personal performance is combined with the increased status this authority implies. Commitment to and responsibility assumed for decisions made are increased.

Personnel development
The devolution of authority provides an opportunity for managers to demonstrate their abilities both as managers and decision-makers. Senior management is able to judge the suitability of junior management for more senior posts, without running the risk that a bad decision would be disastrous for the organization.

Segmental performance comparisons
The identification of separable parts of an organization with responsible managers enables each segment to be separately evaluated and compared against internal or external criteria.

Disadvantages of decentralization

Judging by the growth of decentralization in businesses, the disbenefits cannot be considered as 'weighty' as the advantages. They are nevertheless significant and should not be too easily discounted by management. Disadvantages are believed to be:

Dysfunctional decision-making
The opportunities for suboptimal behaviour are considerable, e.g. where one manager improves his own performance at the expense of the organization as a whole. This is particularly likely to occur when there is a lack of goal congruence between a junior manager and the organization.

Managerial rivalry
Managers may compete with each other in order to impress senior management, rather than working together for the good of the organization as a whole.

Loss of control
Senior management may lose control of the organization and, worse still, be unaware of this loss. Others may feel 'uncomfortable' if they delegated authority.

Increased cost of control
The cost of management information systems to allow senior management to retain control of the organization and check that lower levels of

management are using their delegated authority wisely can be high. There must be a danger of a costly bureaucracy developing purely to control subordinate management.

Lack of competent management
Can senior management select and/or train enough junior and middle managers of sufficient calibre to allow it to delegate the necessary decision-making authority without loss of decision quality.

Risk orientations
To what extent will junior management exhibit similar risk orientations to that of their senior management? Might their lower seniority level discourage them from taking the risks seniors would like them to and hence ignore potentially profitable investments? On the other hand, the reverse may be even more disadvantageous for the organization, i.e. a risk taken by a junior manager might have severe repercussions for the organization.

Diseconomies
Some decisions are best made centrally, perhaps because of economies of scale, the commonality of decisions or the sheer importance of the matter. The raising of finance, for example, is rarely delegated by senior management, even though control of it once it is raised may be delegated.

Divisionalization and segmentalization

Few organizations are totally centralized or decentralized. However, it would be wrong to equate centralization with small functional organizational structures. There are a number of very substantial companies with highly centralized organizations. Examples would include the major banks, many large retailers and certain governmental organizations.

The logical extension of the decentralization concept is the 'divisionalization' of a business. This implies the segmenting of the total business into two or more (relatively) autonomous parts, under separate management, each being responsible for its own corporate objectives and, in particular, profit performance (see Figure 7.1). Such an approach should, it is argued, enable large and/or complex businesses to gain the advantages of decentralization without the disadvantages.

Of course decentralization can take a variety of forms between the 'extremes' of functional and divisional organizational structures. Indeed the concept of segmentalization is applied in many groups to many 'levels' of the business; frequently even relatively small parts of an organization are treated as if they were separate quasi-autonomous businesses. Generalizations can rarely be drawn. The degrees of centralization adopted by businesses, its breadth and depth within and across

A simple functional organizational business structure:

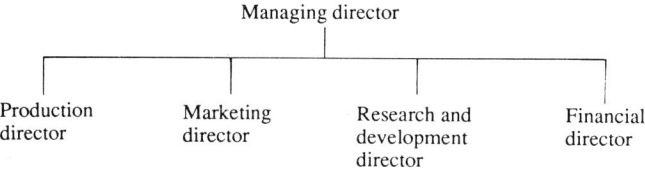

A simple divisional organizational business structure:

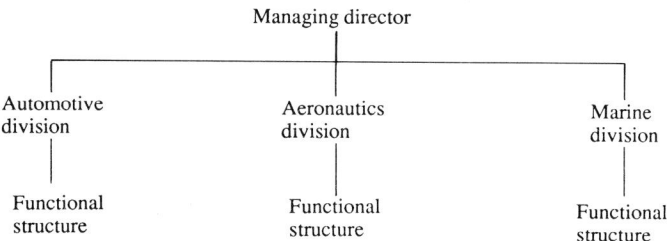

Figure 7.1 *Functional and divisionalized organizational structures*

the organization, and the amounts of responsibility devolved to each level are as various and as variable as there are organizations. A divisionalized structure is probably most suited, however, to businesses with a number of diverse activities, where each can be identified as separable and independent.

Alternative bases for divisionalization

There are a variety of ways in which businesses might logically segment their operations. The more common of these are indicated below.

Markets and customers

It is argued that one of the most vital ingredients of success is the ability to identify and serve market needs. Many firms today therefore create separate divisions specializing in particular areas of the market or for particular types of customer. Thus a large engineering group might create separate divisions specializing in such different industry sectors as automotive, marine, and aeronautic; or a service company might establish divisions specializing in commercial, industrial and governmental work.

Products or product groups

Where the products or services of a business are very different, requiring different business and operational skills, divisionalization by types of product or service would seem appropriate. Thus a manufacturing organization might distinguish between foundry, metal fabrication and electronics divisions, even if they might have, for example, some customers in common.

Technological

If the technological processes of making perhaps very different types of products, for very different types of customers, are similar, it would not be illogical to keep such processes together as one operation. This might occur, for example, where there are joint products such as in sugar refining, where outputs are sold as animal feed, industrial sweeteners and as refined sugar to retail outlets.

Geographical

Segmentalization along geographical lines is perhaps the most common form of divisionalization, particularly within international businesses, e.g. European, American, Asian, Australasian and Middle-Eastern Divisions, the European division being further split between, say, the UK, Germany, France and other EEC countries and the rest. The UK could be further segmented, perhaps between Scotland, N. Ireland, Wales, and North, South, East and West England. As business and competition cross national boundaries, the need to specialize in particular regions becomes increasingly important; the differences in social demands, culture, language, business ethos, law, etc. almost demands that large organizations be prepared to segment geographically whenever practicable.

Of course, many large groups of companies segmentalize by means of more than one of these bases, either at the same hierarchical level of the business or using different bases at differing levels. Figure 7.2 gives examples. Group A is segmented at the highest level by market, at the next two levels by geographical region (continent and nations in which operations are centred) and then by type of product/product group. This approach is not untypical of many large multinational businesses manufacturing and selling a wide range of products. The example of Group B is of a large UK engineering business whose main divisions are separated by means of three different 'bases'. In this specific case the foundry division provides products for both automotive and industrial divisions, as well as for customers outside the group, in these and other industries. As these were a significant proportion of group output, it was decided to retain foundry as a separate division. However, the overseas automotive and industrial divisions were deemed too small to warrant each having a separate representation and organization over-

114 Control and Audit in Management Accounting

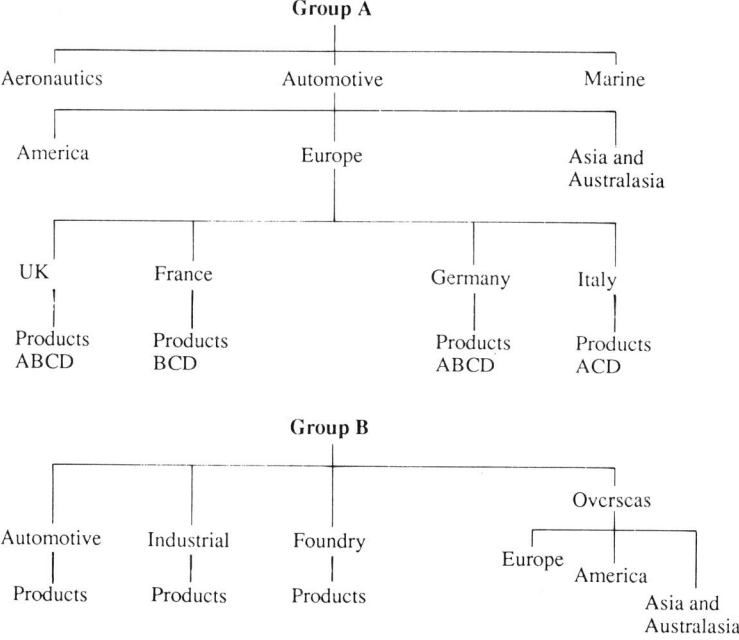

Figure 7.2 *Examples of mixed divisionalized bases*

seas. The amalgamation of these interests into the overseas division enabled local management selling in diverse markets to be more efficient. As overseas sales increase, however, pressure is being exerted to split representation again.

Observers of large businesses will be aware of the almost continual change of divisional/segmental structures of some companies, reflecting, for example, changes in the prosperity of different business sectors, a realignment for improved efficiency or perhaps a political power struggle within the hierarchy of the senior management.

Segments large and small

Although terminology is used very variously and loosely in business, the term 'divisions' is generally used to indicate the first or higher levels of segmentalizations of a large business. However, decentralization of some significance frequently operates in lower levels, with businesses being effectively treated as being just (smaller) subsets of a large division – perhaps with different objectives, etc., but subsets all the same. As many of the approaches to performance measurement of large and small segments of an organization tend to be very similar, the following chapters will use the term 'segment' to imply any part of a business, be it the highest segment/division or the lowest, which a business wishes to assess separately.

Segments or management

One further matter must be addressed before alternative performance measures are examined. The foregoing has examined the segmentalization of a business, which might imply that management wishes to concentrate its controls in that direction. Discerning readers, however, will have realized that each segment of a business must have a manager responsible for it and that senior management would wish to measure the performance of segment managers separately and perhaps in a different way from that of the unit itself. After all, the manager of a 'successful' segment which happens to operate in an area of high economic buoyancy might well not have 'performed' that well himself, and, on the other hand, a manager of a relatively unsuccessful segment might have performed 'miracles' in saving the segment from abject failure. Further, it could and perhaps should be argued that while historic performance measurement may be of value in the evaluation of management, it can be of little relevance to the evaluation of the segment as such. After all, the 'value' of a segment is dependent not on its past performances but on its realizable potential, which can only be evaluated on an ad hoc, future-oriented basis.

In practice, however, common performance measures can be and frequently are applied to the evaluation of both the segment and the responsible manager. For this reason, while recognizing that most performance measures are directed at the measurement of management, such measures will be considered in general before distinctions are drawn as to their adoption and relevance to segments and managers.

Responsibility centres

The term 'responsibility centre' relates to the situation where managers are made responsible for the performance of some aspect of the business's operations. Further, the term implies that (i) the responsibilities and the criteria by which performance will be measured will be clearly stated, and (ii) the requisite and necessary authority will be delegated. Although responsibility centres are usually synonymous with segments of the business, this is not a prerequisite. While the concept of responsibility centres is a simple one, the identification of clearly separate responsibilities is sometimes very difficult. Ideally, allocated responsibilities should not overlap those of other managers nor the decisions of one manager affect the results of another; likewise the measurement criteria should reflect that manager's actions over aspects which that manager can control. In practice, interrelationships and interdependencies in business are frequently such that the isolation of one responsibility centre from another is virtually impossible.

The essence of responsibility centres is that managers are responsible for the outputs of their centre in relation to the inputs into it. Management would therefore logically expect performance criteria to relate, as far as possible, the outputs to the inputs in some way *appropriate to* the operations of the responsibility centre.

Accounting approaches to this problem are to treat activity as one (or more) of the following:

- Cost centre.
- Revenue centre.
- Profit centre.
- Investment centre.
- Budget centre.

Cost centres

Cost centres are suitable in situations where a manager is responsible for the control of cost levels whether or not there are revenue responsibilities. Cost centres can therefore be applied in a wide range of circumstances, from large segments or divisions as a whole to any sub-segment of them down to the smallest responsibility centre to which costs are attributable. The logic would be to identify some suitable expression of output of the cost centre to relate to the cost, so that unit costs may be determined. Trends in these unit costs, perhaps analysed by elements of expense, may be examined to stress cost accountability. Alternatively, unit costs may be compared with those of similar cost centres either elsewhere within the organization or outside.

Sometimes the outputs of cost centres are either not measurable or bear little direct relation to the expenditures. Examples might include research and development, and many administrative departments, such as accounting, industrial relations and the secretariat. Such cost centres are sometimes referred to as 'discretionary expense centres' and are usually 'measured' by the amount of cost expenditure in relation to previous years, expectations or as a percentage of a general indication of activity, such as sales incomes.

Revenue centres

Revenue centres are principally intended to be applied to marketing and selling operations, where the manager's responsibilities relate to the generation of income whether or not there are attributable costs. Such costs could be treated as a separate cost centre if so desired, although it is not uncommon to net these two elements, creating a 'revenue/expense centre', where the aim is to generate revenues but where some expenses will necessarily be incurred. Ideally, in an analogous manner to the calculation of unit cost rates for cost centres, revenues (as a measure of output) would be compared to related inputs and resultant 'earnings rates' calculated. Examples might include sales per representative or sales per marketing £ expended. Such rates might then be compared with trends of past experience or other comparable revenue centres within or outside the organization.

Profit centres

Profit centres are applicable where the object is to earn a profit, i.e. where the responsibility is for the attainment and control of both costs and revenues. Thus such a responsibility centre requires a diversity of managerial skills – the skill to identify what will sell, to whom and at what price; the skill to operate or produce efficiently, and know what to make and how; and the skill to optimize resource utilizations, etc. – to operate a profit-seeking business effectively.

The term 'profit centre' is usually limited to situations where the manager does not have responsibility for the level of investment in the centre. In these instances profit levels would be related to such various factors as sales outputs, cost, machine or labour inputs, and such rates compared with trends over time or against other similar profit centres.

The advantage of the profit-centre approach is that it can be applied to *any* profit-seeking activity, whatever the nature of the goods or services being produced and/or sold. It could therefore be used as a basis for comparison of apparently disparate activities.

Investment centres

Investment centres are profit centres where the responsibility includes the *amount* and management of the investment, in both fixed and working capital. In such cases it would be expected that, in addition to the profit-centre measures described above, profit is related to the capital invested in the business, e.g. return on capital employed (ROCE/ROI) or measured as a profit after the cost of the capital employed (i.e. a residual income approach).

The investment-centre approach is extremely popular today, presumably because the centre managers can be treated as if they were the managing directors or chief executives of the segment, as if it were an autonomous unit and not part of a larger organization. In practice the managers of most profit centres treated as being investment centres have some control over their working capital even if not over their longer-term capital.

Budget centres

Some might consider it inappropriate to discuss budget centres under the framework of responsibility centres. After all, budget centres are usually considered in the context of budgetary control. However, the application of budgetary yardsticks is so interwoven into the fabric of cost, revenue, profit and investment-centre approaches that to neglect it would be fundamentally wrong.

Budget centres, a slightly different concept to cost, revenue, profit and investment centres, compare actual performances with the budget for the same thing, and the resulting variances are analysed with a view to identifying the need for (correcting) actions and to stress the need for control and accountability with the budgeted perameters. As such, budget centres are applicable very widely. Actual and budgeted performances are compared and thus budget centres can be applied to cost, revenue, profit and investment centres as well as being applied in their own right, i.e. where the performances are not measured in monetary terms at all but in such physical measures as labour efficiency and productivity rates, or visits, orders or new customers per sales representative.

Selection of centre bases

As far as possible, segments of a business should be treated on as 'natural' a responsibility basis as possible, i.e. if a segment has both incomes and expenditures, a profit centre basis is likely to be appropriate, while a segment which does not make sales, would logically be measured as a cost centre. Shillinglaw and others (see references) suggest that a centre's performance measurement should be unaffected by actions elsewhere in the organization, and relate to facets of cost and revenue over which the centre manager has some measure of control.

In practice however, many responsibility centres within businesses are established on bases which to some greater or lesser extent are artificial and/or are affected by decisions elsewhere in the organization over which they have little or no control. The reasons for this contradiction of well known and understood managerial logic is probably that:

1 Situations arise, particularly in process industries, with their joint processing costs, where management wishes to segmentalize its organization on a basis other than a 'Technological' basis (see 'Alternative bases for divisionalization', p. 112) A transfer price or apportionment of joint costs to each segment is therefore necessary if each segment is to be treated separately.
2 The profit- and investment-centre approaches are increasingly acknowledged or believed to have considerable advantages over cost and revenue approaches. It is argued that they offer a greater goal congruence with corporate objectives, profit is seen as a better motivation than cost control, and more segments of the organization can be compared on a compatible basis. Thus, for example, the output of a natural cost centre might be 'valued' at a 'transfer price' to derive a figure of sales in order that the centre could be treated as a profit or investment centre.
3 Businesses have expanded through horizontal and vertical integra-

tion and acquisition, which has resulted, as planned, in a perhaps significant degree of inter-company trading. It could be argued of course that these transactions are at a fair, arms' length market price, but management must question whether such a transfer price is ever really 'fair' or 'arms' length', especially where segments of a business are in any way 'required' or 'expected' to trade with each other. Further, as the purpose of growth by merger or acquisition is presumably to gain the advantages of internal trading, it would seem illogical and suboptimal to permit responsibility centre managers the freedom to trade completely autonomously.

4 Centralized group services have increased in many large organizations, effectively creating a similar situation to (3) above. This may have been to gain economies of scale and an increase in negotiating power, or simply to centralize control or gain a uniformity of approach. Such central services would probably include buying, computing, finance, personnel, training, property management, equipment supply and of course head office administration. Whether these central services are treated as cost or profit centres, if charges are made to other responsibility centres, whether it be on a 'work done' or a simple 'apportionment' basis, the charge is effectively a transfer price and therefore an uncontrollable cost from the user's point of view.

5 If a cost centre of an organization has spare capacity, management frequently wants to utilize this opportunity profitably by encouraging its sale (at a profit) to external businesses. A cost centre would then be in the position of being a cost centre for internal work and a profit centre for external work. Sometimes managements resolve this dichotomy of interests by changing such a cost centre into a profit centre, thus requiring internal work to be 'sold' at a price to other responsibility centres. The distinction between internal and external work is therefore potentially resolved.

Thus in all these very common business circumstances a transfer price of some sort is required if a financial evaluation measure is to be applied. As the reader will readily understand, however, the effect of this must be to cast doubt on the resultant measurements of responsibility centres and of their management. If the transfer price is high, the seller is advantaged and the buyer disadvantaged and vice versa if the price is low. Transfer pricing from a control viewpoint will be considered later.

Finally it should be pointed out that there is no logical reason why, in suitable circumstances, a responsibility centre could not be treated as a cost, revenue, profit and investment centre, and as a budget centre for cost, revenue, profit, investment and (some measures of) physical performance. Obviously there would be duplications of 'performance' but each would allow senior management to examine more closely performance in each element as well as overall performance. The more the views, the better the understanding!

Assessment criteria

The alternative types of responsibility centre address different aspects of managerial controls and therefore require different measures of performance. The balance of this chapter will consider performance criteria suitable for profit and investment centres and the following chapter cost- and revenue-centre criteria. Budget centres have been considered in preceding chapters, but their particular relevance to cost, revenue, profit and investment centres will be reintroduced as necessary.

Profit and investment centre criteria

As indicated earlier, most profit-centre managers have at least some responsibility for and impact upon the investment in their profit centre and it might therefore be fair to treat them as an investment centre.[1,2] Such evidence as there is of business practices in Britain and the USA indicates that investment centres are more common than profit centres. This was certainly the experience of the authors in a small sample of divisionalized organizations visited in the generation of case studies between 1980[3] and 1986.[4,5]

There is in any event absolutely no reason why an investment-centre manager could not be assessed as a profit-centre manager as well, although, as will be explained later, this could lead to some conflicts between the various performance measures. A consideration of the situations in which a profit-centre approach might be preferred to that of an investment-centre approach, together with an examination of appropriate performance measures for a profit centre, will be addressed later in the chapter.

The immediate concern here is with possible criteria for the evaluation of investment centres, and the alternatives, variations, advantages and disadvantages and their relevance to the control of responsibility centres.

Return on investment

There can be no doubt that return on investment (ROI) or return on capital employed (ROCE), as it is often termed, particularly when used as an internal measure for the evaluation of investment centres, is the most popular and widely used performance criterion for investment centres and inter-firm comparisons. There would appear to be an intuitive and inescapable logic in drawing together as a ratio (usually expressed as a percentage) two of the most critical aspects of business management – the main objective of profitability and the perhaps major resource constraint of capital availability. If these factors are critical in measuring the business as a whole, surely they must be equally important to each investment centre within the business, if for no other reason than to encourage and emphasize goal congruence. Not only does ROI draw together two such important elements, but the resultant percentage facilitates the comparison of the performances of different investments, whether it be one business with another, one investment centre within a business with another, or an investment centre within one business to that within another, and for that matter whether the businesses are of different sizes or in different lines of business.

The previous chapter mentioned that ROI is frequently used, for inter-firm comparisons, as the apex of a pyramid of ratios. While it is not intended to examine the pyramid as such, it is perhaps germane to examine the two ratios which it is frequently suggested are the constituent ratios forming the next stage down the pyramid, i.e.

$$\text{ROI} = \frac{\text{Profits}}{\text{Investment}} = \frac{\text{Profits}}{\text{Sales}} \times \frac{\text{Sales}}{\text{Investment}}$$

$$= \text{Profit Margin} \times \text{Turnover of Capital}$$

These two ratios demonstrate that ROI can be affected by improvements in profit margin and/or sales volumes for a given level of capital invested, or of course a mix of both, i.e. an increase in either will bring an increased return but so too could a decrease in one if the other increased disproportionately to compensate. For example, a 20 per cent ROI obtained by a 10 per cent profit margin and a TOC of 2 would be improved if, when profit margins are reduced to 9 per cent, sales volumes and therefore TOC increased by more than 10 per cent, say to 2.4. Thus 9 per cent × 2.4 = 21.6 per cent ROI as long as capital invested does not also increase (as it might if sales volumes increase by 20 per cent).

In spite of its popularity as a performance measure, ROI can be interpreted in a large variety of ways, and has a number of inherent limitations which are frequently overlooked or ignored by management. These aspects merit careful consideration.

What profit?

Which figure of profit should be used in the ROI ratio? Should it be operating profit, trading profit, net profit before loan interest or after, before tax or after ... or something else instead? Obviously each has its merits and would give perhaps a different perspective on the business and its management. It depends just what one wants to measure, with what one wishes to compare and why. In comparing one company with another a shareholder might consider net profit after tax to be a sensible profit measure. After all, that is the profit figure available to the shareholder for distribution as dividend or for growth. But would this be a sensible basis to compare the divisions and segments of a business with each other? Possibly. But if taxation planning is considered to be the prerogative of senior management, a pre-taxation basis might be more logical. Similarly, if capital sourcing is a centralized activity, perhaps profit before loan interest would be more appropriate.

However, this assumes that, even for investment centre performance measurement within an organization, a measure of profit compatible with that used in the financial accounts should be used. But why should internal performance measures be restricted to those used in the financial statements? Why should they be prepared to a format and manner proscribed by law and standard accounting practices, and which accountants recognize as having severe limitations as meaningful informative data? Are the traditional accounting conventions really relevant for such measurements? Do we *really* want internal performance measures prepared in a prudent way? Should not 'reality' be the aim for such purposes? Why should we stick rigidly to the historic cost convention, which can provide such meaningless and incomparable data? Surely here is an opportunity to introduce current cost and value data into an internal measurement? Should not internal performance measures concentrate, as far as possible, upon attributability of costs and revenues, i.e. reflect these aspects, which are directly attributable to the investment centre but exclude those which are little more than a sharing out of corporate costs? Likewise, in measuring a manager's performance, should the emphasis not be upon those aspects the manager can control in some meaningful way, while excluding general cost apportionments?

These aspects will be considered shortly, but a similar questioning of the assumptions in the investment element of the ROI ratio is also required.

What investment?

A questioning of the investment/capital employed element of the ROI ratio in a similar manner to that of the return/profit element is necessary. Should the emphasis be upon shareholders' funds alone or include loan capital and other 'creditors over one year'? What figure of capital employed should we use – fixed assets alone, pre- or post-depreciation, or plus current assets or plus net current assets? Should assets remain at historic cost or be increased to reflect current costs of replacement or some other interpretation of value? Do we want to continue using financial accounting conventions? How are shared fixed assets to be dealt with? Are they to be apportioned between investment centres? Can working capital be directly attributed or must this too be apportioned? How much of this capital is truly attributable to investment centres or controllable by investment centre management? How can the anomalies of leased assets, on and off balance sheet, compared to asset ownership be reduced or eliminated for comparison purposes? Should the investment base used be that for the beginning or end of the period, or an average?

As with the profit measure, the investment measure must depend

Table 7.1 A. Freighter – profits and capital employed

	Years			
	1	2	3	4
Profit statement	£000	£000	£000	£000
Sales	50	50	50	50
Operating Costs	(25)	(25)	(25)	(25)
Depreciation	(15)	(15)	(15)	(15)
Net profits	10	10	10	10
Capital employed				
Vehicle at cost	60	60	60	60
Depreciation	15	30	45	60
Net book amount	45	30	15	0

upon circumstances: what one wants to evaluate, why, and with what the comparison is to be made. A shareholder may well be interested in profits after loan interest, pre- or post-tax, compared to shareholders' funds. However, a comparison of the same profit figures with a total of shareholders' funds and loan capital would surely be illogical (in which case a profits before loan interest would be more appropriate). Yet in inter-firm comparisons different capital gearing may make shareholders' funds a poor indicator of managerial utilization of funds. Or would it? And what basis is relevant for a business's investment-centre performance? Gearing differences might make shareholders' funds an anomalous figure, so perhaps fixed assets plus current assets or working capital should be used. Or ...?

ROI inconsistency

ROI can be a ratio that lacks a consistency in proportion over time and can therefore be a misleading measure. Consider the following simplified example.

Arnold Freighter decides to set up in business as a road hauler. He buys a lorry costing £60,000, which he estimates has a business life of 4 years with little or no residual value. His policy is to depreciate the vehicle on a straight line basis. He expects steady sales of £50,000 pa and operational costs, excluding depreciation, of £25,000. A. Freighter's accounting data would appear as in Table 7.1.

What is the ROI likely to be in each of the 4 years? Assuming that it is intended to use net profits as shown, before taxation, the question remains as to which capital-employed figure to use – that at the beginning of the year, end of the year, or an average. Different figures result, as in Table 7.2.

The distinction between the three alternatives is a matter of choice, of policy. There are arguments for using each of them. If capital changes

124 Control and Audit in Management Accounting

Table 7.2 A Freighter – ROI based upon different CE bases

ROI based on CE	1 %	2 %	3 %	4 %
at beginning	16.7	22.2	33.3	66.6
at end	22.2	33.3	66.6	infinity
average	19.0	26.7	44.4	133.3

significantly, year on year, an average may be more appropriate, but practices across industry are very variable.

The principal point to be made, however, is that the ROI percentage increases over time, even though the assumptions of work done/sales volumes are the same over time. The danger therefore is that, if this ratio is used as a control measure, the impression might be gained that performance is improving significantly over the years when it obviously is not.

Additionally, as the ROI percentage increases over time from quite low to perhaps very high figures, managers are likely to become increasingly disinclined to propose new capital investments which would depress the ROI evaluation of their performance. Even if the depression would only affect the short term, managers with an eye to promotion or salary increases in the shorter term may be influenced to defer investment as long as possible.

Residual income

An increasingly popular alternative to ROI is the application of the residual income concept. This measures the net income of an investment after deducting an amount representing the 'required' rate of return on the capital invested in the business. The required rate may represent the minimum required by the organization, perhaps some target or expected level of returns, or, in some businesses, the weighted average cost of capital of the organization. In this latter case the sum of the residual incomes of all segments of the business could equate with the business's net profit after loan interest.

The argument for residual income (RI) is that it encourages investment-centre managers to explore any investment with the potential of obtaining a return in excess of the business's required rate of return. As mentioned earlier, this motivation does not always exist where ROI is used as a performance measure, particularly if the percentage is high with an ageing capital base.

An illustration of the residual income approach is shown in Table 7.3.

It could be argued that, even if the ROI percentages shown were a consistent annual measure, not prone to increase over time, if ROI were the main preference measure, investment managers of A and B are likely to act suboptimally from the business's viewpoint. Suppose A and

Assessing segmental performance 125

Table 7.3 ROI and residual income calculation for business segments

	Segment A	Segment B
Capital invested	£3,000,000	£10,000,000
Annual profit	£540,000	£1,400,000
ROI percentage	18%	14%
Required return (10%)	£300,000	£1,000,000
Residual income (at 10% required return)	£240,000	£400,000

Table 7.4 Residual income for differing rates of required return

	Segment A	Segment B
Capital investment	£3,000,000	£10,000,000
Annual profit	£540,000	£1,400,000
ROI percentage	18%	14%
Residual income		
at 10% return	£240,000	£400,000
at 13% return	£150,000	£100,000
at 16% return	£60,000	£(200,000)

B identified new investment propositions for £1m with a return of 17 per cent and 15 per cent respectively. The manager of B is likely to propose such an investment, as it would increase his segment's ROI performance measure, and if the required rate of return is 10 per cent, this would be good for the business as a whole. The manager of A, however, is unlikely to propose such an investment, even though it has a higher return than that identified by B, because it would depress his segment's ROI performance of 18 per cent, an action which would not be in the business's best interest. At worst, A is being encouraged to be beautiful (in ROI terms), even if small!

If, however, residual income was the performance measure of A and B, *both* segments would be likely to propose the £1m investments.

This does mean, however, that the judgement of management in setting the required rate of return can be of critical importance to the operation of the residual income performance measure and to decisions made. If, for example, the required rate of return had been set not at 10 per cent, as earlier, but at 13 per cent or 16 per cent, very different performance measures would result (see Table 7.4).

The repercussions are significant. From a control viewpoint the relative performances of A and B vary with the requirements for return. Is segment A performing better than unit B or not? Is it sensible to argue that if the required return of the business is 10 per cent, B is performing better than A, while at required returns of 13 per cent and 16 per cent the reverse is true? After all, if the required rate was 10 per cent, the manager of B would argue that, even though his rate of return on capital was lower than that of A, by taking on investments with returns over 10 per cent he has increased corporate profits to a greater extent than A. A, it could be argued, has perhaps ignored opportunities to expand and obtain an increase in residual income. Was this a good decision? Apparently not, if capital is freely available at a rate of 10 per cent or less.

What then should the required rate of return represent? Ideally, as RI could be considered as an abbreviated NPV approach from an economic decision making viewpoint, the opportunity cost *of additional sources of capital* should be used. However, once expenditures have been made, it would be more logical to apply a rate approximating to the opportunity value *of those assets required*. As (a) this rate may be difficult to determine, (b) using two different rates is likely to lead to confusion and (c) changing the rate used to reflect changes in opportunity can distort performance measurement over time, businesses tend to adopt one rate and stick to it over time. This should mean of course that business management ought to take a long-term view of opportunity cost in its industry(ies). It should be noted, however, that if the availability of capital is effectively nil, then the residual income measure is irrelevant, and profit maximization alone is relevant.

Finally, the reader should be aware that RI is as prone as ROI to the increase of the performance measure over time. If A. Freighter, for example, was a segment of a business using residual income at a 10 per cent required rate of return, the performance would appear as in Figure 7.5.

Suppose, however, that the investment was less profitable than as shown. Say that periodic net profits were only £5,000 pa and resultant residual incomes were £(1,000), £500, £2,000, and £3,500 in each of the four years. Bearing in mind the negative RI in the first year and a second year of only £500, would A. Freighter have proposed the investment?

Annuity depreciation

Annuity depreciation is an attempt to equalize the cost of asset purchases over time, asset costs being defined as depreciation and the required rate of return on the capital expended to buy the asset. Perhaps the most obvious analogy is that of a building society mortgage, where repayments are made in *equal* instalments over time. In the early years repayments represent mostly interest and a small amount of capital. In later years the interest element declines and the capital repayment increases.

To illustrate, a simple example is shown in Table 7.6, continuing the A. Freighter residual income approach example shown in Table 7.5. The 'equal annuity rate' of £18,930 required to repay £60,000 over 4 years at an 'interest' rate of 10 per cent may be calculated from the formula illustrated below:

Table 7.5 A residual income example showing improving RI over time for A. Freighter

	Years			
	1	2	3	4
Profitability statement	£000	£000	£000	£000
Sales	50	50	50	50
Operating costs	(25)	(25)	(25)	(25)
Depreciation	(15)	(15)	(15)	(15)
Net profit	10	10	10	10
Required profit	6	4.5	3	1.5
Residual income	4	5.5	7	8.5
Capital employed				
Vehicle at cost	60	60	60	60
Depreciation	15	30	45	60
Net book amount	45	30	15	0

Note that the required profit is based in this example upon the *opening* balance of *depreciated* assets. Different depreciation assumptions will therefore affect the notional profit requirement.

Table 7.6 A. Freighter – residual income calculation using annuity depreciation and cost of capital of 10%

	Years							
	1		2		3		4	
Profitability statement	£000		£000		£000		£000	
Sales	50		50		50		50	
Operating costs	25		25		25		25	
Gross margin	25		25		25		25	
Annuity costs:								
Depreciation$^{(ii)}$	12.93		14.22		15.64		17.21	
Interest$^{(i)}$	6.00	18.93	4.71	18.93	3.29	18.93	1.72	18.93
Residual income$^{(iii)}$		6.07		6.07		6.07		6.07
Capital employed								
Cost		60.00		60.00		60.00		60.00
Depreciation		12.93		27.15		42.79		60.00
Net book amount		47.07		32.85		17.21		0

Notes (i) 10% of opening book amount.
(ii) The balance between the interest charge and the annuity repayment of 18.93 (£000) pa.
(iii) NPV of 6.07 (£000) for 4 years @ 10% = 19.240 (£000)

$$A = I \times \frac{(1+r)^n \times r}{(1+r)^n - 1}$$

where

A = annual investment
I = invested sum
r = required rate of return, expressed as a decimal
n = number of years (life of asset/projected)

Thus for example using the Figures as in Table 7.6

$$A = 60,000 \times \frac{(1+0.1)^4 \times 0.1}{(1+0.1)^4 - 1}$$

$$= 60,000 \times \frac{1.4641 \times 0.1}{1.4641 - 1}$$

$$= £18,930$$

In year 1 only £12,930 of this is depreciation, while in year 4 £17,210 is depreciation (see Table 7.6).

Annuity depreciation enables the RI performance measure to reflect a consistent figure over time (rather than a rising one), when margins before depreciation are at a constant level. Of course if gross margins vary, so will the RI, but that is presumably a relationship that management is not unhappy to reflect in resultant residual income levels. The point is that the total cost of buying equipment in terms of depreciation and interest remains constant.

A further advantage is that the resultant RI is consistent with the NPV approach to capital investment appraisal. In our example the NPV of the original investment at 10 per cent (£25,000 in four annual instalments less £60,000 invested) is £19,240, the same as the NPV of £6,070 in four annual instalments shown in Figure 7.7. Thus annuity depreciation offers management the potential to measure investment-centre performance by the same criteria that its expenditures were (probably) approved by. Further, it should continue to encourage investment-centre managers to put forward proposals which are expected to beat the company's required rate of return and/or opportunity cost. However, it may not show consistently positive residual incomes if cash flows from the investment are erratic, and therefore investment centre managers may be deterred from proposing such an investment.

However, annuity depreciation is apparently rarely adopted in practice. The reason is probably because the effect of low depreciation in early years goes against both managers' instinctive belief about depreciation and the accounting prudency principle of asset 'valuation', in as much as depreciation is lower in the early years and therefore the net book amount is likely to be higher than the assets' potential resale value (although the 'going concern' concept could counter this argument).

Table 7.7 A. Freighter – residual income calculation using the NPV value of the vehicle as the basis for depreciation

	Years			
	1	2	3	4
Profitability statement				
Sales	50	50	50	50
Operating costs	(25)	(25)	(25)	(25)
Gross margin	25.000	25.00	25.00	25.000
Depreciation	17.075(i)	18.78	20.65	22.275
Profit before interest	7.925	6.22	4.35	2.275
Interest	7.925(ii)	6.22	4.35	2.275
Residual income	–	–	–	–

Value at start: (25 × 0.909) + (25 × 0.826) + (25 × 0.751) + (25 × 0.683) = 79.225
Value at end of year 1: (25 × .909) + (25 × 0.826) + (25 × 0.751) = 62.150
Value at end of year 2: (25 × .909) + (25 × 0.826) = 43.375
Value at end of year 3: + (25 × 0.909) = 22.725

(i) Value at start £79.225 less value at end of year 1 £62.15.
(ii) 10% of the value at start of £79.225, adjusted slightly to allow for rounding of discounting.

Valuing assets at net present value

An interesting variant of the annuity depreciation approach values investments at their NPV, using the required rate of return. Thus in the A. Freighter example (Figure 7.7) the vehicle would be valued at its NPV of £19,240. This vehicle could therefore be 'sold' by the Group to the A. Freighter investment centre at £19,240. The management of A. Freighter would then, for performance evaluation purposes, depreciate and charge interest on £19,240, reducing periodic residual income to nil. Thus Table 7.7 indicates the performance statements. The advantage of this approach is that (i) investment managers would be more careful in putting forward exaggerated cash flows for favoured investments, (ii) managers' performance against investment proposals are consistently measured, and (iii) irregular cash flows would still allow a consistent residual income (of nil) to be produced. However, the authors know of no example of this approach in practice, which perhaps is not surprising, as it is not likely to motivate managers to propose new investments when resultant RI would not increase. Further, the method would require a separate set of managerial records from those of the financial accounts.

Table 7.8 A. Freighter – ROI using sum of digits depreciation

	Years			
	1	2	3	4
Profit statement	£000	£000	£000	£000
Sales	50	50	50	50
Operating costs	(25)	(25)	(25)	(25)
Depreciation	(24)	(18)	(12)	(6)
Net profits	1	7	13	19
Capital employed				
Vehicle at cost	60	60	60	60
Depreciation	24	42	54	60
Net book value	36	18	6	0
ROI% based on opening CE	1.7%	19.4%	72.2%	316.7%

Accounting conventions and policies

The reason for the ROI etc. inconsistencies is of course that a depreciating figure of capital employed is used as the denominator in the ROI ratio. This might be logical if the asset was decreasingly utilizable year on year (in the A. Freighter example, reducing by 25 per cent each year). However, while an asset may well be decreasingly useful over time, because (i) it reduces in efficiency as it wears, and (ii) it requires more frequent stoppages for repairs and maintenance and therefore has reduced availability, such is not likely to reduce utilizability as substantially as most assets depreciation rates would imply.

It should be pointed out that the anomalies stem partly at least from the use of financial accounting conventions and policies. Consider the profits and ROI over time of, say, a 'sum of digits' or 'reducing balance' depreciation method had been adopted. The financial statements might (at worst) appear as in Table 7.8.

Of course no account has been taken of increasing repairs and maintenance and reducing utilizability over time. However, it would appear that such a system is likely to provide even bigger variations in the ROI percentage over time than a straight line approach.

The above examples have all been based upon the original assumption that the vehicle will have a 4-year life and no residual value. It would not be surprising if these estimates were somewhat pessimistic, based upon the need to be prudent and conservative in calculating profitability for financial accounting purposes. Suppose a more 'realistic' assumption is that the vehicle will last 5 years and will have a residual value then of £5,000. Depreciation then would be £55,000 over 5 years or £11,000 pa on a straight line basis. In these eventualities, if the

Table 7.9 A. Freighter – contrast between 4- and 5-year assumptions of asset life

	Years					Profit on sale
	1	2	3	4	5	
	£000	£000	£000	£000	£000	£000
Net profits						
original	10	10	10	10	25	5
revised	14	14	14	14	14	0
Capital employed[(ii)]						
original	60	45	30	15	0	
revised	60	49	38	27	16	
ROI %						
original	16.7%	22.2%	33.3%	66.6%	infinity	
revised	23.3%	28.6%	36.8%	51.9%	87.5%	

(i) Profit on sale of assets = sales value less WDV. Does this become a below the line or above the line profit? A central or a segmental profit?
(ii) Capital employed using straight line depreciation, taking the opening figure for each year.

vehicle lasts for 5 years, the financial figures when compared to the original assumptions might appear as in Table 7.9.

Different figures of ROI emerge of course, but increasing at a lower rate, simply because a less conservative/more realistic view of depreciation is taken. This is particularly important if assets are likely to be retained beyond their book life, as ROI percentages in later years could appear to be very high indeed.

One possibility to reduce the anomaly would be to use an undepreciated figure of fixed assets for capital-employed calculations. This would give a constant figure in this example of 16.7 per cent. However, as in practice assets do become less utilizable and more costly to repair over time, this approach would probably lead to a *reducing* ROI over time, even if other efficiencies, e.g. excluding utilizable vehicle capacity, remained the same.

Some observers might argue that the increasing ROI percentages are not likely to happen in practice, as most businesses own more than one fixed asset: if, for example, the business owned four vehicles, one purchased each year, every year the total figures would be made up of one vehicle each of 1, 2, 3 and 4 years old and therefore a consistent percentage over time would arise. This of course would be essentially true *if* businesses replaced assets regularly and equally year on year. Some business may well do so of course, but an examination of the accounts of businesses shows clearly that this is by no means a universally adopted practice. The financial director of one large asset leasing/rental business has abandoned the ROI percentages as a performance measure for his investment centres because in his words, 'they are meaningless ... they go up over time, and when we replace assets to

Table 7.10 A. Freighter – effects of inflation upon ROI %

	Years			
	1	2	3	4
Profit				
Sales less operating costs	25	27.5	30.25	33.275
Depreciation	(15)	(15)	(15)	(15)
Net profits	10	12.5	15.25	18.275
Capital employed (as originally)				
Vehicle at cost	60	60	60	60
Depreciation	15	30	45	60
Net book amount	45	30	15	0
ROI %	16.7	27.7	50.8	121.8

modernize our equipment, in response to customer demands for the latest models, the percentages go back down again'.

Depreciation is not the only element affected by accounting policies and conventions. Consider, for example, alternative stock valuation approaches and the treatment of goodwill and R & D expenditures. Are the accounting conventions adopted for external financial statements appropriate for internal performance measurement purposes? For inter-firm comparisons figures have to be taken in the form in which they are available, but within a business it is possible to adopt a different approach to attempt to reflect 'reality' or, at least, policies that are not overly prudent and conservative.

Historic or current cost

The historic cost convention underpins most businesses' external financial statements, although revamped versions adopting current costs are frequently provided nowadays. This is one accounting convention, however, which tends to be ignored in the preparation of many aspects of management accounting data such as budgets and standard costs – the principal exception regrettably being segmental performance measurement. Perhaps this follows from the felt need to segmentalize not only the organization but its objectives and financial measures as well.

Some drawbacks of an historic cost measure in an inflationary period can perhaps be illustrated by considering again A. Freighter/ROI example. Table 7.10 takes the original figures but assumes an annual 10 per cent increase in operating costs, vehicle costs and selling prices.

This results in net profits increasing at a rate of over 20 per cent because (a) depreciation remains static, being based on the original cost of the vehicle in spite of the vehicle's replacement cost increasing annually, and (b) gross margins are increasing in line with inflation. This simply makes the ROI percentage increase even faster than when there was no inflation.

If, however, inflation adjustments were made to the performance measurements in a similar way to those adopted for the published financial statements, performance criteria would be at least no less steady than if there were no inflation, thus reducing the possibilities of invidiously comparing different segments with very different effective inflation rates. Bearing in mind that most companies have this information available for external disclosure purposes, why should management feel it needs even less information than that provided to shareholders?

Asset hire or ownership

One fundamental problem in comparing the relative performance of investment centres within an organization (or indeed of entire businesses) has been the differences in practice on the ownership of assets. One business/segment may have decided to buy the assets it uses, another business/segment to rent, hire or lease business assets whenever possible. In such situations, the former is almost certain to have a much lower ROI than the latter, particularly in the earlier years, given relative similarity in other respects. Consider again the A. Freighter example, this time with a working capital of £10,000, compared with an otherwise identical operator, B. Freighter, which hires its vehicles at an annual cost of £21,000. A comparison of operating ROI is shown in Table 7.11. In this particular case A. Freighter's ROI is worse than B. Freighter's until the last year. Thus A may appear less profitable than B simply because of its assets financing practices/policies.

If, however, a residual income approach were adopted, a different, perhaps fairer, view could be obtained. Table 7.12 illustrates this, using again a 10 per cent required rate of return. In this particular case the measured relative profitability is reversed, looking better than B in all but the first year.

The extent to which businesses own or hire/lease assets varies considerably, even in the same industry. Even within particular organizations different practices may exist, although many would consider the decision to be a centralized one, related to capital sourcing. This is particularly so where leasing assets is considered to be an 'on balance sheet' item, i.e. where the asset is treated for financial accounting purposes as if it were owned, the capital cost and related depreciation being separate from the interest element, which is written off in the accounts over the leasing period. In such a situation the financial accounting policies may well be reflected in the management performance measures, and thus any anomaly between owned or leased assets is effectively removed. Additionally, the financial gearing of the business as a whole will be affected.

Table 7.11 A. Freighter – comparison of ROI-owned and hired fixed assets

	Years			
	1 £000	2 £000	3 £000	4 £000
Profit statement				
Sales	50	50	50	50
Operating costs	(25)	(25)	(25)	(25)
Depreciation	(15)	(15)	(15)	(15)
Net profit	10	10	10	10
Capital employed				
Vehicle at cost	60	60	60	60
Depreciation	15	30	45	60
Net book amount	45	30	15	0
Working capital	10	10	10	10
Total capital employed	55	40	25	10
ROI Percentage	4	18	25	40
B. Freighter				
Profit statement				
Sales	50	50	50	50
Operating costs	(25)	(25)	(25)	(25)
Hiring charges	(21)	(21)	(21)	(21)
Net profits	4	4	4	4
Capital employed				
Working capital	10	10	10	10
ROI percentage	40	40	40	40

NB ROI based on asset figures at the beginning of the period. Working capital being treated as an opening balance.

However, by no means all hiring/leasing contracts are 'on balance sheet'. For example, for some segments/businesses property is a substantial part of their fixed asset expenditures. Others rent or lease their business premises. In such cases ROI and RI measures can still result in invidious comparisons between investment centres.

Apportionments, attributability and controllability

Profit concepts

When making inter-firm comparisons, the alternative profit concepts available to the analyst are somewhat limited – essentially to those available in published data, which, with few exceptions, relate to some variation of net profit. Indeed all examples of investment centre performance used in this chapter have consistently used net profit as the profit measure.

Table 7.12 Comparison of residual incomes – owned and hired fixed assets

	Years			
	1 £000	2 £000	3 £000	4 £000
A. Freighter				
Profitability statement				
Net profit[i]	10	10	10	10
Required return[ii]	7	5.5	4	2.5
Residual income £000	3	4.5	6	7.5
B. Freighter				
Net Profits[i]	4	4	4	4
Required Return[iii]	1	1	1	1
Residual Income	3	3	3	3

Notes (i) Figures ex Table 7.5
        (ii) 10% of opening capital employed for A. Freighter, e.g. in year 1, 10% of 60 + 10 = 70.
       (iii) 10% of capital employed of £10,000 working capital.

It is necessary, however, to consider the value of net profit as the basis for both segmental and managerial performance measurement across all investment centres within a business. The investment centre approach can be applied within businesses to segments both large and small: from large divisions of conglomerates to small sections of operating units. Should such different segments, even if both are treated as investment centres, be measured on the same basis or can some appropriate differentiation be found? Some investment centre managers have the ability to control most, if not all, of the costs, revenues and investments constituting their performance measure; others may have relatively little control over perhaps significant aspects of cost, revenue and investment. Should both these managers, then, be measured by similar criteria or should some differentiation be considered to reflect their different situations?

Segment or manager

As indicated earlier, there must always be a danger that management and its business segment become so associated in the minds of senior management that the performance of the segment is effectively treated as being the performance of its managers. It could be argued that, if the managers' responsibilities are to manage an investment centre, the requisite duties are effectively analogous to those of the segments' objectives and that therefore the same measure should be applied to each. However, as indicated earlier, good managers may be responsible for poorly performing segments, perhaps if the industry the segment is in, is in a slump or a highly competitive state. In the circumstances the manager may be performing very well indeed. In contrast, a manager of a higher performing segment may be failing to manage the segment as successfully as he might. Additionally, the risk orientation of the business must be considered in relation to the return: a business in a high risk industry or one which adopts a high risk profile could be expected to have higher returns than those in low risk industries or with a low risk profile.

It is surely apparent that the measures applied to the manager need to be different from those applied to the segment. But in what respects should the measures differ? Suggestions over recent years (see Solomons,[6] Shillinglaw,[7] Amey and Eggington[8] have concentrated on distinguishing between controllability in the measurement of managers and attributability in the measurement of investment centres.

Controllability and attributability

It would be reasonable to assume that management would wish to measure an individual manager on the basis of those aspects of the business the manager is able to control, which presumably would reflect the autonomy and decision-making authority delegated to the manager. Although, as discussed earlier, this will vary from centre to centre, for an investment centre manager significant aspects of revenues, costs and investment are likely to be included.

The controllability approach suggests therefore that a variety or range of profitability measures be considered. Investment centre managers may then be evaluated by the profitability measure which best suits their delegated authority and ability to control.

The attributability approach follows a similar reasoning and suggests that differing degrees of attributability of costs may be relevant for different management comparison, control and decision-making purposes.

Shillinglaw[9] has suggested four profit concepts:

1. Sales margin, or total revenues less total variable costs to make or sell.
2. Controllable profit, or sales margin less all the division's fixed costs controllable by the manager.
3. Contribution margin, or controllable profit less all other costs directly traceable to the division.
4. Net profit, or contribution margin less some share of general management and service centre costs.

As he points out, 'No one of the four profit concepts is 'best'. None is superior for all purposes'. Each has a value for differing control and/or decision-making purposes.

'Sales margin' concentrates on sales volume and price and production efficiency responsibilities. 'Controllable profit' emphasises the profit margins controllable by the manager while 'contribution margin' measures profit on attributability bases – attributable that is to the business segment. 'Net profit', however, is described by Shillinglaw[10] as appearing to be a logical basis on which to judge investment centres but summarized as the least useful of the four concepts. Its usefulness for both evaluation and guidance is destroyed by the arbitrary allocations of extra divisional expenses that must be made in order to derive a net profit figure'.

Emmanuel and Otley,[11] adapt the approach of Amey (1969),[12] Solomans (1965)[13] and Amey and Eggington (1973)[14] and suggest a wider range of profit classifications (Figure 7.3). Their first two profit concepts are similar to those suggested by Shillinglaw[15] though with 'sales margin' called 'controllable contribution'. Thereafter two alternative sets of profit concepts are adopted, one relating to profit attributable to the segment (traceable profit, net profit and net profit after tax) and the other profit controllable by the manager (controllable residual income before and after taxes and net residual income after taxes).

The principles on which these profit concepts are based appear to be well accepted in accounting texts, although Amey (1969)[16] suggests that 'in the interests of achieving the firm's overall objective, divisions should not ... have the power to determine their own capital investment'.

The academic argument against apportionments and far more emphasis on attributability and controllability is by no means accepted in business. In those companies of which the authors have recent experience,[17,18] the willingness to view profit measures in more than one way is common, although most businesses retain the net profit concept as either the main objective for their investment centre managers or to remind them of those costs which are incurred on their behalf, even if they are not directly attributable or controllable. This widely held view in business today makes the point that if investment centre managers are not regularly reminded of their segments' non-attributable/controllable costs, there is a danger that they will ignore them from an operating decision viewpoint. However, for control, it should surely be argued that these costs can only be managed at a senior level and therefore should not be included in investment centre management's routine control information. If they are, there must be the danger that managers' attention is distracted away from the aspects they can control, or that their energies are given to arguing the unfairness of these changes, with demotivational effects. Do investment managers think like that? Some certainly do. The important aspect, however, is that the segmental/management performance measures used and the detailed information given to those managers should be agreed upon by senior management and not left to be decided by default.

The Investment Base

The same arguments which apply to controllable and attributable profit also apply to the investment base. If investment centre management or

Sales to outside customers				XXX	
Internal sales				XXX	
				XXX	
	Less	Variable costs of goods sold externally and internally		XXX	
		Variable divisional expenses		XXX	
		Controllable contribution		XXX	
	Less	Controllable divisional overhead		XXX	
Controllable profit				XXX	
Less	Depreciation and expenses on divisional fixed assets		XXX	Less Depreciation and controllable fixed assets	XXX
	Non-controllable divisional overheads		XXX	Expenses (e.g. leases) relating to controllable fixed assets	XXX
				Interest on controllable investments	XXX
			---		---
	Traceable profit		XXX	**Controllable residual income before taxes**	XXX
Less	Allocated central expenses		XXX	Less Depreciation on non-controllable fixed assets	XXX
				Allocated central expenses	XXX
				Interest on non-controllable investments	XXX

	Net profit		XXX	**Net residual income before taxes**	XXX
Less	Taxation on divisional income		XXX	Less Taxation on divisional income	XXX
	Net profit after tax		XXX	**Net residual income after taxes**	XXX

Figure 7.3 *Alternative forms of divisional profit measures (Adapted from Emmanuel and Otley, 1985)*

segments are to be fairly measured, the investment base must be as appropriate as the profit concept. Thus, for any given manager, controllable profit can be related to controllable investment, and, for any given segment, attributable profit can be related to attributable investment.

In administrative/accounting terms this may of course require some changes in the information system, which would need to identify, as far as practicable, the fixed and current assets of each investment centre. While fixed assets and the depreciation may not be too difficult to identify with particular segments, the same may not be true of current assets. Are debtors recorded and controlled centrally? Can the actual debtors of each segment be identified, especially where segments have the same customers? Are stocks held locally and/or centrally? Is cash considered to be a controllable item at segment level or are any such surpluses controlled centrally? Are creditors relatable to each segment or are they controlled centrally?

Of course the information system would ideally need to reflect asset controllability as well as attributability, but in many, perhaps most, cases these are likely to be similar. However, this does raise the question of just how controllable by investment centre managers are the fixed assets? Can the manager, for example, identify a surplus asset and either physically or book-wise have it excluded from their accountability and returned to a 'central pool'? It is not uncommon in building and contracting industries, for example, to have a central plant and equipment stock through which management can change its fixed asset investment levels according to requirements. Not only does each investment centre manager recognize his accountability for such fixed assets, but he is thereby encouraged to return surplus fixed assets rather than have them standing idle. This makes them available to other investment centre managers, and economies in plant and equipment cost and utilization are therefore obtained.

One specialist haulier known to the authors has a pool of vehicles which are attributed to the segment that operates them. They are controllable in that vehicles not required in the long term are appropriated elsewhere and extra vehicles required are either transferred to the segment or bought for it. This forms a controllable investment base perhaps, but the costs are perhaps not controllable. It is central management's policy to place newer vehicles in the busier segments of the business and older ones in the less busy. A busy segment therefore usually has disproportionately high depreciation and fixed asset investment costs than one that is less busy. Of course the advantage of lower repair and maintenance costs and higher utilization rates helps to compensate, but the effect on the busy segments' profitability is almost certainly negative.

The other side of the coin, however, is that, if attributability and controllability are practised, the problems of apportioning the fixed assets of the business to each investment centre is unnecessary. Such apportionments can be time-consuming, arbitrary and frequently the cause of discontent among segment managers. Apportionments will not be seen as fair by those who feel they are adversely affected by them.

However, if central management is interested in comparing the performance of investment centres with organizations outside the business, it may be necessary for some apportionment of fixed assets to be made. If not, the controllable and/or attribute investment base is unlikely to be comparable with the data available on these external entities.

Short-term measures, long-term goals

By definition, an investment centre is a business entity, small or large, responsible for profitability and investment. As a large proportion of investment is likely to be of a long-term nature – fixed assets, new products, new markets, etc. – the appropriate performance measure should logically be a long-term one, at least in part.

Profitability indices such as ROI and RI are potentially capable of reflecting long-term performance of *past decisions* but *not recent* or current decisions. The measures are for a particular period but not of the future. They are therefore effectively short-term measures, which if overemphasized as a measure of performance can only lead to short-term decision-making, dysfunctional in the longer term. The potential for such decisions will be apparent from the foregoing.

It could be proposed of course that those ROI and RI measures be applied only to longer-term profitability – by using, for example, 3- or 5-year rolling/average profitability indexes. But this is likely to be both impractical and misleading. Is a new manager to be held responsible for the decisions of his predecessor? If a manager expects to be in a particular post for only 2 or 3 years before being promoted or leaving for pastures new, of what relevance is a long-term measure, even if a fair one were found? Would errors of judgement affecting the long term not be as apparent as with shorter-term performance measures?

It is the use made of this profitability index which is the critical factor. If it is not overemphasized, but perhaps used as just one of a range of measures, the impact upon managers' behaviour should not be dysfunctional. If businesses place an undue emphasis on such profitability indices, adverse behavioural effects aimed at achieving short-term results will surely be encouraged. Worse, those managers who do take a longer term view at the expense of shorter-term performance may well not be allowed by the company to survive long enough to be judged upon the long term benefits. Further, that manager is likely to have missed out on the rewards of shorter-term performance in terms of personal salary and promotion. Those who gain promotions are perhaps more likely to be those who achieve short-term results than those who strive to achieve such in the longer term.

Is therefore the concentration by management on profitability indices which are not seen by managers as fair or relating to attributable and controllable features likely to have demotivational effects on investment centre managers? Will such controls simply discourage managers from long-term planning and decision-making and cause them to settle for the achievements of shorter-term performance measures. If senior management closes its eyes to this problem, it is quite likely, perhaps inevitable, that those managers who achieve senior management status are those who will have been motivated towards shorter-term measures and therefore will not see any need to change the control measures. Naturally, once this situation is reached, it is likely to be self-perpetuating.

Profit centres

As discussed earlier, a profit centre is the term used for 'a segment of the business entity by which both revenues are received and expenditures are caused or controlled, such revenues and expenditure being used to evaluate segmental performance'.[19] The presumption therefore is that the manager is responsible for both the sources of supply and the sale thereof. 'Sources of supply' may well include the manufacture or the buying in of goods or operation of services; 'sale' is likely to include decisions as to markets (perhaps within constraints so as not to trespass on the allotted areas of other segments of the business) and the marketing mix – pricing, promotion, product design and perhaps distribution networks. The autonomy, however, that profit centre managers are given may well be restricted by internal trading requirements – the sourcing of goods and service supplies and the sale of selected customers, including probably the prices of any such trading. A profit centre is not related to the level of investment in the segment, although of course its manager's decision-making may well have investment repercussions, if only on working capital. Thus performance measures must be of profitability unrelated to investment *per se*.

The profit measure

Essentially a profit centre's performance is judged upon the level of profit earned and the trend thereof, perhaps related to some aspects of output, e.g. profit as a percentage of sales, or as a percentage of input (profit per vehicle, machine or employee). The profit to sales percentage is by far the commonest measure, although this is usually used in addition to the growth trends in absolute amounts of profit.

However, in the same way that the ROI measure was questioned as regards its components 'what return?' and 'what investment?', so here the challenge must be made concerning 'what incomes?' and 'what costs?' In other words, 'what are the profits?'

In fact interpretations of profit for profit centre purposes are similar in many respects to those considered earlier for investment centre purposes. Operating and trading profits, and net profits before loan interest, are logical measures, but not of course after loan interest or post-tax, as these have capital gearing implications. The relevance to these interpretations of profit of accounting conventions and policies, including that of historic versus current costs and the hiring versus leasing argument, are also important considerations in profit-centre performance measurement.

Such profit concepts as controllable contribution margin, controllable profit and traceable profit, discussed earlier, probably have at least as great a significance in profit centre measurement, as they may be appropriately tailored to the specific responsibility aspects of profit centres, large and small, within a business. The arguments for these approaches will not be repeated here, except to suggest that the arguments against their use on investment centre measurement are less strong in a profit centre context. While it could be argued that a net profit figure is needed to compare against total invested capital, no such objective exists in profit centres, where net profit is of no special significance. Hence some interpretation of controllable or attributable profit before apportionments could be expected to be more popular in practice within profit centres than investment centres.

The contradiction between the short- and long-term nature of profitability measures is also relevant to profit centre performance assessments.

The added value concept

The added value concept, probably more appropriate to profit centres than investment centres, is an increasingly popular measure of profitability. Although various methods of calculations are used, the basic theme is that profitability is measured by the differences between sales and the cost of bought-in goods (and sometimes services). The difference is the amount of value added to the material inputs by the operation of the business, the bulk of which is usually the employment of staff, whether direct or indirect. This concept is particularly useful in situations where the sales value of items can be high or low, depending primarily on the cost of material inputs. If the sales value does not vary proportionately with resource inputs such as direct labour or machine time, sales value and such measures as profit as a percentage of sales are poor and inconsistent indicators of performance. In such circumstances 'added value' can replace profit as a profitability measure in absolute terms or as a ratio in relation to resource inputs such as machine labour hours, or be the base against which some interpretation of profit is compared.

Profit to sales percentage

This ratio simply expresses the size of the profit to the output, expressed at sales value, and together with 'turnover of capital' forms the first two elements of the ROI pyramid of ratios. The components effectively being compared of course are the levels of sales revenues and costs (sales − costs = profit), and it could thus be argued that the measure is soundly based. As with all performance measures, however, there is always a danger that the profit to sales ratio will, in motivating a manager towards its achievement, cause dysfunctional behaviour. In this case the emphasis of the ratio is on the size of profit margin. This may be achieved by a number of actions which to some extent pull in different directions, e.g. cost reduction, increased volumes and increased prices.

Cost reductions achieved by improvements in efficiency is an excellent means of increasing the sales margin, because it need have no repercussions elsewhere and gives the profit centre more flexibility for pricing in periods of high competition or low industry activity. If, however, cost reductions are achieved by a reduction in the quality of the product and/or service available to the customer, any increases in margin may be short-lived.

Changes in the volume of output can have a sometimes significant effect on the measured unit cost and therefore on resultant sales margins, as fixed costs spread more thinly across larger volumes. If sales volumes are increased without a reduction in sales prices, higher margins should result. If the higher output levels require additional fixed cost expenditures, the long and short term aspects may again be important in that incremental fixed costs resultant from increases in output may not be easily removed if volumes subsequently decrease. If volumes are increased by a reduction in sales prices, however, significant longer-term implications may ensue. Will reductions invite retaliation from competitors? For how long will the additional volumes be retained? What are the longer-term prospects in the market and in particular the effects upon the profit centre?

If prices are increased to achieve higher margins, this may or may not prove a desirable action. If the centre's prices were low for some or all customers, a change in price may well have no serious long-term effects on volume. The danger of increased prices is that the higher margins are achieved on small sales volumes. Although of course smaller volumes, by increasing average unit costs, can decrease resultant margins, it is quite possible that a profit centre can unconsciously become a high price/low volume business, with resultant lower levels of total profit. No doubt for this reason the objective of increase sales volumes is frequently linked with the profit to sales percentage measure. It is perhaps the fear of the opposite effect, i.e. achieving volumes by low prices (what is sometimes called 'chasing marginal business'), that makes the profit to sales percentage so popular.

As would be expected, the sales price: volume: cost: profit relationship is of critical importance in managing profit centres. The major concern, however, must be that in the achievement of higher margins, profit in relation to investment is not also optionally achieved. If higher margins are achieved by lower prices and increased volumes, additional investment may result either from an earlier than expected exhaustion of fixed assets or the need for incremental capacity. If higher margins are achieved at the expense of lower volumes, the danger is more of a contraction in long-term volumes and market share, resulting in lower total profitability with a fixed investment base.

Profit growth objectives

The objective of profit growth in absolute terms is frequently used as a profit centre measure, either as the principal measure or in conjunction with profit/sales or other ratios. If capital investment is effectively fixed, profit maximization, i.e. making the best of what you've got, is the obvious and optimal business objective and therefore performance measure. However, as capital is unlikely to be fixed in the longer term, the measure would be logical only as a short- or medium-term indicator.

Measures which compare profit with resources inputs such as employees or equipment may be seen as a surrogate for ROI, i.e. resources could be seen as financed by the investment. Their use in practice, however, tends to be limited to that of an ancillary measure, unlikely to be used as a measure of prime importance except perhaps in businesses where management expertise or specialist equipment are in scarce supply and are effectively limiting factors as far as profitability is concerned.

Why profit centres?

Profit centres tend to be used relatively rarely in practice, the extension into an investment centre being overwhelmingly popular and in many cases more logical. Although investment centres may also be measured as a profit centre, i.e. in profit to sales percentage and sales growth terms, profit centres tend to be used where the investment centre approach is seen to be either less relevant or inapplicable to a particular segment.

When a company makes an investment in plant and equipment, especially if it is flow- or process-oriented say a steel mill or motor assembly line, such an investment is effectively a sunk cost, with relatively little sale or alternative use value. The object therefore must be to use that equipment as profitably as possible. In such circumstances ROI, whether it be high or low, is of little relevance to decision-making or control except in a post-audit of investment sense. The treatment of the segment as a profit centre may therefore be more appropriate in that it directs management's attention to the one objective, whereas ROI may add concern over the investment (which is effectively more relevant from a decision-making point of view) and worry the managers unnecessarily.

The owning or hiring/leasing of assets was discussed earlier as a problem of investment-centre performance measurement. If one segment owns and another leases assets, their respective performances as investment centres are likely to differ, perhaps considerably. In many industries there has been a trend away from the ownership of business assets towards the hiring and leasing of operating assets, the sale and perhaps leaseback of property, the discounting of debtors; obtaining stocks 'just in time' by requiring your suppliers to hold stock or by having such on a 'sale or return' basis. Although there have been some tax advantages in these actions, the principal benefit has perhaps been in the areas of cash flow – the release of funds for other parts of the business.

The effect of these actions is that many businesses effectively have relatively few owned assets and therefore capital invested either in some or all of the segments of their business. When this occurs, the investment centre approach is not, effectively, an available option, but as the profit objective remains, a profit centre approach is the only logical responsibility centre basis.

An example of this is the Central Freight Co. This haulier operated a large number of depots situated in large British conurbations, each of them treated as an investment centre. Even at this time there were anomalies between owned premises old and new and rented premises. As the business expanded, the pressure on capital and liquidity became significant. Operating assets, especially vehicles, were frequently leased if cash was not available, and this soon became the normal means of acquiring such assets. Further, in order to release capital some depots with a high market value were sold and either leased back or moved to a rented site. The attributable fixed assets of many depots therefore became negligible, while others were little changed. In such a situation ROI was of little relevance as a basis for comparison across the group or indeed of trends over time and against other similar organizations. Although the investment centre concept had effectively broken down, the profit centre concept was unlikely to be an acceptable alternative basis in such circumstances. Comparison was impossible between depots when some rented and others owned their property and therefore had no rental, or between those which leased vehicles and those which operated owned assets now depreciated perhaps wholly or only to a small extent.

If a profit centre approach was to be adopted, an equalization of ownership/rental/leasing was required. Central divisions were established to 'own' all operating assets and property. These were then rented/leased back to the depots on a 'going rate' basis. Thus all depots were treated in a similar fashion, but the capital base per depot had disappeared. Profit performance measures of profit percentage of sales and sales volume growth were established. Interestingly, however, some responsibility for investment remains. New operating assets can be applied for and surplus assets reassigned to other depots, such actions being reflected in the charge made for assets used. Stocks are under depot control although much of these are on a sale or return basis. Debtors are considered to be a depot responsibility, although debt collection is organized centrally, and only slow payers are referred to depot management for collection. Poor working capital control is therefore not reflected in the profit centre performance measure, which might therefore encourage a laxity in this area. However, management performance is also assessed via a number of performance measures, including those for stock and debtor control.

Budgeted profit and investment centres

It can be argued that many of the deficiencies of profit and investment centre measures discussed in this chapter can be remedied or ameliorated if a budget centre approach is adopted, i.e. if segments are measured against a budgeted level of performance. Thus, for example, the increasing ROI percentage over time is not a problem, it is argued, if such is compared against a budget for the increase, which might reasonably be anticipated, as asset depreciation rates are known at the budgetary stage.

As discussed earlier, to compare one profit or investment centre's performance against another's may well be illogical if each segment is operating under different circumstances – industry, location, market etc. – certainly in the shorter term. To be 'fair' a segment performance needs to be compared against a comparable parameter, of which a budget is likely to be the most applicable and appropriate. The popularity of budgeted profit and investment centre measures can be seen as an acceptance of the need for budgets as a comparator, but in some respects it is applied somewhat illogically. If a budget makes allowance for the special circumstances of a segment, what is the logic of comparing such a profit budget against capital employed whether actual or budgeted? Indeed is not the logical measure controllable or attributable profit or residual income? The asset base in the shorter term is surely irrelevant even if, say, working capital is considered to be controllable or attributable. Surely such can be better measured by separate, more specific, measures.

As a control measure therefore, while budgets add an extra dimension to the measurement of profit and investment centres, the use of the same ratios/comparisons in a budgetary terminology may not be so logical. However, the projected ROI over, say, the 5 years of a segment's corporate plan may be a very useful measure for decision-making and be the basis for a longer-term post-audit of the performance of a segment or, in particular, its management, especially if the budget incorporated new developments or the ideas of new management.

Non-financial criteria

The foregoing has concentrated upon the financial aspects of performance, appraisal and control. Non-financial measures should not, however, be forgotten.

Key results analysis

In 1952, The General Electric Co. in the USA, following extensive decentralization of its operations, recognized the need for an improved system of management control and evolved a set of eight 'key result areas' for the measurement of departments (not managers), as follows:

1 Profitability, defined as residual income.
2 Market position, measured in terms of market share.
3 Productivity, recognized as being difficult to define, but broadly based on the inputs of capital and labour versus outputs of sales, added-value, or other suitable measure.

4 Product leadership, i.e. being a market leader in product innovation and development.
5 Personnel development, i.e. the 'bringing-on' of staff to fill vacancies, allow expansion, etc.
6 Employee attitudes, i.e. employee attitudes which might influence future behaviour and thus objective achievement.
7 Public responsibility, an ethical objective to stakeholders – the public, shareholders, customers, suppliers, employees – and the environment in general.
8 Balance between short-range and long-range goals, of survival and growth over 5, 10, 15 and more years.

The company's planning, budgeting and forecasting programme then incorporated these key result areas by reviewing the recent and present levels of achievement, setting standards for each department, planning their achievement and establishing their periodic reporting.

As will be apparent, such a multi-faceted approach may have considerable merits in (i) recognizing the breadth of organizational objectives, and (ii) being widely adaptable to a variety of managerial situations. Its implementation, however, may be fraught with difficulties.

Definition

The most obvious problem perhaps is that of clearly and unambiguously defining the objective. 'Market share', for example, may be defined in many ways and 'public responsibility' may be definable in only general terms.

Measurement

If performance is to be appraised, achievement must be measured. The extent to which the GE key results areas may be objectively evaluated is likely to vary considerably. Given a definition, profitability and productivity are likely to be relatively straightforward to measure, and market position and product leadership somewhat more complex. But how would one measure personnel development, employee attitude and public responsibility.' The use of subjective judgement is likely to be an essential ingredient in the evaluation of non-quantifiable and perhaps some quantifiable performances.

Objective ranking and suboptimality

Objectives such as those proposed may to some extent be mutually exclusive: market position may be achieved at the expense of profitability, productivity may be achieved with the expense of employee attitudes, personnel development may be achieved at the expense of long-term goals. This problem may be mitigated perhaps by establishing a hierarchy or ranking of objectives, e.g. (i) Profit (ii) Market position ...

Alternatively, each objective may be given a weighting, reflecting top management's perceived valuation in relation to the others. Another possibility is the establishment of minimum criteria in each area, below which super performance in other areas will not be considered a sufficient compensation.

A departmental measure?

The key results areas established by GE were specifically aimed at measuring the performance of parts of the business (departments) and not necessarily their management. However, as discussed earlier in the chapter, the separation of the performance of a segment and its manager is not always that clear.

In a subsequent study at GE, Meyer, Kay and French[20] concluded that:

- Criticism has a negative effect on achievement of goals.
- Praise has little effect, one way or the other.
- Performance improves most when specific goals are established.
- Defensiveness resulting from critical appraisal produces inferior performance.
- Coaching should be day to day, not a once-a-year activity.
- Mutual goal setting, not criticism, improves performance.
- Interviews designed primarily to improve a man's performance should not at the same time weigh his salary or promotion in the balance.
- Participation by the employee in the goal setting procedure helps produce favourable results'.

Most managers have responsibility for a wide range of activities, some of which may well not lend themselves to objective measurement. The fact that financial measures lend themselves readily to objective evaluation should not necessarily imply that they should be the sole or prime performance measure. The evaluation of non-quantifiable and non-financial objectives may, depending upon the situation, be at least as important as those of a quantifiable financial nature. Evaluation complexity or difficulty should not be an excuse, but merely a challenge.

References

1   Coates, J.B., Smith, J.E. and Stacey, R.J., 'Results of a Preliminary Survey into the Structure of Divisionalised Companies, Divisionalised Performance Appraisal and the Associated Role of Management Accounting', in *Management Accounting Research and Practice*, ICMA, 1983.

2. Coates, J.B., Rickwood, C.P. and Stacey, R.J., 'Examination of the Differences Between Academic Concepts and Actual Management Accounting Practices', Report to ESRC, British Library Document Supply Centre, August 1987.
3. Coates, Smith and Stacey, op. cit.
4. Coates, Rickwood and Stacey, op. cit.
5. Rickwood, C.P., Coates, J.B. and Stacey, R.J., 'Managed Costs and the Capture of Information', *Accounting and Business Research*, Vol. 17, No. 68, Autumn 1987.
6. Solomons, D., *Divisional Performance Measurement and Control*, Richard D. Irwin Inc., 1965.
7. Shillinglaw, G., *Managerial Cost Accounting*, Richard Irwin, 1961.
8. Amey, L.R. and Eggington, D.A., *Management Accounting – A Conceptual Approach*, Longman, 1973.
9. Shillinglaw, G., 'Guides to Internal Profit Measurement', *Harvard Business Review* Vol. 35, No. 2 March/April 1957, pp. 82–94.
10. Shillinglaw, G., *Managerial Cost Accounting*, op. cit.
11. Emmanuel, C.R. and Otley, D.T., *Accounting for Management Control*, Van Nostrand Reinhold (UK), 1985.
12. Amey, L.R., *The Efficiency of Business Enterprises*, G. Allen and Unwin, 1969.
13. Solomons, op. cit.
14. Amey and Eggington, op. cit.
15. Shillinglaw, *Managerial Cost Accounting*, op. cit.
16. Amey, op. cit.
17. Coates, Rickwood and Stacey, op. cit.
18. Rickwood, Coates and Stacey, op. cit.
19. Coates, Smith and Stacey, op. cit.
20. Meyer, H.H., Kay, E. and French, J.P.R., 'Split Roles in Performance Appraisal', *Harvard Business Review*, January/February 1965.

Questions

1. ABE Ltd and KIM Ltd are two newly established divisions of RAT plc. They operate as independent trading units, though some of their final product markets overlap.

   Their managing directors each agreed an initial plan based on a 20 per cent per annum charge for capital by RAT plc. The plan showed both divisions to be capable of meeting the 20 per cent target.

   During the first year's operation ABE Ltd secured a contract to supply items to LO plc, a company not within the RAT group and a direct competitor in KIM Ltd's market. KIM Ltd could have bought the same supplies from ABE Ltd but preferred to buy from a supplier outside the RAT group.

   In the first year of operation LO plc secured a 5 per cent increase in its share of the market at the expense of KIM Ltd. A major factor in LO plc's success was considered to be the superiority of ABE Ltd's product over those of its competitors.

KIM Ltd and LO were each initially expected to have a 50 per cent share in the final product market, the latter being KIM Ltd's sole market outlet.

The key elements of the budgets agreed at the outset by ABE Ltd and KIM Ltd are:

	ABE Ltd	KIM Ltd
Initial investment in plant and equipment (£m):	10	15
Cost of capital charge	20%	20%
Expected new cash flows in £m:		
First year	1.9	3.2
Years 2–8 pa	2.9	4.2

Assume that:

1 The operating efficiencies of KIM Ltd and LO plc are broadly the same.
2 The 5 per cent increase in the market share made by LO plc results are in a pro rata 5 per cent increase in ABE Ltd's net cash flow.

You are required to:

(a) Evaluate the two divisions' expected performance as seen by RAT plc at the time of their establishment.
(b) Evaluate the actual performance of the two divisions in their first year of operation, giving a reasoned interpretation of the outcomes.
(c) Discuss the performance measures applicable to assessing the success or otherwise of the divisions. Identify further issues which may be deemed relevant but beyond the information given by the question.
Note: Taxation is to be ignored.

2 (a) Discuss the nature of the problems presented for the creation and transmission of planning to control information at (i) the top management level, and (ii) the divisional level, when a previously centrally managed organization decides to reorganize the management of its operations into a group of autonomous divisions.

(b) Many indicators may be used to assist in the appraisal of the performance of divisions within a company. However, they must be designed to ensure that divisions' activities are directed toward the achievement of corporate goals. Discuss the above statement and

support your answer by reference to particular performance measures.
(a) What are the potential strengths and weaknesses of the profit centre approach to performance appraisal?
(b) Why has the popularity of cost centres declined in recent years in favour of profit centres.

4 'The linking of budget performance to the individuals' reward package is a natural development of control via budget centres.' Consider this assertion and identify the positive and negative aspects of such an approach.

5 IVY plc manufacture invalid vehicles in Birmingham, England, for sale worldwide. The vehicles are marketed in Britain and Eire by the UK Division; in Europe by the Europe Division, based in Switzerland; and in North and South America by the Americas Division, based in New Orleans.

Although there is currently only one model, the need to comply with safety and other requirements of overseas countries creates substantial additional manufacturing costs over and above those of the basic UK model.

Vehicles are sold overseas at estimated cost price. Although it is difficult to record all the additional costs of overseas models, this is estimated by reference to the time and materials booked on to production batches. These are added to the standard product costs of the UK model. In both cases overheads are recovered at the budgeted blanket overhead recovery rate, currently 200 per cent of direct labour.

Included in the Budgeted Profit Statement attached are assumptions regarding tax rates and currency exchange rates in the UK, Switzerland and the USA.

Expert advice received is conflicting, reflecting the current state of uncertainty in politics, oil prices, the British and world economies and therefore currency exchange rates. Likely scenarios are briefly as follows:

1 The US dollar will lose 10 per cent value against European currencies and US sales volumes reduce by a similar percentage.
2 The £ sterling will lose 20 per cent value against the US dollar and 10 per cent against European currencies. Overseas sales will increase by a similar percentage in both cases.
3 A change in British Government influences a 25 per cent £ sterling currency reduction against European and US currencies and will result in the introduction of exchange control and currency regulations.

Matters for consideration
(a) Which performance measures should IVY plc consider for the evaluation of its three Divisions.

(b) Invalid vehicles are currently sold within the group at standard/estimated cost. Which transfer price method would you recommend:
1 To facilitate the performance measures chosen.
2 In order to maximize after tax profits for the group.
3 In order to maximize liquidity
   (i) overseas, and
   (ii) in Britain?
(c) What legal and operating constraints need to be considered?

6 If ROCE has so many inherent deficiencies, why do you think it is so popular among senior managers?
7 (a) Consider the difficulties in applying key results analysis to the performance evaluation of segmented managers.
(b) Why might it be desirable in spite of these difficulties?
8 As a junior consultant with Stokes Consultants you have gleaned the following information about a client company, Central Freight. The new managing director of the Elco Group has expressed concern about the relevancy and adequacy of the operating statements and appraisal measures both for Central Freight's internal purposes and as a basis for the management and control of CF by the Elco Group. He has given Stokes Consultants a wide ranging brief to examine and criticize the existing approach and to recommend such alternatives as it thinks fit. However, he expects that any alternatives or changes proposed will be appropriate and that the likely implications of their imposition will be clearly stated.

CENTRAL FREIGHT

Central Freight, a subsidiary of the Elco Group, is a large goods haulage company. It is organized on a regional basis, each region consisting of a number of operating depots which provide the services/products of the company. Regional and company head office staff act as a back up to and control of the depots.

Before 1974 the company offered only a general haulage service, although it also operated a separate 'contracts' company. However, following a change in strategy of the organization, it was decided to add 'new products', hopefully synergistically, stemming from a conversion of their main general haulage product. As a result each depot was then able to offer the following products:

1 *Contracts* – where an organization's road haulage function is taken over by Central Freight.
2 *General haulage* – a national service, although now on a much smaller scale, previous haulage work having been converted to other products, especially contracts.
3 *Warehousing* – a storage facility to other companies, perhaps related to distribution or general haulage products.
4 *Property* – the rental of surplus storage space to a third party.
5 *Truck rental* – the hire of trucks of various sizes and types either on a self-drive or with-driver basis to individuals and organizations.

Assessing segmental performance   153

IVY plc
Budgeted profit statement

	UK division		Europe division			Americas division			Consolidated Group Total
Sales volume	3,000		5,000			3,000			
	Total £000	Per unit £	Total £000		Per unit £	Total £000		Per unit £	Total £000
Sales – internal	24,900								
Sales – external	10,500	3,500	20,000		4,000	13,500		4,500	44,000
	35,400		20,000		4,000	13,500		4,500	44,000
Cost of manufacture (all in UK)				MEMO ONLY					
Variable costs:									
materials	12,600		6,000	1,200		3,600	1,200		12,600
labour	6,600		3,000	600		2,100	700		6,600
Fixed costs	13,200		6,000	1,200		4,200	1,400		13,200
Total	32,400		15,000	3,000		9,900	3,300		32,400
Cost of sales	(24,900)		15,000		3,000	9,900		3,300	
Selling and admin. costs	2,100	700	3,500		700	2,100		700	7,700
Profit before tax	900	300	1,500		300	1,500		500	3,900
Effective tax rates	35%		20%			45%			
Assumed Exchange Rate To £ sterling			2.75 Swiss Francs			1.40 US dollars			
Capital employed (historical)	13,200		2,000			1,500			16,700

6 *Engineering* – the maintenance workshops for the company's fleet, surplus capacity being sold to the market place.
7 *Distribution* – the distribution of goods either held in Central Freight's or client companies' warehouses, which could involve a 'breaking of bulk' service.
8 *Rescue* – roadside assistance to commercial vehicles on motorways and elsewhere and providing an on the spot repair service, or bringing a vehicle into the engineering depot for more serious repairs.
9 *Trailer rental* – the rental of trailers with or without the truck rental.
10 *Miscellaneous*, covering any items of income or expenditure not covered under any other head.

A depot may have had any or all of these products, depending upon local demand. Thus in any one area one product may predominate, while others may be insignificant or non-existent.

Each depot was treated by the company as a budgeted investment centre, as in turn were each of the products within each depot. Additionally, performance was compared with that budgeted for the investment centre as a whole and for its component parts.

While depot managers had an overall responsibility for all products within their depot, some products, depending on their nature or significance within the depot, also had individual product managers. Thus the engineering product invariably had an engineering manager, owing to the specialist nature of the product, while other products were managed directly by the depot manager with some assistance from subordinates.

Each product and depot, as indicated above, was expected to sell its services to the market at a profit, according to the local market conditions at any point in time. However, a considerable amount of inter-region, inter-depot and inter-product group (intra-depot) trading occurred. While wishing to retain the profit motivation for such internal trading while encouraging (in theory requiring) the use of such facilities (rather than that of outside suppliers), fixed internal charge rates were agreed centrally for some products. These rates were designed such that intra-depot trading had the lowest margins, with increasing margins for inter-depot and inter-region transactions, the latter still being lower than the current market price, or at least no lower than a favoured customer.

The above resulted in an investment centre's revenues being generated from four different sources in terms of price structure, i.e. sales to other products within the same depot, sales to other depots in the same region, sales to other regions and sales to the general market. The proportions of these sales were largely dependent upon the particular location of a depot, the extent to which it had a variety of products, spare capacity for sale to the outside market, etc.

There were also directives on a number of expenditure items over which profit centres had little or no control. These included rates of pay (and to an extent the hiring and firing of staff) and the source and/or price of a number of expenditures such as fuel, tyres and insurance. Capital equipment was authorized at regional and/or company level, depending upon the size of expenditures proposed. There were also company policies regarding such factors as depreciation rates and the apportionment of depot, regional and head office overhead expenses across depots and product investment centres.

Operating statements
A periodic trading statement was produced for each depot, analysed between the ten product investment centres. This statement analysed revenue into eight categories of sale, as follows:

1 External sales – to own customers
2 External sales – to own customers, storage only
3 External sales – transportation work subcontracted to another depot, e.g. backloads
4 External sales transportation subcontracted to outside contractors
= Total customer revenue
5 Internal sales transportation work for other depots, e.g. backloads
6 Internal sales – intra depot/products revenues
7 Internal sales – inter depot revenues
8 Internal sales – inter-company revenues
= Total revenues

Expenditures included the costs of inter-group services, subcontracting and the various operating expenses of each investment centre, including depreciation, and *shared* depot overheads. The margin between these expenditures and revenues was defined as the 'gross operating profit'. Thereafter apportioned charges were subtracted to provide a 'trading profit or loss', which was then expressed as a percentage of (i) capital employed and (ii) revenues.

Capital employed itself contained a number of apportionments, being composed of (a) directly attributable fixed assets, i.e. those assets which could be specifically identified with a particular product investment centre, (b) fixed assets directly attributable to a depot (though apportioned to product investment centres and (c) working capital and regional and company head offices fixed assets, apportioned over depots and thence product investment centres. In outline therefore a depot operating statement appeared as follows:

Table 1

Revenue:	Sales to outside customers
	Sales to outside customers – storage only
	External sales – transportation work subcontracted to another depot, e.g. backloads
	External Sales – transportation subcontracted to outside contractors
	= Total customer revenue
	Internal Sales – transportation work done for other depots, e.g. backloads
	Internal sales – Intra-depot/products
	Internal sales – Inter-depot and Sales inter-company
	= Total revenues
Expenditure:	Subcontracting – own company
	Subcontracting – other contractors
	Total subcontracting
	Vehicle hire charges – medium- to long-term
	Vehicle hire charges – short-term

	Drivers' wages
	Depot and warehouse wages
	Fuel and lubricants
	Tyres
	Other operating expenses
	Vehicle and equipment maintenance depreciation
	Insurance and damages
	Licence duties
	Direct property charges
	Direct property depreciation
	Direct branch management and administration
	Direct branch miscellaneous
	= Total operating expenses
Gross operating profit:	Apportioned property charges
	Apportioned property depreciation
	Apportioned branch management and administration
	Apportioned branch miscellaneous
Net activity profit:	Regional company/group head office expenses
	Trading profit/loss
	Trading profit as a percentage of revenue
	Capital employed(£)
	Trading profit as a percentage of capital employed

The above was compiled on a 4-weekly basis showing a total for the depot as a whole and for each of the product investment centres. A number of regions introduced incentives schemes based upon the achievement of budgeted profitability and other 'key target areas', particularly the level of debtors and certain cost ratios such as the fuel and maintenance costs per mile.

Management appraisal

Management was assessed primarily on actual return on capital employed and profit percentage to revenue figures against budget, as well as certain physical/cost centre ratios such as maintenance cost per mile and fuel cost per mile.

Some regional accountants produced a league table for senior management based upon the ROCE figures of the depots within their region. Although not published as such, depot managers were usually made aware of their relative position in the table: those at the bottom end of the table could expect more 'attention' and 'visitations' than other depots, while those at or near the top received relatively fewer.

Profit as percentage of revenue was considered to be of secondary importance to the ROCE ratio. Its trends were followed and considered to be an important indicator of the pricing practices adopted and of the present and future market situation. Low margins were in general considered with extreme concern.

9 As a result of entry into new products and markets, a company is adopting a divisionalized organization structure and is considering its accounting information system (AIS). You are required to
   (a) discuss the requirements such a company faces in developing

an AIS which provides and communicates information for planning and control at the levels of both
(i) top management, and
(ii) divisional management;
(b) assess the main features to be recognized in the operation of performance measures which seek to ensure the achievement of corporate objectives in this divisionalized organization.
(CIMA November 1987)

10 Residual income and return on investment are commonly used measures of performance. However, they are frequently criticised for placing too great an emphasis on the achievement of short-term results, possibly damaging longer-term performance. You are required to discuss
(a) the issues involved in the long-term:short-term conflict referred to in the above statement;
(b) suggestions which have been made to reconcile this difference.
(CIMA November 1988)

8 Assessing performance – expense and service centres

Introduction

A thorough understanding of responsibility-centre concepts is fundamental to good organizational and managerial control. This chapter will examine control of those parts of a business which service directly or indirectly the business's profit or investment centres or expend resources that provide benefits for the business as a whole. The former may well be termed service centres and the latter expense centres.

While the outputs of a profit or investment centre are quantifiable in monetary terms in relation to monetary inputs, thus providing a ready measure of performance, i.e. profit, the same is not true of expense and service centres. While inputs to service and expense centres may be measurable in monetary terms, their outputs are not. Indeed it may sometimes be difficult, impracticable or impossible to quantify in any meaningful way the outputs of some centres, let alone measure the qualitative aspects of the service provided. After all, not all such outputs are tangible. How, for example, would an organization quantify employee morale, pride or disaffection?

Effectiveness and efficiency

In establishing measures of expense/service-centres' performance a distinction needs to be drawn between those that measure effectiveness and those that measure efficiency. Effectiveness is a measure of performance outputs against objectives, while efficiency is a measure of the creation of outputs in relation to inputs.

The danger of course is that expense/service-centre managers may achieve efficiency at the expense of effectiveness. The implications for managerial control therefore are to identify measures for the evaluation of such responsibility centres which encourage the desired *balance* between effectiveness and efficiency, i.e. between efficiency and the supply and usage (by other managers) of a service provided.

The word balance is emphasized, because the pressures for effectiveness and efficiency may pull in different directions. Consider, for example, a plant maintenance department. It may be effective at reducing machine breakdowns and keeping machine downtime to a minimum by employing large numbers of maintenance engineers, even if from time to time they are underemployed or overservicing equipment – 'Rolls-Royce' service maybe but surely they are unlikely to be *efficient*. For that they may need perhaps to provide, say, a 'Sierra', 'Cavalier' or even a 'Mini' service – reduce staff to a 'sensible' minimum, so that all are kept fully stretched and occupied, though at the expense of some effectiveness in terms of machine downtime. Of course line/production/ operational management would probably prefer the Rolls-Royce service, as that would make their job easier, but senior management is likely to be looking for both efficiency and effectiveness. That balance, however, needs to be defined?

Expense or cost centres

A distinction is sometimes drawn between expense and cost centres. Anthony, Dearden and Vancil argue, for instance, that 'The cost centre is an accounting entity, a device for accumulation of costs to be charged to products or services; the expense centre is an organizational entity'.[1] Although terminology in accounting is often applied very loosely, the distinction raised is an important one.

The cost centre approach is an accounting measure to control those parts of an organization whose outputs are not expressible in monetary terms. As such, it may be equally applicable to the measurement of both service and expense centres. Distinction, however, needs to be drawn between various types of expense centre, e.g. engineered, committed and managed costs.

Engineered, committed and managed costs

Engineered costs are those for which an input:output relationship may be defined, e.g. the direct material and labour costs of manufacture may be expected to have a direct relationship to output volumes. *Committed costs* are costs which have already been incurred, of which depreciation is the best and most obvious example. *Managed or discretionary costs* are those categories of expense incurred at the discretion of management at a point in time, and may vary quite widely in size. The 'right' amount of expense, say, on research and development is impossible to determine on any scientific or engineered basis, and management must use its 'nous' in deciding what level to authorize.

Control can be exercised over engineered costs by the measurement of cost rates (the relation of physical outputs to cost inputs), the objective being that of rate reduction within some parameters of the minimum desired/specified quality of goods or service. Managed costs, however, may not be controlled in such a manner; the relation between outputs and inputs is not meaningfully calculable. The levels of expense must therefore be at the discretion of management.

Cost centres and control

Cost centres are parts of an organization to which costs are attributed for purposes of management and control. If possible, some suitable expression of output of the cost centre is established, compared with the costs, and cost rates per unit of output calculated. These are then compared with the cost rates of previous years or of cost rates of similar units elsewhere in the organization.

The control implications of cost centres vary between the circumstances under which each operates, i.e. whether or not service or expense costs are allottable or chargeable to beneficiaries of the service or expense, engineered, committed or managed costs.

Control of engineered costs

As indicated earlier, engineered costs are those where there is a specific and specifiable relation between the outputs and the cost inputs, i.e. those costs which lend themselves to standardization via methods and work-study engineers. Most but not all variable costs are of this nature, as (i) by definition there is a linear relation between the cost input and the volume of output, and (ii) engineered standards for such costs are usually creatable.

Such costs lend themselves neatly to the cost centre approach. Cost rates can be derived and compared with those of previous years, other similar cost centres, or budgeted/standard cost rates.

Although the term 'engineered costs' may give the impression that such are necessarily manufacturing-oriented, it must be stressed that this need not be the case. *Any* cost, whether it be in manufacturing or service organizations or segments, where the output: input relationship exists can be treated as an engineered cost. Nor necessarily need methods and work measurement techniques be applied, although these techniques are increasingly applied to non-manufacturing/service-oriented situations, though not without some difficulties, owing to the varied nature of the work in many non-manufacturing business segments.

Allotment of service costs

It is difficult to plan and control any part of an organization whose goods or services are not sold to a customer outside the organization. There are no market forces which indicate the profitability of the segment and the outputs are not easily expressible in monetary/financial terms. Many organizations resolve this quandary by establishing transfer prices for the segment's goods and services. Where these transfer prices are above cost, a pseudo-profit or investment centre is created. However, where the price is at or below cost, a cost centre is established.

The reasons for the charging or allotment of costs tend to be negative in that they stem from the problems believed to exist if the costs were not charged or allotted. Many managements believe that if recipient managers are not aware that they will be charged for a supply, they will use it uneconomically, perhaps by demanding more or of a higher quality than they really need, in an unplanned manner or simply by being wasteful in its use. Further, as it is difficult for management to know what volume and quality of service to provide, a charge acts as a surrogate for a market price, and in effect regulates the demand to calculate the supply, against which the price of an external supplier can be compared. Of course such a system also has the 'advantage' of deriving data to calculate a total product/service cost of the business.

Although we are primarily concerned here with the control of the supplying cost centre, the control upon the recipient cannot be ignored. Thus a distinction needs to be drawn between charges based upon some realistic measure of consumption or usage and those of an arbitrary apportionment nature. In the former case there is an implication that control is likely to be more meaningfully exercisable than in the latter case.

Charging on consumption

If a measure of consumption or usage is available, the input cost of the cost centre can be compared with total usage to derive a cost rate as a basis for evaluation. Likewise the recipients may be more readily controlled in respect of their consumption. However, this control may only be fair if the calculation base of the charge is consistently calculated. In principle the charge and the suppliers' cost rate should not be affected by the demands, actions and efficiencies of other segments of the business or factors that cannot be anticipated or lie beyond the centre's control.

Thus, for example, the charge per unit to users should not increase if the total demand in a period falls, nor because the costs of the supplier be higher than anticipated. On the other hand, management would certainly want to know the reasons for the change in demand and the effect on cost rates both in the short and long run.

For those reasons, budget cost rates are used in many organizations as the basis for charges, perhaps reflecting the fixity and variability of costs, actual cost rates being compared with the (flexed) budgeted cost rates of the supplying cost centre.

Although charging on a usage basis has a number of advantages, in some circumstances it may be counter-productive. Many large groups, for example, operate an internal consultancy service and have found that charging for their services on a usage basis dissuades some managers from using the service, an event which senior manager neither intended or desired. Possible alternatives are not to charge at all or to charge a fixed (apportioned) rate whether the service is used or not.

Apportioned charges

Charges of a fixed nature not reflecting consumption may, however, have adverse effects. Why should a manager control the usage of a service if the charges made to the using segment will not increase? Further, those managers who believe that their charges are inequitably high might be demotivatived, blame all their segments' ills upon such perceived inequality and be diverted from their real problems.

However, many managements believe that any such demotivations are overstated and that recharging of costs, even on an arbitrary basis, provides a positive motivation (i) in that the user will demand a good service, and (ii) that the supplying managers attain a higher status (in their eyes) not dissimilar from that of managing a profit centre. Again, the use of budgeted costs as the basis for charging, reflecting fixed and variable cost elements, is popular among businesses for the reasons outlined earlier.

In terms of a control on the supplying managers, however, the recovery of costs via apportioned changes may mislead management into believing that the cost centre is 'paying its way'. In fact of course the effect of apportioning costs to user segments is, *per se*, no control at all. However, if the fact of charging persuades users to criticize the service, and thereby create an environment under which improvements are encouraged and made, a control of a sort may be achieved.

Management is likely to seek alternative means of controlling such cost centres. If costs had a direct *causal* relation with some measure of output, the need for apportionments would presumably not arise, for they would be chargeable on a consumption basis. If possible therefore, management should consider alternative bases – bases, which, having no direct causal link, can be viewed as a surrogate for them. Such activity levels might include numbers of units sold, sales value, standard hours produced or worked, customers' enquiries or orders received, purchase requests received, and invoices received or issued. Actual cost centre costs may then be related to those measures to derive unit cost measures for comparison and, thereby, control.

Such an approach is not possible for many cost centres, particularly where the costs are committed or managed, and must therefore be controlled by other means.

Committed costs

Committed costs are those which will be expended by an organization to maintain a minimum level of competence if normal activities ceased for a period (such as a strike). Such *fixed* costs, as they must most surely be, would include the depreciation on fixed assets, property costs (rent, rates, repairs and maintenance), equipment costs (repairs and maintenance to maintain workable capacity) and such minimum organizational costs as minimum staffing levels, especially key staff and senior managers.

Such costs are not controllable in the short term, although of course the utilization of them may be. In the short term therefore 'control' can perhaps be best achieved by excluding such costs from routine reports or making it clear in reports that such costs are provided 'for information only'.

In the longer term, however, no cost is committed permanently. Control can be exercised (i) by carrying out a post-audit of capital expenditure authorizations to learn from past decisions and to indicate the need for future decisions, and (ii) by considering the desirability or not of retaining/reducing/removing existing levels of committed costs, e.g. by selling assets representing any excess capacity.

Managed/discretionary costs

Managed or discretionary costs are those which are neither committed or engineered and which therefore, by definition, are expended at the discretion of management. Such expenditures are a considerable problem to management in that there is no way of knowing how much expenditure on such costs is warranted in terms of the benefits it would bring, nor of the relative benefits of one such expense type over another, e.g. of £1m on research and development and over £1m on promotion.

Logically this might be interpreted as implying that these costs could be reduced or eliminated should the organization hit 'hard' times, suffering profitability, liquidity and survival problems. Curiously, while this may be true of some discretionary costs, particularly in the short term, and is a practice exhibited by many managements, the very reverse may be the case in respect of other costs. Thus, for example, management might reduce expenditure on research and development when resources were low, without sufficiently damaging the short-term results, but at the risk of the long-term prospects. Should management, however, reduce marketing and promotion costs when market size or market share falls? Perhaps the very reverse would be more rewarding in both the short and longer term. It would be a gamble of course, but that is in the nature of such discretionary costs. The output for a given input is not predeterminable in any scientific sense: Output forecasts from 'experts' are likely to be 'best' information available to assist such decision-making.

Discretionary cost decisions are usually made as part of the budgetary process, as a matter of policy/tactics. While the actual expenditure decision may take place subsequently, as the expense is presumably an integral part of the plan, actual expenditure is unlikely be deferred – unless of course management decides to rethink the strategies/tactics of the business.

Control over such costs is necessarily of a somewhat different nature to that of engineered and committed costs. It must reflect as far as possible the decision-making processes, assumptions and decision data.

Decision practices in relation to managed costs are likely to be made on one or more of the following bases:

1 Treating past years as the 'norm', adjusting annually for inflation.
2 Treating the expenses as a percentage appropriation of budgeted or previous years' sales.
3 Treating the expenditure of competitors as the 'norm' either in absolute or percentage terms.
4 Consideration on a 'what we can afford basis', as a 'residual' of the budgetary process, i.e. sales less committed and engineered costs and the profit requirement.
5 Evaluation on a case by case basis, using past experience and expert opinion to answer such questions as the following. Why spend any money at all? What alternative ways are there of obtaining the same objectives? What are the estimated costs, benefits and viabilities of each, and what priorities should be given to each alternative?
6 Negotiation, as part of the budgetary process, on the basis of any of the other 'approaches'.

Such expenditures, once agreed, are effectively budgeted fixed costs, although some would argue that if such expenses are authorized on the basis of a fixed percentage of sales values, they are thereby variable costs. Control, it may be argued, can be established by a comparison of actual with budgets, and depending on whether the budget is considered to be a maximum, minimum or a guide, variances may be examined accordingly. However, in all but the fifth decision base outlined above, the authorization itself is the only yardstick and must be considered somewhat arbitrary. Higher or lower levels of budget might well have been agreed, and therefore neither an overspend or underspend against budget is necessarily good or bad. Control therefore is purely a measure of managers' ability to manage their expenditure within the agreed budget. That is not to say, however, that comparisons with expenditure levels of other companies are completely arbitrary. It must surely always be reasonable to question why competitors spend more or less on discretionary costs.

However, in situations where discretionary expenditures are evaluated individually (the fifth basis outlined above), more points for control are likely to exist. The opinions offered by line managers in the formation of the budget can be the yardstick against which actual events, performances, costs, etc. can be compared. Thus, for example, in the case of the S Co.[2] discussed in Chapter 6, the marketing assumptions put forward during the budgetary/tactics process in deciding between alternative marketing strategies/tactics were used subsequently to 'control' the costs and outcomes. In this instance it is believed the commitment by marketing managers to their estimated input:output relationships encouraged them to ensure, as far as they were able, that the results matched that forecast.

The potential outputs of some managed costs may be better known than others. The aim for control purposes must be to engineer as many or as much managed costs as possible. Expenditures on such areas as research, management training and public relations are probably among the most difficult areas to control, as the outputs are not only impossible to predetermine but also to measure in respect of past expenditures. The control of managed costs as regards both effectiveness and efficiency of quality and quantity of expense and outputs must therefore remain subjective, but that is no reason not to exercise such controls as are possible.

Revenue centres

The revenue centre concept is a marketing measure/control. The implication is that marketing/sales segments are measured on their sales volumes and values. However, such could be a dangerous application of this approach, as managers might be encouraged to obtain sales at almost any price. However, if sales prices are fixed, and are not at the discretion of sales management, the measure could be practicable, although the mix of products sold might distort the value of the revenue centre measure.

Perhaps a more logical approach would be to attribute the contribution or gross margin of sales to the revenue centre rather than the sales value as such. In such a situation flexibility could still be devolved to sales management without its objective being incongruent to that of the business as a whole. Indeed such an approach could be developed into a revenue/expense centre, where marketing and sales managers are measured on the net contribution created, i.e. the contribution from the sale of products/services less marketing and selling expenses. Thus marketing management could itself authorize, say, some promotional expenditure which it believes would generate more additional contribution than its cost, and be itself measured on the net effect of its decisions.

This perhaps attractive idea could, however, lead to problems if marketing/sales managers expanded their sales volumes by selling marginal business. They would also of course need to be aware of the organization's productive capacities, the relevant range under which product contribution is calculated and incremental effects on fixed costs and liquidity reasources, e.g. of additional working capital as sales volumes increase.

The problems for control in such situations is not likely to be one of measurement as such. As outputs are known in terms of sales volume and resource inputs identifiable, performance measures are calculable and practicable. However, what may not be so easy is to draft performance measures in such a way that the actions of marketing/sales management are congruent with that of the organization as a whole, its segments and its resources.

Budgeted performance measures

The successful application of the cost centre approach to the control of services, engineered, committed and managed costs relies substantially upon the use of budgets, i.e. the budgeted cost centre approach. Additional or alternative measures in the control of services and cost centres may be available through the application of budgeted performance measures.

Budgeted performance measures may also be expressed in terms of physical, non-financial indicators, such as machine downtime rates, scrap rates, distribution response rates and enquiry/order conversion rates. Their advantage is that (i) managers may well feel that such indicators are more realistic than monetary expressions, which in any event can be distorted over time, (ii) such may be possible in situations where financially oriented cost rates are impossible or inapplicable, and (iii) budgeted performance can address facets of a segment's objectives that are not measurable in financial terms.

References

1. Anthony, R.N., Dearden, J. and Vancil, R.F., *Management Control Systems: Cases and Readings*, Richard D. Irwin, 1965.
2. Coates, J.B., Rickwood, C.P. and Stacey, R.J., 'Examination of the Differences Between Academic Concepts and Actual Management Accounting Practices', Report to ESRC, British Library Document Supply Centre, August 1987.

Questions

1. (a) How would you assess the performance of the maintenance department of an organization of your choice?
   (b) How, and why, would your view differ if it was allowed to sell its spare capacity to other organizations?
2. (a) By what measures may the operations of the research and development function be controlled?
   (b) How would you assess the long-term performance of the R & D function?
3. 'Charging, even if arbitrary, for the assumed consumption of service centres is the only means by which management can dissuade other managers from mis-using the service.' To what extent and why would you agree or disagree with the statement?
4. What are the arguments for and against the recharging of service and expense centre costs?
5. Contrast the methods by which committed and managed fixed costs may be controlled.
6. Why are 'budgeted performance centre' measures (as against budgeted cost or profit centres) an important element of multi-variant performance analysis?

9 Assessing performance in public sector organizations

Introduction

The idea of the value for money (VFM) audit has already been introduced in Chapter 5, as a source of information to assist in budgetary planning in not-for-profit (NFP) organizations. In this chapter the concept is taken up once again, this time from the point of view of the provision of control information. Public sector organizations are numerous and varied and are not wholly not-for-profit. The present discussion will concentrate on local authorities, public enterprises and nationalized industries, the last two being ones where more commercial targets may be set alongside the less tangible ones normally associated with a not-for-profit activity. It should be remembered throughout, though, that increasingly in business generally the adopted measures of performance are either intangible, such as the level of customer service provided and the speed and accuracy of the provision of information, or give an additional measure of success beyond profit-based measures, such as growth in sales, reputation in the community and so on. In other words, it is not the case that one set of measures applies solely to private sector profit-oriented organizations and another totally separate set to public sector NFP organizations.

The '3 Es' are widely accepted as the basic measures to be applied in VFM studies and their definitions were given in Chapter 5. However, having a definition is not an infallible guide to solving a problem, and in the case of the application of the '3 Es' concept there are often difficulties in measuring both inputs and outputs and relating the latter to the achievement of an imprecisely defined objective. To give some examples:

- It is difficult to give precise meaning to qualities such as health, welfare, education.

- Benefits from expenditure may not arise altogether immediately, but be rather diffusely and imprecisely spread over a period of time; this clearly applies again to health as well as to most other normally recognized social services.
- Additionally, a number and variety of benefits may arise from expenditure programmes. A healthy population could be more generally economically productive; campaigns to reduce smoking, if successful, produce not only a more healthy population, but save costs in provision of health services, reduce working days lost, and improve output.
- The benefits claimed will frequently be difficult to measure in monetary units. This applies to the success of the forces of law and order in combating crime, to the success of the armed forces in preventing war, and to measuring the outputs of many of the traditional social services such as those instanced above.
- In the pursuit of law and order, for example, several services may at times combine to prevent problems, with police, fire and ambulance services acting together on many occasions. It would be difficult therefore to ascribe individual benefits to individual services, even if they were measurable.

There are numerous other aspects which could be introduced to illustrate the point further. The above items should suffice, though, to underline the main issue of the substantial difficulties faced in tracing benefits and costs to specific activities in order to produce an initial appraisal and subsequently a measure of performance.

Acceptance of the serious nature of the problem of course does not mean it cannot be usefully tackled. The principal means adopted to this end have been the employment of wide ranging performance measures, indices and indicators, which provide both historical perspective and the basis for comparative analyses. This approach is not without problems itself:

1. How to obtain an impression of what the totality of the performance indicators convey.
2. Where there is some conflict between almost commercial objectives which may be imposed and a simultaneous requirement to meet certain social obligations, as is the case in many nationalized industries and public enterprises, there is likely to be a considerable problem of reconciliation.

The chapter contains illustrations of measures of performance taken mainly from local authorities, nationalized industries and public enterprises. There is also a short reference to approaches made by central government to evaluate performance within its spheres of activity. It may be noted that 'public sector' organizations need not be always thought of in the context of a simple private/public sector dichotomy, but as part of a 'range of organizational forms with completely private and completely public forms being at each end of the range', as Tomkins[1] suggests. He also suggests a possible continuum of organizational forms, and comments that since 1979 a considerable development of this (latter) notion has been seen:

A – Full private
B – Private with part state ownership
C – Joint private/public ventures
D – Private regulated
E – Public infrastructure/private operating
F – Contracted out
G – Public: with 'managed competition'
H – Public: without competition.

This suggestion is related to his assessment that 'there is no clear cut economic logic which states that private sector organizations must be more efficient'. Nor is 'ownership, per se, ... the key issue'. 'The important matter is to examine each type of activity and consider exactly what form and extent of social control is needed'.

Altogether it will be seen that the measures used in practice are in the main pragmatic in nature and do not derive or form part of a theoretical construct. Hence there is little to guide their application and interpretation other than practicality and common sense.

The significance of the public sector

Tables 9.1 and 9.2 summarize Central Statistical Office data on employment in the public sector and government spending as a proportion of GDP.

Table 9.1 Government spending as a proportion of GDP (%)

	1980	1981	1982	1983	1984
Total	45.2	46.0	46.4	46.1	45.8
Purchases	23.7	23.6	23.4	23.9	23.8
Transfers	21.5	22.4	23.0	22.2	22.0

Source: Economic Trends Annual Supplement, 1986.

Table 9.2 Government employment as a share of total employment (%)

	1980	1981	1982	1983	1984	1985
Central Govt.	9.4	10.0	10.0	10.1	9.8	9.7
Local Govt.	11.7	11.9	12.2	12.2	12.0	11.9

Source: Economic Trends Annual Supplement, 1986.

These statistics exclude public sector corporations, which accounted, for example in 1982, for a further 7 per cent of employment. Roughly one in five of employees worked in central and local government over the period quoted. With the addition of the public corporations, the figure could be seen to be rising toward three in ten. The public sector is clearly by any standard both an important contributor to the wealth creation process as well as a major consumer of resources. How it operates towards the realization of maximum benefits from its activities while keeping resource usage as low as is feasible will obviously have considerable impact on the economy as a whole.

Ratio analysis

This is widely used in this and other evaluation and appraisal applications. In the following sections value for money (VFM) repeatedly emerges as the underlying test of public sector services. Within VFM, as noted in Chapter 5, lie the basic concepts of Economy, Efficiency and Effectiveness, the '3 Es', which also continually surface as key criteria by which to measure.

Ratio analysis can be a valuable aid to understanding how elements are linked together, which greatly improves the exercise of effective control as well as assisting in measuring the degree of achievement of activities and programmes. Intelligently applied, and observing the strict need to employ wholly compatible data, ratio analysis is again seen as a useful tool, not conclusive in itself of any issues and in public sector organizations limited by the many inherently qualitative aspects of the services they are required to provide.

The 'value for money' ratio is essentially:

$$\frac{\text{The value of the objectives of policy actually achieved}}{\text{The cost of their achievement}}$$

While the denominator of this ratio may be aggregated in part at least from recorded data, it is quite possible that the numerator may not be, since subjective judgement could play a large part in its valuation. However, measuring the degree to which programme outputs achieve the objectives is possible and this could be the starting point for the development of a ratio 'tree' (Figure 9.1).

The most straightforward of the '3 Es' ratios relates to economy, which in turn can be broken down into price and quantity factors (Figure 9.2).

It is a development of analysis very similar to a variance tree. The main complications rest with a clear understanding of the '3 Es' concepts and how they are to be measured. Efficiency in this framework is regarded as an output:input ratio (which would sometimes also be thought of as productivity); the output numerator is expressed as 'ex-

Assessing performance in public sector organizations 171

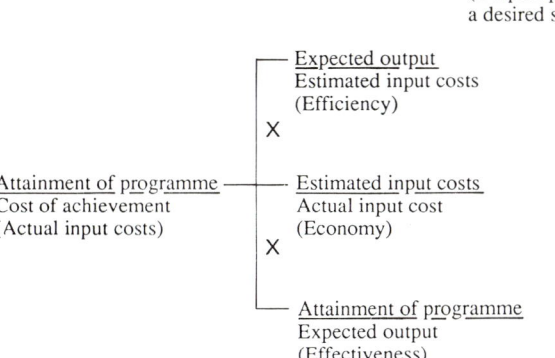

Figure 9.1 *'Ratio' tree*

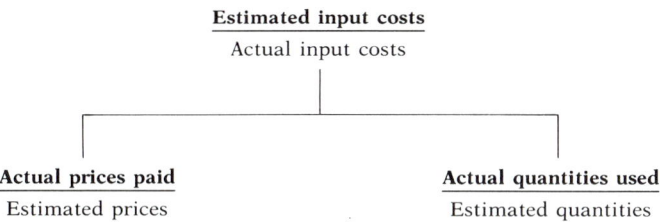

Figure 9.2 *'Economy' breakdown*

pected output', which may be measured in standard hours, teaching hours, patient hours, but each related to a budgeted amount. 'Effectiveness' gives the greatest difficulty, for at the outset the planned ratio could be expressed as 100 per cent i.e. outputs of a service fully meeting objectives. This may not always be so if the numerator really expresses longer-term objectives. One has to be clear on the basis of the figures, though each at some stage will be concerned with a comparison of actual against expected. Subsequent sections contain a number of illustrations of the adoption of a ratio presentation of results, though nowhere has there been found a standard practice.

Many points need to be settled before a ratio scheme can be implemented and interpreted:

1. A clear recognition and understanding of policy objectives.
2. The order of priorities to be attached where multiple objectives exist.
3. Recognition and understanding of the objectives of schemes designed to meet 1 and 2.
4. The sequence in which schemes relate to each other to meet 1.
5. How objectives are to be measured.

172   *Control and Audit in Management Accounting*

6   How costs are allocated and apportioned between areas of the authority.
7   Managerial responsibility for and control over costs (particularly in relation to 6).
8   The relation between organizational structures and objectives, with particular reference to 6 and 7.

These are broad areas of investigation aimed primarily at clarifying objectives, authority and responsibility before the conduct of the detailed audit. It would be an approach equally at home in profit-oriented commercial enterprises.

Nationalized industries

In the UK the list of nationalized concerns and public enterprises and those where the state has the major and majority shareholding, such as the Rover Group, is steadily shrinking under the auspices of the current government's privatization programmes. Nonetheless the list of industries presently remaining constitute an impressive group, the main ones being:

> The Electricity Council
> Water Authorities (England and Wales)
> British Railways Board
> British Waterways Board
> Civil Aviation Authority
> National Coal Board
> North of Scotland Hydroelectric Board
> Post Office
> South of Scotland Electricity Board

The list is not entirely complete, and does not include public corporations such as the Bank of England, the BBC, the Audit Commission and so on. It does indicate the significance that nationalized industries still retain within the economy, though the first two on the list are among further ones targeted for return to the private sector in the near future.

Space precludes much detail on the background to the nationalised industries and readers are referred to Henley *et al.*[2] for this purpose. Briefly the legislation setting up each industry contains a broad reference to its financial objectives and additionally there are statements concerning non-financial obligations such as those imposed on British Rail. The Transport Act of 1962 states the Railway Board has duties to 'efficiency, economy and safety of operation'. Statements of this kind are not clear, but do convey the possibility of conflict with the pursuit of purely financial objectives in all aspects of an industry's business.

Nationalized industries report to Parliament via the ministers of the so-called 'sponsoring' departments. In the cases of the National Coal

Board and the Electricity Council, this is the Department of Energy, with the Treasury also concerned about financing and capital expenditure.

The 1978 White Paper[3] provided a framework for reference as to the financial and non-financial objectives of these industries, in particular the means by which their achievement was to be judged:

- Financial performance could be measured by ratios targets, some but not all of which would be commonly used in private industry, such as (i) return on (net) assets (the most usual ratio target), (ii) percentage profit margin on sales, and (iii) a target profitability or loss.
- Non-financial measures, such as percentage of letters deluered on time, output per man-shift, equipment dounture: actual to estimated.

Details of these measures are given by each industry in its annual report. One apparently seen as important by nationalized industries, though not stated as a requirement by the White Paper is the self-financing ratio, which may be considered as a significant measure of ability to operate independently of government. Basically it can be formulated as:

$$\frac{\text{Capital expenditure for year}}{\text{Retained profit plus depreciation}}$$

Capital expenditure could include working capital. A measure broadly along the same lines in cash flow terms would certainly be regarded as important in the private sector. Cash limits (or external financing limit, EFL) imposed by governments from time to time also have to be observed by nationalized industries and have given rise to conflict in that their imposition could well preclude the achievement of other targets, financial and non-financial. To some extent their impact has been less than would appear at first sight, since, *de facto*, industries have exceeded limits supposedly imposed.

This is not the only major source of conflict in the policies laid down for these industries to operate to. Another major one is the financial earnings target taken in relation to the required rates of return (RRR). The RRR refers to capital expenditure projects and relates to average returns foreseen over the life of a project. As is well appreciated, the nature of investment projects generally means a high cash outflow initially, followed by various phases of earning levels over the project life. It is never likely that the average will ever be realized in fact, but the financial targets will incorporate the RRR in their figures. This is compounded by the fact there may be several separate projects, as well as returns from the existing body of assets. The scope of project assessments themselves is much wider than would be the case in private enterprise, evaluating both tangible and intangible, direct and indirect costs and benefits.

Finally on conflicts, there is the obvious problem that meeting a financial return may be achieved at the expense of cutting out certain activities such as services (including ones with a wider social significance) or reducing their standard. Examples of these possibilities are exceedingly numerous, among the obvious ones being the cut-backs in rail services to outlying districts and the change in frequency of post deliveries and collections.

Clearly the value of the ratios which utilize accounting information depends on the standard of accounting within the industries. So far as published reports are concerned, their aim has been to match 'best accounting practice'. For example, though not required to, public bodies observe SSAPs (in part) and the accounts are audited as to their 'true and fair view'. The form of their presentation is decided by the minister responsible for them, and of course, because of the nature of their differences with private sector firms, their results are not necessarily assessable in the same light as they would be if they were in the private sector.

The 1978 White Paper[4] has attracted a number of criticisms concerning its coverage of targets and performance indicators in nationalized industries. In an appraisal of performance measurement in nationalized industries Kayastha[5] quotes several authors, among them Redwood and Hatch,[6] and Perks and Glendinning,[7,8] to the effect that guidance on the subject given in the White Paper is not as clear or coherent as it might be and that the actual publications in the annual reports of nationalized industries indicate 'patchy' progress by individual industries in their development and presentation. In other words, the information which could be derived from them is less than the potential of properly specified, carefully linked ratio analysis framework would be. In particular the need for a well-defined framework into which price and quality (of service) performance indicators would fit'[9] is highlighted as a major improvement required.

Kayastha was concerned to use the UK nationalized industries' experience to develop the case for a 'well organized and well thought-out framework that enables decision makers and others to appreciate the significance of the indicators', and apply this to certain public enterprises in Nepal. Of special concern is the provision of consumer performance indicators which would reflect many of the social aspects of these enterprises, and although subject to government financial targets, nonetheless would provide key objectives for pricing, investment and quality of service decisions.

Ratio analysis is normally presented in the form of a pyramid, linked together at various levels. It is easy to state that a logical linkage would start with a primary objective to be fulfilled, breaking down from this into a series of supporting subsidiary ratios, but one of the problems in public enterprise at the outset could be the measurement of the top level objective, which need not always be a return on capital. Lack of precision in definition or a multiplicity of objectives leads to the expan-

Assessing performance in public sector organizations 175

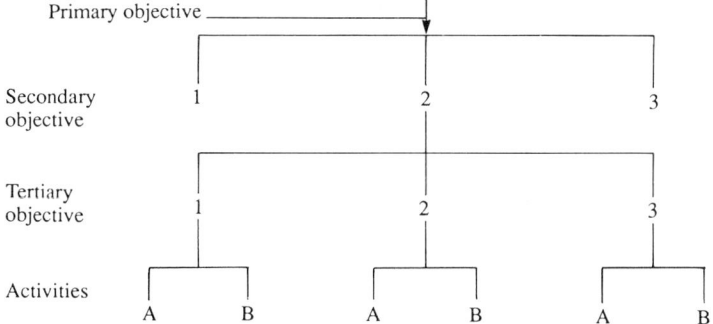

Figure 9.3 *Layers of objectives*

sion of the pyramid into secondary or tertiary objective layers in order to provide the expansion of information necessary to obtain a measure of particular achievements.

Given that the primary objective was indeed difficult to measure, then judgement as to how well an enterprise had performed would rest on satisfactory fulfilment of the next highest level and so on.

In the Nepalese situation Kayastha indicates that there is considerable lack of consumer performance indicators in public enterprises. He quotes Redwood and Hatch[10] as providing guidance on the provision of such measures:

> First, a service is no use to people unless they can obtain it. Targets are therefore required for availability. Secondly, the service must be competent. Targets are needed for quality, reliability, timeliness, and for maintenance and repair. Thirdly, a service should be convenient to use. Standards should be set for design, instructions in use and methods of payment. Fourthly, pricing is important. Criteria must be established for determining the 'entry' price (for installing a telephone, for example) for remaining in the system, and for making use of the system. Fifthly, unpleasant side-effects should be avoided. Standards are needed on safety and pollution. Finally, consumer control systems are needed. Formal procedures should be established and monitored, to ensure choice, representation, and complaint and redress.[1]

Several illustrations of the way a hierarchy of ratios may be built up for a number of important Nepalese public enterprises are given. Among them are ones for the Drinking Water and Sewerage Corporation (DWSC) and the Nepal Electricity Authority (NEA), the suggested schemes which are reproduced below by kind permission of the author. His work serves simply as an example of the general transferability of this kind of analysis – in this case to an overseas situation.

DWSC: major functions and objectives

The main function of the Corporation is to develop the drinking water supply and sewerage system in an area specified by the Nepalese

Government. Currently the Corporation confines its activities to Kathmandu Valley and Pokhara. Its other functions are to maintain and regulate the drinking water supply system for the community and to construct, manage and control the sewerage system.

The detailed hierarchy of objectives of DWSC, together with their associated output measures/performance indicators, is presented in Figure 9.4. As shown in the hierarchy, A1, B2 to C14, A, B and C represent each of the three levels of objectives of DWSC and the associated number indicates the present hierarchy has got 14 objectives. D1...D39 represents the output measures, performance indicators and the number means that all together there are 39 of these.

Nepal Electricity Authority (NEA)

'State ownership and control over the supply and distribution of basic utilities, namely water, electricity and gas has been a common practice in most of the developing countries because competition in these sectors is generally regarded as technically unsound and economically wasteful. In Nepal, generation and distribution of electricity have long been undertaken directly by His Majesty's Government.

'The Three Year ⌐lan (1962/63–1964/65) contained a programme of establishing an autonomous public corporation to manage electricity generation and distribution in the Kathmandu Valley. This measure was taken in conformity with HMG's policy to gradually transform all departmental enterprises into autonomous corporations. It was contemplated that such an act of organization and legal transformation would bring about operational efficiency in the enterprises and generate a financial surplus that could gainfully be used for financial development programmes.' Thus Nepal Electricity was incorporated by the Nepal Electricity Corporation Act, 1962.[12] The Nepal Electricity Corporation was converted into the Nepal Electricity Authority (NEA) in July 1985.

Major functions and objectives

The Act specified the following functions and objectives:

1   To generate and distribute electricity in a secure, efficient, economical and orderly manner in the areas approved by HMG.
2   To endeavour to develop an electricity distribution system so as to yield greater benefits to consumers at a reasonable price.
3   To promote the generation and distribution of electricity with a view to fostering industrial development and economic welfare of the people.
4   To fix electricity tariff rates and realize other dues for electricity services.

The Act explicitly mentioned that the Corporation, while discharging its functions, should adopt commercial principles without ignoring the interests of the economy and the general public.

Figure 9.4 Drinking Water and Sewerage Corporation (DWSG)

Hierarchy of objectives along with their output measures/performance indicator

A1   To provide adequate provision of potable water and proper management of sewerage system for the protection of public health and hygiene

    D1 Annual potable water distribution
    D2 Water supply unit costs
    D3 Total length of sewer
    D4 Sewerage unit costs

B2   *To supply potable water efficiently*
    D5   Annual potable water distributed
    D6   Supply of water per day per customer (litres)
    D7   Water supply unit costs
    D8   Minimum water charge (Rs.)

B3   *To manage sewerage system efficiently*
    D9   Percentage of population connected to sewer
    D10 Total length of sewer
    D11 Total sewage works
    D12 Sewerage unit costs

C4   To process more water   C5   To increase the supply of water   C6   To rectify biological and chemical quality of water   C7   To rectify unacceptable water quality

C8   To reduce amount of unaccounted for water   C9   To reduce unreliability of supplies   C10 To reduce water unit costs

C4   *To process more water*
    D13 Annual quantity of water processed
    D14 No. of reservoirs
    D15 No. of water treatment works

C5   *To increase the supply of potable water*
    D5   Total quantity of potable water supplied annually
    D6   Total quantity of water supplied per day customer (litres)
    D16 No. of new connections i.e. new customers
    D17 Capital expenditure per head of population

C6   *To rectify the biological and chemical quality of water*
    D18 Estimated quantity supplied failing to comply with bacteriological quality standards
    D19 Estimated quantity supplied failing to comply with certain chemical standards

C7   *To rectify unacceptable water quality*
    D20 Estimated quantity supplied failing to comply with certain acceptability standards
    D21 Unacceptable water quality percentage because of taste and odour
    D22 Unacceptable water quality percentage because of discoloration or appearance

C8   *To reduce the amount of unaccounted for water*
    D23 Water leakage percentage

C9   *To reduce the unreliability of supplies*
    D24 Number of customers suffering complete loss of piped supply for a period of 12 hours or more
    D25 Percentage of severe cut-offs
    D26 Percentage of severe pressure deficiencies

C10 *To reduce water unit costs*
    D7   Water supply unit costs
    D8   Minimum water charge (Rs.)
    D27 Administrative expenses per Ml/d potable water distributed
    D28 Operating expenses (excluding administrative costs) per Ml/d potable water distributed
    D29 Manpower numbers per 1,000 customers.

Figure 9.4 cont.

B3 TO MANAGE THE SEWERAGE SYSTEM EFFECTIVELY

| C11 To extend the sewerage system | C12 To improve existing old or overloaded sewerage system | C13 To reduce foul flooding | C14 To reduce sewerage unit costs |

C11 *To extend the sewerage system*
    D30 Population served by the sewerage system
    D10 Total length of sewer
    D11 Total sewage works
    D31 Capital expenditure per head of population

C12 *To improve existing old or overloaded sewerage system*
    D32 Number of sewers at risk of frequent flooding
    D33 Length of renewed or enlarged sewer to reduce overload or old and dilapidated
    D34 Number of significant sewer collapses

C13 *To reduce foul flooding*
    D35 Number of storm overflows deemed unsatisfactory
    D36 Length of renewed or enlarged sewer to reduce foul flooding problem

C14 *To reduce sewerage unit costs*
    D12 Sewerage unit costs
    D37 Administrative expenses per head of population
    D38 Operating costs (excluding administrative expenses) per head of population
    D39 Manpower numbers per 1,000 head of population.

A detailed hierarchy of objectives of the NEA together with their associated output measures/performance indicators consistent with the statutory objectives and obligations, is presented in Figure 9.5. As shown in the hierarchy, A1 to E16, A to E represent a sequence of operating objectives arranged in descending order of importance. 'A' relates to the mission statement, the number indicating that there are altogether sixteen objectives in the present hierarchy. P1 to P33 represent the output measures/performance indicators and the number indicates that the present hierarchy has got thirty-three output measures/performance indicators.

The predominantly service-oriented DWSC may be contrasted with the financially oriented NEA ratio structures. Interpretation of the ratios would follow the traditional rules of ensuring that a proper understanding of their derivation and aims exists and that attention to the time period within which progress toward their achievement is made appears in managerial performance appraisals. Comparisons could be made with corresponding organizations in other countries if a valid basis for comparison exists.

Evaluation still presents a problem. How can one take a global view of a substantial number of performance indicators to arrive at a conclusion as to whether the industry has performed successfully or not? A complete answer is not possible using ratio outcomes alone, since variations may range from political intervention to economic difficulties caused by changes in world trade levels. As would be the normal case in variance analysis, a commentary is needed to explain and interpret the actual outcomes, but some numerical benchmarks could be provided,

Figure 9.5 Nepal Electricity Authority (NEA)

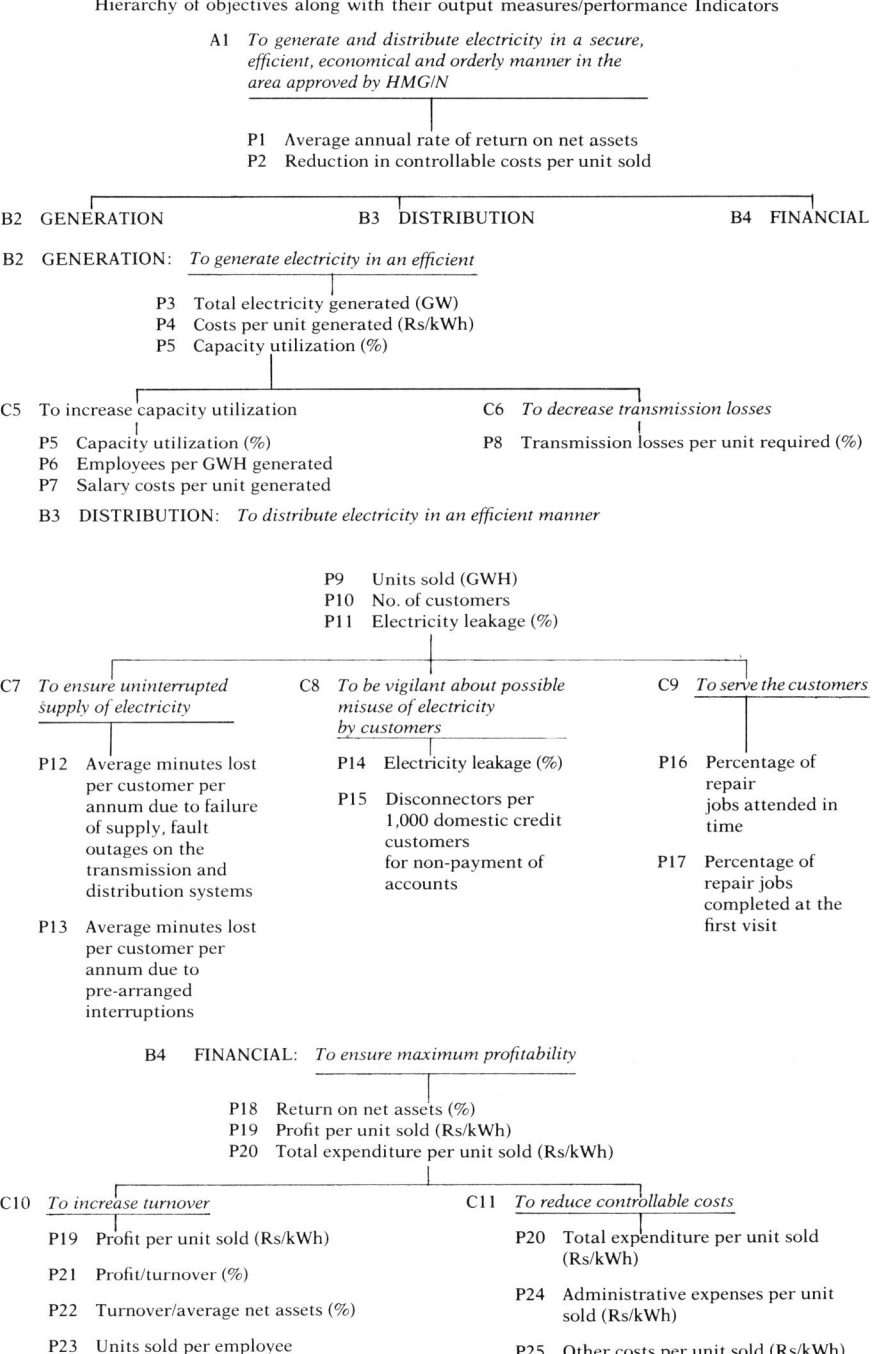

180 *Control and Audit in Management Accounting*

Figure 9.5 cont.

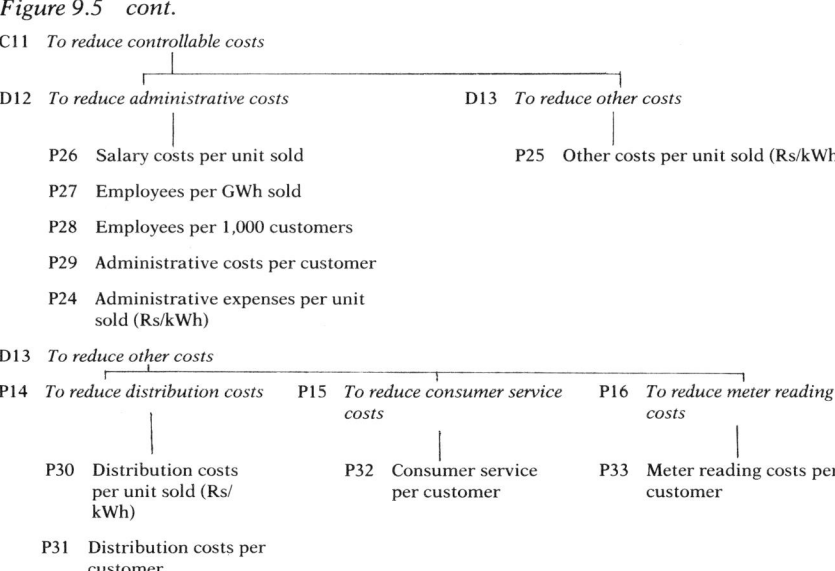

apart from trends applicable to both financial and non-financial measures. For example, the degree of achievement could be expressed in percentage form: a target 5 per cent return on capital and a 4 per cent actually achieved return could be expressed as an 80 per cent achievement. In turn such achievement could be weighted in relation to a priority ranking, and the total used as an indicator of the general extent to which targets had been met. Similar constructions could analyse the individual secondary and tertiary objective levels as well as groups of activities.

The extensive nature of the performance indicators published by nationalized industries and public enterprises is further illustrated through those produced by the Thames Water Authority.

Thames Water Authority

This Authority produces a list of performance ratios in common with each water authority in England and Wales. In its 1985–6 accounts it compares its own results with a weighted average of all water authorities over a 5-year period. In a commentary on the ratios it points to the adjustment of previous years' costs to a current cost basis in order to make effective comparisons by repricing to 1985–6 on the following basis:

(a) Rates and power costs – actual price increases as recorded by each authority.
(b) All other operating costs – retail price index.
(c) Capital expenditure – Public Works Non-Roads outturn index

To obtain a basis for comparison with other authorities, it divides operating and management costs by 'equivalent populations'. For each service the latter 'comprises the resident population who receive the service plus allowance for holiday visitors and for the service provided to industry commerce and agriculture'. This, the Authority considers, may not be an ideal measure for output, particularly in comparative analysis, but does give consistency to time series results.

It adds its own interpretation of the internal comparisons, which really amount to no more than a comment: 'the continuing search for greater efficiency is reflected in the improved operating and management costs results for all services ... the efficiency improvements have contributed to the increase in current operating profit on all services, but the required increase in the financial target specified by the Government was the *major* (authors' *italics*) factor in these particular results'.

Among its comparisons with national averages it comments: 'Operating and management costs per head of equivalent population in Thames Water ... for ... water supply were above average, but over the last 5 year period Thames has achieved the greatest percentage reduction in costs'. A similar level of comment is made about each of the main sections of the performance report, namely:

Water supply
Sewerage
Sewerage treatment and disposal
Environment services
Manpower
Capital expenditure

The full performance ratio statement and review is contained in Appendix 9.1 (p. 190), together with the financial review, which gives details of Thames's financial targets, performance aim, the external financing limit and capital expenditure. Almost identical schemes of information construction and analysis are to be found in other water authority reports. (Appendices 9.2 and 9.3 relate to the Seven Trent Water Authority.)

Local authorities

The work of the Audit Commission, district and local auditors has already been referred to in Chapter 5. The objective of achieving value for money enshrined in the 3 Es was referred to as setting the scene for guidance of local authorities in their planning.

All three bodies referred to conduct studies aimed at securing improving value for money either in the form of special studies or as part of the normal audit of local authority accounts carried out by appointed auditors. The duties of the latter, including their responsibility for value for money, are set out in an Audit Commission publication on a code of practice for auditing in local government.[13]

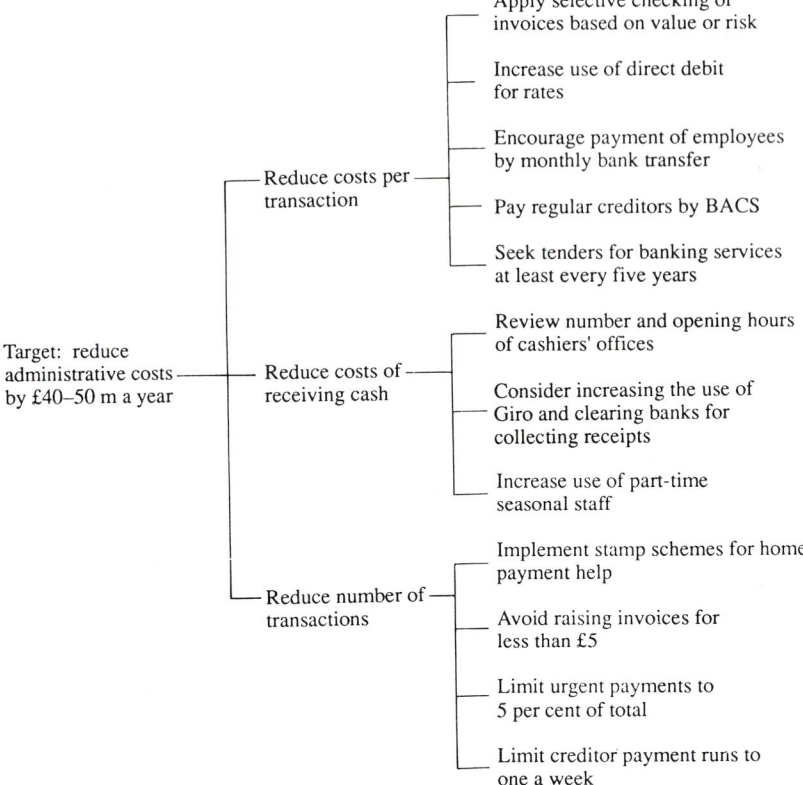

Figure 9.6 *Recommended steps to reduce costs of cash flow administration*

The source of much information defining how performance may be measured in the many and varied areas of local authority activities is contained in the special studies conducted by the Audit Commission. By way of example, we give extracts from studies of cash flow management,[14] housing management,[15] and the statistical profile of Birmingham City Council.[16] Beyond the measures themselves, the reports also draw conclusions which provide pointers as to how, where and with what potential effect authorities can act to improve their performance.

Cash flow management[17]

Based on 1985, the report states the local authorities in England and Wales handled cash flows of some £60b. Administration of this cash cost some £500m. It was estimated that about £60m annual savings could be made from better management of cash flow and a further £40m to £50m a year could come from wider application of current good practice in administering cash flows.

Table 9.3 Summary of performance indicators for cash flow management – efficiency

Indicator	Benchmark of good practice
Rate collection	
Direct ratepayers per FTE staff	>3,500
Sundry debtors	
Accounts per FTE staff	>5,000
Mortgagaes	
Mortgages per FTE staff	>950
Pay and display car parking	
Spaces per patroller	>500, <1000
Cashiers	
Transactions per FTE staff	>30,000
Creditors	
Invoices per FTE administrative staff	>7,000
Invoices per cheque	>2.5
Payroll	
Employees per FTE staff	>260

The basic element of the performance indicators in the latter case is the 'Full-Time Equivalent' administrative staff unit (FTE). Table 9.3 and Figure 9.6 respectively list the performance measures usable to measure various aspects of efficiency and provide a breakdown of recommended steps to reduce costs of cash flow administration.

A questionnaire completed by 370 authorities and their auditors, together with Rating Statistics published by the Chartered Institute of Public Finance and Accountancy (CIPFA), formed the basis of the analytical work and visits were made to some authorities 'exhibiting particularly interesting practices'. The benchmark of good practice is derived from the study of the FTE resource inputs to the individual classes of output, being founded on what is achieved in practice. Without undertaking some fundamental work measurement studies itself, the Commission's report has to rely principally on what is observed to happen, but it does support its analyses by illustration and commentary on the statistics. For example, as part of the drive to reduce costs per transaction, payment of creditors by the Bankers Automated Clearing Services (BACS) is recommended. Among the supporting arguments for introducing this system, the Commission reported that BACS charged about 3p per transaction, compared to a charge of up to 20p per cheque by bank charges – 'there is therefore scope for reduced bank charges'.

For cash flow management itself, a further set of indicators is proposed, as shown in Table 9.4.

Again these benchmarks are backed up by recommended steps to secure objectives of increasing the speed with which income is collected, reduce the level of arrears and make explicit the policy for paying invoices. The stated target is to reduce interest charges by £60m

184 Control and Audit in Management Accounting

Table 9.4 Summary of proposed performance indicators for cash flow management – effectiveness

Indicators	Benchmark of good performance
Rate collection	
Interest 'lost' per £100 rates collected	£4.70
Date of despatch of straightforward demands	by 31st March
Reminder action within arrears as a % of amounts collected	2 months
District council	1
Metropolitan authority	2
Sundry debtors	
Debit outstanding (annual average) as % of annual debit	13
Accounts outstanding for more than 4 weeks as a % of annual debit	5
% of accounts referred to legal department	2
Mortgages	
Arrears as % of amount due in the year	2
% of accounts more than one month in arrears	5
% paid by cash/cheque	30
Pay and display car parking	
% of excess charge notices collected	75
Payments	
Timings controlled to maximize benefits to the authority	Policy made and monitored

a year and, for instance, one recommended step is to (actively) manage overnight bank balances to ±£100K.

It may be noted that Table 9.4 is in terms of the concept of effectiveness, whereas Figure 9.6 deals with efficiency.

Managing the crisis in council housing[18]

An example of performance indicators where the emphasis is on economy in respect of resource input is taken from this report. A benchmark of adequate performance is given, this time associated with a level which would give 'cause for concern' (Table 9.5).

These measures are refined to match local circumstances, but the Commission suggests that a reduction in total of around 8,000 staff could be achieved without any decline in service levels if all authorities performed as well as the best 25 per cent (which is really the efficiency benchmark).

Table 9.5 Proposed housing management performance indicators – economy

	Benchmark	Cause for concern
FTE staffing:		
– general supervision and management per 1,000 dwellings	6.2	9.5
– waiting list admin./1,000 applicants	1.4	2.8
– rent collection/1000 payments		
door to door	1.8	3.5
cash office	1.0	2.7
– rent accounting/1,000 new lets	2.8	6.6
– housing benefit admin./1,000 recipients	0.7	1.4
– homeless admin./1,000 applicants	3.0	7.9
– hostel staff/10 units	0.5	1.9
– housing advice/1,000 cases	0.4	2.7
– administrative support/10,000 dwellings	5.1	13.9
– central management/10,000 dwellings	3.1	10.3
– caretaking and cleaning/1,000 dwellings serviced	6.0	12.7

Profile of Birmingham City Council[19]

Much of the data used in the profile comes from CIPFA compilations of estimates for the 1986–7 period, though not all.

In its introduction the Audit Commission comments, 'Please bear in mind that cheap is not necesarily efficient and that generous is not necessarily effective', a remark of course referring to interpretation in general. The profile itself is primarily a statistical comparison of the authority compared to the metropolitan districts' average. The presentation is in the form of a tree diagram (see Figure 9.7).

The figures are supported by further analyses showing, for example, in the case of schools the number of pupils per 1,000 of population, cost per pupil and the total cost of the difference between the city council and the metropolitan average. Then various segments are expanded further. For instance, the expenditure per head on primary schools is subdivided into cost per pupil and pupils per 1,000 of the population; the former is then broken down into teaching and non-teaching costs and so on into more and more refined detail.

The purpose of this exercise is to guide investigators to the most important items revealed by the comparisons. There are no accompanying benchmark targets as described in relation to the preceding reports, though graphical comparisons show, for instance, expenditures per pupil for the Inner London Education Authority, Other London Boroughs, Metropolitan Authorities, and Shire Counties. A given authority can use the standarized base of the data to see how it compares with these four groupings, and gain an impression of how well they are performing relative to them.

186 *Control and Audit in Management Accounting*

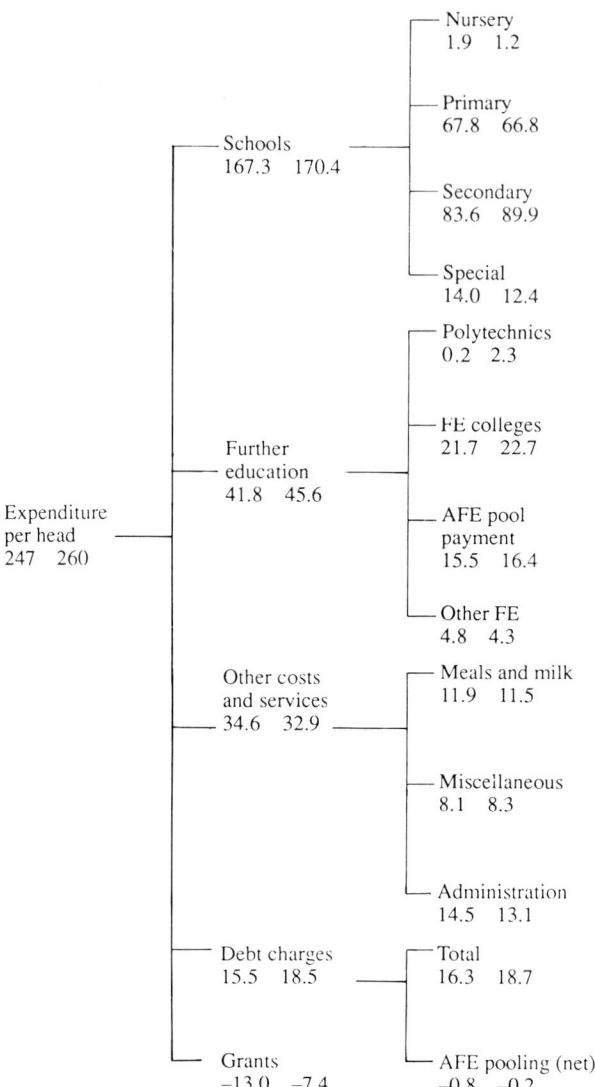

The figures show the expenditure per head for the council on the left and the metropolitan average on the right

Figure 9.7 *Education – summary 1986–7 estimates. Birmingham compared to Metropolitan Districts' average (£)*

There is in fact a wealth of information about local authority expenditure, besides the reports emanating from the Audit Commission. The CIPFA statistics have been mentioned earlier;[20] another useful work is the *Local Government Value for Money Handbook*.[21] The District Audit Service also publishes its own reports, for example on policing in the West Midlands,[22] which, *inter alia*, pointed to the need for good management practices as complementary to good policing, indicating that the former were rather neglected.

Although the preceding extracts from the Commission's reports have been quoted without much comment, investigations and reports of this nature can be controversial and, in any event, their recommendations do not have legal backing. Only the way their investigations have been conducted can give compelling force to their arguments and conclusions. Neilson,[23] in an article on VFM auditing in local government, reports the results of a survey into how ten authorities had apparently responded to the era ushered in by the creation of the Audit Commission. Each authority had experienced one full audit under the 1982 Act. It is an early days survey, reflected by reported mixed reactions among those interviewed. The conclusions stress cultural, political and organizational obstacles to be overcome:

1. Getting value for money is partly a technical issue – as with performance indicators – but is even more about political and cultural factors. Questions about what constitutes value for money must be viewed within the context of a particular organization.
2. Value for money auditing has been found to be useful in suggesting items for examination, though these have had to fit in with the prevailing values of the organization. Suggestions for change have to be seen as feasible for that particular organization.
3. Value for money requires both the development of an appropriate culture and adequate management systems. Helping in this process will call for a greater range of skills from auditors than has been needed so far.
4. Members will need to be brought into the value for money process much more if the auditor's findings are to have a chance of making any major impact. The important point is not where policy options come from, but who makes the choice.

Whitehead,[24] in a comment on the Audit Commission's Housing report,[25] points to several potential problems relating to how well the report (and, by inference, others) succeeds in achieving an objective base for its conclusions. It is possible that the Commission simply did not reveal sufficient about the factual basis for the report, but the author concludes it risks its reputation for objectivity by not doing so.

Central government

Only a short commentary is given here in respect of more recent initiatives in this area. The general ideas of value for money and the '3Es' are as relevant to central government as anywhere else, but concerted efforts to have them introduced in a coherent fashion over a broad range of activities are not really in evidence. The office of the Comptroller and Auditor General and the National Audit Office (NAO) have of course been in existence for some time (though until 1983 the latter was called the Exchequer and Audit Department). Its reports are taken up by the Select Committee on Public Accounts of the House of Commons, which may raise issues with ministers and their departments, leading to House of Commons debates. However, these audits are not designed essentially to highlight value for money issues in particular, but are more concerned with the traditional purposes of auditing and to concentrate on lapses in these areas.[26]

Since 1979 there have been changes, at least to the visible conduct of efficiency studies, in this sector, as follows:

(a) The establishment of the Efficiency Unit in 1980.
(b) The Financial Management Initiative (FMI), launched in 1982.

The former Unit was headed until 1983 by Lord Rayner, and the programmes of study of government expenditures he initiated became known as the 'Rayner Scrutinies'. In a report on these programmes the National Audit Office[27] records only limited success, with scrutiny reports having indicated around £216m potential savings, but only a part of the recommendations, amounting to £99m, accepted. The process of scrutiny appears to have been largely ad hoc, and carried out by a very small investigatory unit.

The FMI was introduced as part of the then government's strategy to improve efficiency in the civil service, by improving 'the allocation, management and control of resources throughout central government',[28] Managers in all departments at all levels were to have:

1 A clear view of their objectives; and means to assess, and wherever possible measure, outputs or performance in relation to those objectives.
2 Well defined responsibility for making the best use of their resources, including a critical scrutiny of output and value for money.
3 The information (particularly about costs), the training and the access to expert advice which they needed to exercise their responsibilities effectively.

Although the UK government has not explicitly attempted to introduce PPBS or ZBB (Chapter 5), the requirement for clear statements of the objectives of (departmental) activities comes through strongly both as a means to improve budgetary planning and control and as the basis for the development of performance measures. The FMI is still proceeding and, according to the NAO conclusions,[29] should eventually produce the required results.

The annual Public Expenditure White Papers contain certain justifications to the Treasury, Parliament and taxpayers for departments' proposed expenditure programmes. The Treasury provides guidelines, but does not impose requirements on departments, which in turn can exercise their own initiatives in this area. Suffice it to say that, as yet, these do not appear to have advanced very far and currently may be judged to provide adequate performance measures, according to Beeton,[30] who deals in particular with the Departments of Health, Education, Social Security and Defence.

Finally a feature of recent government policy toward the public sector has been the programme of 'privatization' – selling certain public sector organizations back to the private sector in the belief that such a move will improve their efficiency. 'Market forces' are seen to be the main source of inducing this improvement, but again it is still rather early to pronounce on the success of the move in general (although in terms of business growth, share price growth, many do not appear to be performing well), and whether success in any event is attributable to the programme.

Summary

Sufficient has been said to indicate that achieving 'value for money' does not come through the adoption of uniform schemes of approach, and success does require rather more than a diffuse notion that it would be a 'good thing'. All schemes need clarity of purpose and a proper, responsible structure of organization and authority to carry them through. Since they may well call for substantial changes in traditional practices and possibly organizational groupings, they are likely to encounter a certain degree of resistance in implementation, which will only be overcome if the sense of their purpose is backed by a rigorously based and tested case for introduction and continued application.

References

1. Tomkins, C., *Achieving Economy, Efficiency and Effectiveness in the Public Sector*, Institute of Chartered Accountants of Scotland, 1987.
2. Henley, D., Holtham, C., Likierman, A. and Perrin, J., *Public Sector Accounting and Financial Control*, Van Nostrand Reinhold, 2nd ed., 1986.
3. White Paper, 'The Nationalised Industries', Cmnd. 7131, 1978.
4. *Ibid.*
5. Kayastha, A., 'Performance Measurement in Public Enterprises of Nepal: Some Lessons from British Nationalised Industries', unpublished MSc Dissertation, University of Aston, 1987.
6. Redwood, J. and Hatch, J., *Controlling Public Industries*, Basil Blackwell, Oxford, 1982.
7. Perks, R. and Glendinning, R., 'Performance Indicators Applied to the Nationalised Industries', *Management Accounting*, October 1981.
8. Perks, R. and Glendinning, R., 'Little Progress Seen in Published Performance Indicators', *Management Accounting*, December 1981.
9. Mayston, D., 'Performance Indicators: Are They Performing?', *Public Domain*, Peat Marwick and Public Enterprise Foundation, 1986.
10. Redwood and Hatch, *op. cit.*
11. *Ibid.*, p. 110.
12. Ministry of Finance, HMG, Kathmandu, 'Performance Review of

Public Enterprises in the Nepal Corporation Coordination Division', June 1981. p. 124.
13 Audit Commission, *Code of Local Government Audit Practice for England and Wales*, 1984.
14 Audit Commission, *Improving Cash Flow Management in Local Government*, October 1986.
15 Audit Commission, *Managing the Crisis in Council Housing*, March 1986.
16 Audit Commission, *Profile of Birmingham City Council 1986/87*.
17 Audit Commission, *Improving Cash Flow Management in Local Government*, op. cit.
18 Audit Commission, *Management the Crisis in Council Housing*, op. cit.
19 Audit Commission, *Profile of Birmingham City Council, 1986/87*, op. cit.
20 Chartered Institute of Public Finance and Accountancy (CIPFA), *Statistical Information Service. Management and Maintenance Statistics*, published annually.
21 CIPFA, SOLACE and LAMSACC, *Local Government Value for Money Handbook*, Vol. 1, 1982, Vol. 2. 1983, Vol. 3, 1985.
22 The District Audit Service, *Review of the Management of the West Midlands Police*, October 1985.
23 A. Neilson, 'Value for Money Auditing in Local Government', *Public Money*, Vol. 6, No. 1, June 1986.
24 C. Whitehead, 'Local Government Housing Audit', *Public Money*, Vol. 6, No. 1, June 1986.
25 Audit Commission, *Managing the Crisis in Council Housing*, op. cit.
26 Coates, J.B., Rickwood, C.P. and Stacey, R.J., 'Examination of the Difference Between Academic Concepts and Actual Management Accounting Practices', Report to ESRC, British Library Document Supply Centre, August 1987.
27 National Audit Office, *The Rayner Scrutiny Programmes, 1979–1983*, HMSO, London, 1986.
28 National Audit Office, *The Financial Management Initiative*, London. October 1986.
29 *Ibid*.
30 Beeton, D., 'Justifying Departmental Expenditure Programmes', *Public Money*, Vol. 6, No. 3, December 1986.

Appendix 9.1 Thames Water Authority

Performance ratios

Thames in common with the other water authorities, has again produced a series of nationally agreed performance ratios.

As in previous years, priority has been given to speed of publication rather than detailed refinement of the data and this has required the use of some estimated figures.

In order to enable more effective comparisons to be made between the various years' figures, expenditure of earlier years is repriced to 1985/6 prices on the following basis:

(a) Rates and power costs – actual price increases as recorded by each authority.
(b) All other operating costs – retail price index.
(c) Capital expenditure – Public Works Non-Roads outturn index.

Operating and management costs are converted to ratios by dividing them by 'equivalent populations'. The equivalent population for each service comprises the resident population who receive the service plus allowances for holiday visitors and for the service provided to industry, commerce and agriculture.

Equivalent populations are not ideal measures for output, particularly when comparing Thames' ratios with those of other authorities, but they do provide a consistent basis on which some series of results can be constructed and compared.

The Thames' results – internal comparisons
The continuing search for greater residency is reflected in the improved operating and management costs results for all services. It is also reflected in the further significant reduction in manpower numbers. The efficiency improvements have contributed to the increase in current cost operating profit on all services, but the required increase in the financial target specified by the Government was the major factor in these particular results. Overall capital expenditure in the year increased compared with 1984–5, but whilst there was increased investment in water supply and sewerage assets, there were reductions in investment in the sewage treatment and disposal and land drainage services.

The Thames' results – comparison with the national averages
Operating and management costs per head of equivalent population in Thames Water compare as follows:

- Water supply – above average, but over the last five year period Thames has achieved the greatest percentage reduction in costs.
- Sewerage – above average, but performed significantly better than the national average over the last five year period.
- Sewage treatment and disposal – just above the average, but Thames has not performed as well as the national average over the last five year period.
- Environmental services – continues to be below the national average.

Current cost depreciation is below the national average for all services, but the trends in the Thames' figures are similar to the national trends. With regard to current cost operating profit, on clean water services Thames Water is earning more profit than the national average, but that position is reversed on dirty water services. However, the percentage increase in profits for dirty water services is higher in Thames than nationally in making comparisons with 1984–5.

The percentage of supplies in Thames which are unmetered remains the highest of all the authorities, despite the numbers of commercial customers in particular who are transferring voluntarily to the metered tariff. Decisions in relations to possible compulsory metering will therefore be monitored closely by Thames.

Manpower numbers for Thames are now at or about the national averages and reflect the very significant reductions in employee numbers compared with 1981/82.

Capital expenditure in Thames per head of equivalent population continues to be significantly below the national average. This is shown in the following table for 1985–6 which shows Thames' investment per service as a percentage of the national average.

Water supply	67%
Sewerage	79%
Sewage treatment and disposal	48%
Land drainage	73%

Financial review

Profit and loss
Financial results for the year showed an improvement on the budget – key figures from the profit and loss account are given in Profit and Loss table.

The summary shows that trading profit was £10m greater than budgeted. This resulted largely from a turnover which was £8m higher than targeted, and reduced operating costs.

Results also compared favourably with the previous year, as shown below:

	1985/86 £m	1984/85 £m
Turnover	501	455
Trading Profit	184	145
Profit after Interest	150	105

Financial target
Thames Water was set a financial target by Government which required a rate of return of 1.37 per cent on the net current cost value of assets in use throughout the year. The target does not apply to land drainage services. Variations against targets are required to be carried

forward from year to year. The Financial Target table shows the position as compared with the budget and the target mentioned.

The rate of return actually earned in the year was 1.68 per cent on net current asset values of approximately £4,732m.

Performance aim

Government also sets a performance aim which acts as an efficiency target on operating costs. For Thames Water this covered a two-year period ending in 1985–6. The 'aim' was for a figure of £241m at 1982–3 prices. Performance in the year showed an improvement on this as follows:

Performance aim £241m
Achievement £237m

Profit and loss

	1985–6 Results £m	1985–6 Budget £m
Turnover	501	493
Expenditure		
Operating costs	275	278
Depreciation	39	38
Exceptional items	3	3
Trading profit	184	174
Interest	34	37
Profit after interest	150	137

The trading profit of £184m shows an improvement of 26.9 per cent compared with 10.1 per cent on turnover. This was largely planned in the original budget by allowing for a reduction in the level of operating costs in real terms. The results confirm the successful achievement of the plan.

Financial target

	1985–6 Results £m	1985–6 Budget £m
Current cost operating profit	80	64
Amount brought forward from earlier years	26	26
	106	90
Less financial target set by Government	65	63
Amount available to be carried forward	41	27

	Thames					All water authorities weighted average				
	1981–2	1982–3	1983–4	1984–5	1985–6	1981–2	1982–3	1983–4	1984–5	1985–6
Water Supply										
Expenditure per head of equivalent population:	£	£	£	£	£	£	£	£	£	£
1 Operating and management expenses	11.54	11.52	11.18	10.79	10.30	9.17	9.10	9.12	9.11	8.85
2 Current cost depreciation	2.54	2.35	2.67	2.61	2.75	3.30	3.18	3.29	3.44	3.48
3 Current cost operating profit	2.33	2.06	2.19	2.43	3.60	1.93	2.35	2.23	1.87	2.58
Percentage of water put into supply from:	%	%	%	%	%	%	%	%	%	%
4 Ground sources	26.6	25.1	25.8	25.3	25.7	27.6	27.5	27.6	27.8	27.4
5 Surface sources	73.4	74.9	74.2	74.7	74.3	72.4	72.5	72.4	72.2	72.6
Percentage of supplies which are:										
6 Metered potable	16.9	16.9	17.1	17.9	17.7	25.1	25.0	24.2	24.2	23.7
7 Metered non-potable	0.0	0.0	0.0	0.0	0.0	4.0	3.8	3.6	3.7	3.8
8 Unmetered	83.1	83.1	82.9	82.1	82.3	70.9	71.2	72.2	72.1	72.4
9 Percentage normal population on supply	99.96	99.96	99.96	99.96	99.96	99.0	99.0	99.0	98.9	98.9
Sewerage										
Expenditure per head of equivalent population:	£	£	£	£	£	£	£	£	£	£
10 Operating and management expenses	3.64	3.64	3.43	3.39	3.32	2.86	2.97	2.94	2.86	2.79
11 Current cost depreciation	4.88	4.40	4.84	4.85	4.97	5.12	4.76	5.25	5.34	5.39
12 Current cost operating profit	−0.01	0.49	0.43	0.84	1.31	1.29	1.56	1.23	1.72	2.33
	%	%	%	%	%	%	%	%	%	%
13 Percentage of population connected to a sewer	99.7	97.7	97.8	97.8	97.8	95.5	95.6	95.7	95.8	95.7
Sewage treatment and disposal										
Expenditure per head of equivalent population:	£	£	£	£	£	£	£	£	£	£
14 Operating and management expenses	6.86	7.03	6.78	6.92	6.78	7.24	7.17	7.02	6.90	6.75
15 Current cost depreciation	3.24	2.71	2.98	2.65	2.77	3.58	3.18	3.48	3.51	3.52
16 Current cost operating profit	−0.01	0.58	0.46	0.90	1.38	1.68	2.00	1.36	1.32	1.95
17 Pollution load (BOD) removed per head of equivalent population	kg 29.5	kg 29.5	kg 29.5	kg 29.5	kg 29.5	kg 23.8	kg 23.8	kg 23.2	kg 23.1	kg 23.4
18 Average size of works – equivalent population	30,698	30,623	31,108	31,066	31,253	7,958	7,935	8,092	8,050	8,069
19 Length of Class 3 and 4 rivers	km 184	km 125	km 210	km 159	km 243	km 3,598	km 3,427	km 3,769	km 3,787	km 3,907
20 Total length of classified rivers	2,408	2,408	2,418	2,418	2,418	37,846	37,763	37,921	37,932	38,657

	£	£	£	£	£	£	£	£	£	£
Environmental services										
21 Expenditure per head of equivalent population	0.81	0.73	0.74	0.69	0.67	0.83	0.79	0.80	0.79	0.77
Manpower										
Manpower numbers per thousand of equivalent population:										
22 Water supply (including appropriate part or water resources)	0.44	0.42	0.38	0.33	0.31	0.36	0.35	0.33	0.32	0.30
23 Sewerage	0.20	0.19	0.18	0.17	0.16	0.15	0.15	0.14	0.14	0.14
24 Sewage treatment and disposal	0.27	0.27	0.25	0.22	0.22	0.33	0.32	0.29	0.27	0.26
25 Land drainage	0.07	0.06	0.06	0.06	0.06	0.08	0.07	0.07	0.06	0.06
Capital Expenditure										
Capital expenditure per head of equivalent population:										
26 Water supply	2.36	2.96	3.80	3.11	3.20	3.56	4.43	4.83	4.57	4.80
27 Sewerage	2.69	3.19	3.66	3.54	3.67	3.50	4.01	4.43	4.44	4.67
28 Sewage treatment and disposal	1.57	1.78	2.05	1.87	1.49	2.91	3.13	3.11	2.97	3.09
29 Land drainage	0.71	0.75	0.89	0.81	0.77	1.68	1.58	1.53	1.28	1.05

Notes:

1 The classification of rivers (items 19 and 20) follows that set out in the former National Water Council's report 'River Quality – The Next Stage – Review of Discharge Consent Conditions', published in April, 1978. Class 3 rivers are those which are polluted to such an extent that fish are absent or only sporadically present. Such rivers may be used for low grade industrial purposes. Class 4 rivers are those which are grossly polluted or are likely to cause nuisance.

2 The financial figures used for the calculation of ratios exclude exceptional and extraordinary items in the accounts.

External financing limit
Finally, Government also sets an External Financing Limit (EFL). For Thames Water this was a negative figure of £60m. This meant that all capital expenditure had to be financed from charges and also required a net reduction in outstanding debt of £60m. The year's results show that the actual reduction was £76m, which was well in excess of the target. The EFL table shows how this was achieved by comparison with the budget.

Capital expenditure
Capital expenditure in the year 1985–6 amounted to £116m.

Government EFL

Capital expenditure and financing

	1985–6 Results £m	1985–6 Budget £m
Capital expenditure	116	114
Working capital movement	4	2
Total capital requirement	120	116
Internal sources of finance (mainly after interest profit and depreciation)	196	177
External sources of finance	(76)	(61)
	120	116
Government EFL	(60)	(60)

Appendix 9.2 Performance ratios – extract from Severn Trent Water Authority Annual Report

A common series of key performance ratios was called for in the White Paper on Nationalized Industries in 1978. The basis of some calculations continues to be refined, leading to minor amendments to the figures published in previous years.

Equivalent population

The equivalent population for each service comprises the total resident population who receive the service, plus an allowance for holiday visitors to the Region and for the service provided to industry and commerce.

River Classification

The Classification of rivers follows that set out in the National Water Council's Report 'River Water Quality – the Next Stage – Review of

Water supply ratio

	1981–2	1982–3	1983–4	1984–5	1985–6	Industry average 1985–6
1 Unit costs at 1985–6 prices (£s per head)						
(a) Operational and management expenses per head of equivalent population						
(i) Authority unit costs	8.65	8.55	8.65	8.54	8.27	
(ii) Industry average unit costs	9.17	9.10	9.12	9.11	8.85	
(b) Current cost depreciation per head of equivalent population						
(i) Authority unit costs	3.59	3.30	3.30	3.31	3.47	
(ii) Industry average unit costs	3.30	3.18	3.29	3.44	3.48	
(c) Current cost operating profit per head of equivalent population						
(i) Authority unit costs	1.51	2.06	1.72	1.67	2.05	
(ii) Industry average unit costs	1.93	2.35	2.23	1.87	2.58	
Significant items included 1(a)(i) above:						
(d) Manpower	4.09	4.02	3.70	3.57	3.35	3.55
(e) Power costs	1.35	1.35	1.39	1.41	1.37	1.23
(f) Chemical costs	0.17	0.17	0.16	0.15	0.15	0.24
2 Percentage of water put into supply from:						
(a) Ground sources	40.2	39.9	39.6	39.0	39.7	27.4
(b) Surface sources	59.8	60.1	60.4	61.0	60.3	72.6
3 Percentage of supplies which are:						
(a) Metered potable	27.2	26.9	25.6	26.0	26.6	23.7
(b) Metered non-potable	0.1	0	0	0	0	3.8
(c) Unmetered	72.7	73.1	74.4	74.0	73.4	72.4
4 Normal population on supply as a percentage of total normal population of the supply area	99.2	99.2	99.3	99.4	99.3	98.9

Sewerage and sewage
Treatment and disposal ratios

	1981–2	1982–3	1983–4	1984–5	1985–6	Industry average 1985–6
5 Sewerage unit costs at 1985–6 prices (£s per head)						
(a) Operational and management expenses per head of equivalent population						
(i) Authority unit costs	2.22	2.32	2.43	2.35	2.33	
(ii) Industry average unit costs	2.86	2.97	2.94	2.86	2.79	
(b) Current cost depreciation per head of equivalent population						
(i) Authority unit costs	5.11	4.78	4.93	5.02	4.99	
(ii) Industry average unit costs	5.12	4.76	5.25	5.34	5.39	
(c) Current cost operating profit per head of equivalent population						
(i) Authority unit costs	3.26	3.03	2.73	2.34	2.94	
(ii) Industry average unit costs	1.29	1.56	1.23	1.72	2.33	
6 Sewage treatment and disposal unit costs at 1985–6 prices (£s per head)						
(a) Operational and management expenses per head of equivalent population						
(i) Authority unit costs	7.53	7.36	7.12	6.81	6.93	
(ii) Industry average unit costs	7.24	7.17	7.02	6.90	6.75	
(b) Current cost depreciation per head of equivalent population						
(i) Authority unit costs	3.91	3.00	3.36	3.44	3.39	
(ii) Industry average unit costs	3.58	3.18	3.48	3.51	3.52	
(c) Current cost operating profit per head of equivalent population						
(i) Authority unit costs	0.80	1.03	0.12	0.33	1.01	
(ii) Industry average unit costs	1.68	2.00	1.36	1.32	1.95	
Significant terms included in 6 a) i) above						
(d) Manpower costs	4.25	4.10	3.69	3.56	3.45	3.08
(e) Power costs	0.71	0.73	0.67	0.64	0.67	0.80

to sewer	96.0	96.5	96.8	97.6	97.3	95.7
8 Pollution load removed (BOD) kg per head of equivalent population served by works removing BOD	27.1	26.8	23.8	23.4	23.5	23.4
9 Average size of works (population equivalent divided by number of works)	9021	9108	9490	9281	9361	8069
10 Length of Class 3 and 4 rivers (km)	565	511	497	502	497	3907*
11 Total length of classified rivers (km)	6202	6202	6202	6202	6202	38652*

Environmental services ratio

12 Operating and management expenses per head of equivalent population (£ per head)

(i) Authority unit costs	0.79	0.83	0.85	0.86	0.81
(ii) Industry average unit costs	0.83	0.79	0.80	0.79	0.77

Manpower ratios

13 Manpower numbers per thousand head of equivalent population

(a) Water supply (including appropriate part of water resource)	0.35	0.35	0.33	0.32	0.30	0.30
(b) Sewerage	0.11	0.10	0.10	0.10	0.10	0.14
(c) Sewage treatment and disposal	0.38	0.36	0.33	0.32	0.31	0.26
(d) Land drainage	0.06	0.06	0.05	0.05	0.05	0.06

Capital expenditure ratios

14 Capital expenditure per head of equivalent population at 1985/6 prices (£s per head)

(i) Authority unit costs					
(a) Water supply	3.12	6.39	4.03	3.78	3.82
(b) Sewerage	3.11	3.69	3.57	3.64	3.52
(c) Sewage treatment and disposal	1.75	1.55	1.56	1.35	1.34
(d) Land drainage	0.68	0.62	0.69	0.76	0.60
(ii) Industry average unit costs					
(a) Water supply	3.56	4.43	4.83	4.57	4.80
(b) Sewerage	3.50	4.01	4.43	4.44	4.67
(c) Sewage treatment and disposal	2.91	3.13	3.11	2.97	3.09
(d) Land drainage	1.68	1.58	1.53	1.28	1.05

Discharge Consent Conditions', published in April 1978. Class 3 rivers are those which are polluted to such an extent that fish are absent or only sporadically present. Such rivers may be used for low grade industrial abstraction purposes, Class 4 rivers are those which are grossly polluted and are likely to cause nuisance.

The financial figures used for the calculation of ratios exclude exceptional and extraordinary items in the accounts. Current cost accounting depreciation and operating profit in earlier years (at 1985–6 prices) are shown for the first time.

Appendix 9.3 The Water Authorities (Return on Assets) Order 1985

The Secretary of State for the Environment, with the approval of the Treasury, in exercise of the powers conferred on him by section 29(2)(a) of the Water Act 1973 and of all other powers enabling him in that behalf, hereby makes the following order

1 *Title, commencement and application of powers*

This order may be cited as the Water Authorities (Return on Assets) Order 1985 and shall come into operation on 14th February 1985.

2 *Interpretation*

In construing, for the purposes of this order, 'current cost' and 'current cost operating profit' regard shall be had to the requirements for the preparation of current cost accounts contained in the publication entitled 'Statement of Standard Accounting Practice No. 16' issued in March 1980 by the bodies represented on the Consultative Committee of Accountancy Bodies.

3 *Definition of 'the value of its net assets' for the purposes of section 29 of the Act*

'The value of its net assets' is defined, for the purposes of section 29 of the Water Act 1973, as the mean between the total net value, at current cost, of the assets held by the Authority for the purposes of its functions (other than functions relating to land drainage) on 1st April 1985 and of the assets so held on 31st March 1986.

4 *Return on value of net assets*

   (1) In this article, 'the 1985 balance' means the amount by which the Authority's 1985 achievement, as defined in the Water Authorities (Return on Assets) Order 1984 exceeded or fell short of the rate of return specified in that order; and
   'the 1986 achievement' means the aggregate of
   (a) the 1985 balance
   (b) the current cost operating profit of the Authority earned for the financial year 1985/86 from the Authority's functions other than functions relating to land drainage, and
   (c) any amount transferred to its appropriation account in respect of that year from any tariff equalisation fund maintained by the Authority

(2) 1.47% is specified as the rate of return on the value of its net assets which the Secretary of State considers it reasonable for Severn-Trent Water Authority to achieve in respect of the financial year 1985/86 (in this article referred to as 'the specified rate')

(3) It is hereby directed that during the financial year 1985/86 the Severn-Trent Water Authority shall discharge its functions with a view to securing that its 1986 achievement expressed as a percentage of its net assets is not less than 1.47%

Patrick Jenkin
Secretary of State for the Environment

24 January 1985

We approve the making of this order.

Donald Thompson
A G Hamilton
Two of the Lords Commissioners
of Her Majesty's Treasury

10 Internal audit and control

Internal control

A pervasive theme found throughout this book has been that of control. The management of any organization is charged with the responsibility of ensuring adequate control exists. To be effective, controls should ensure that the entity's activities maintain a degree of coordination, that activities are complementary and that the individual pursues the goals of the organization, suppressing, if necessary, his own interests. In this context internal control and internal audit play a vital part.

Internal control is defined as 'the whole system of controls, financial and otherwise, established by the management in order to carry on the business of the enterprise in an orderly and efficient manner, ensure adherence to management policies, safeguard the assets and secure as far as possible the completeness and accuracy of the records'.[1,2]

Types of control

Internal control defined in this way covers a broad range of management functions. This is amplified by the Auditing Practices Committee (APC), which identifies eight types of control[3] which may be commonly found:

- *Organization*. This provides the general structure for control, identifying the location and extent of authority and responsibilities within the structure and defining reporting channels and the existence of control mechanisms.
- *Segregation of duties*. The separation of duties and responsibilities for the recording and the processing of a complete transaction provides a prime form of control, reducing the risk of error or deliber-

ate manipulation without the existence of collaboration. It permits the checking of one individual's work by another. The APC indicates that the following functions should be separated: 'authorization, execution, custody, recording and in the case of computer-based accounting systems, development and daily operations'.[4]

- *Physical*. These are the security measures and procedures which restrict direct and indirect access to assets to authorized personnel. They play a role in relation to the custody of assets, particularly those which are readily exchangeable, valuable, or portable.
- *Authorization and approval*. This control specifies the individuals responsible for approving transactions and the extent of their authority.
- *Arithmetical and accounting*. As part of the recording function, these controls check the correct and accurate recording and processing of transactions verifying the proper authority is present. Examples include reconciliations, control accounts, trial balances, document controls and check totals.
- *Personnel*. The quality of control systems is dependent upon the competence and integrity of those who carry out control operations. This control factor requires attention to be given to selection, training and qualifications of personnel, as well as personal qualities, including honesty, reliability and conscientiousness.
- *Supervision*. 'The supervision by responsible officials of day-to-day transactions and the recording thereof'.[5]
- *Management*. In addition to day-to-day supervision, management should provide control through analysis and review of management accounts, including comparison of achievement with budgets, by other special reviews and through the provision of internal audit procedures.

Use of controls

These controls may be utilized in various combinations, and what is appropriate will vary between organizations with, *inter alia*, company size, the nature of the business and the assets, the volume of transactions and the geographical distribution and remoteness of company operations.

The effect of increasing numbers of people within an organization is to decrease the degree of personal contact with management and increase the need for formal controls. Segregation of duties is likely to be more extensive in large organizations; those controlling large quantities of cash or other valuable exchangeable assets will find more need for controls which provide for the security of its assets. The senior management of the organization will need to consider the extent of the risks faced by the organization and to install the control systems appropriate to the particular situation, taking into account the system's costs.

The function of the system of controls instituted by management is to enable an organization:

(a) To operate in an efficient and orderly manner.
(b) To safeguard its assets.
(c) To check the accuracy, reliability and completeness of records.
(d) To permit the preparation of financial and other reports.
(e) To ensure compliance with the law.
(f) To promote pursuit and observation of management policies.

It may be useful to classify controls as either administrative or accounting controls.

Administrative controls are particularly concerned with the achievement of objectives and implementation of policies. Attention is directed to the provision of a suitable structure, including the division of managerial authority and job descriptions, channels of communication and reporting responsibilities.

Accounting controls aim to achieve accountability and provide records. They cover the recording of transactions, establishing responsibilities and maintaining authority, including that for assets. Specific procedures are applied to:

cash and cheques
stocks including work in progress
sales and debtors
purchases and creditors
investments
fixed assets
capital expenditure
debt and equity capital

These procedures are the subject of the following chapter.

Limitations of controls

It must be recognized that, whatever the extent of the internal controls in operation, the resulting control system cannot be regarded as 100 per cent effective, automatically achieving efficiency and accurate reports and providing full protection for assets. The APC identifies a number of ways in which controls may fail:[6]

1 Segregation of duties avoided by fraudulent collusion, especially by those in authority.
2 Authorization controls abused by the person in authority.
3 Competence and integrity of personnel undermined by pressures from inside or outside the organization.
4 Human errors of judgment or interpretation due to misunderstanding, carelessness, fatigue or distraction undermining the effective operation of internal controls.

Internal audit and the internal auditor

When we considered internal controls, reference was made to internal audit as a key element. This managerial function plays an important part in the maintenance of all other controls. This is evident in the definition of internal audit provided by CIMA quoted on page 8. 'It is a control which functions by examining and evaluating the adequacy and effectiveness of other controls'.[7] Similarly the APC definition[8] includes reference to internal audit's role in 'examining accounting and other controls on operations'.

The CIMA definition extends to identifying the scope of internal audit: 'Originally concerned with the financial records the investigative techniques developed are now applied to the analysis of the effectiveness of all parts of the entity's operations and management'. The work of the internal auditor may have originally been restricted to the checking of accounting and other records to identify mistakes, and disclosure of errors continues to be a part of the important controls which ensure duties are carried out in accordance with policies and instructions. He/she continues to provide protection for the organization and its assets.

However, the internal auditor's independent position and access to all parts of an organization enable him to perform a wider role. He/she is able to provide an integrating service, particularly with his knowledge of the accounting system, which itself plays an important coordinating role. He/she no longer limits his attention to narrow compliance but is concerned with promoting efficiency in the implementation of policy. He/she can make use of his/her broad organizational perspective to identify corporate risks and opportunities.

Status and capacity

It is important that the internal auditor is given the appropriate status to enable him/her to carry out these functions. He/she is responsible to senior management, and if he/she is to have the authority required to support his/her access to all parts of the organization, he/she needs to be able to report any findings to senior management. However, it must be recognized that the role is one of reporting and recommending; it is not the internal auditor's job to make and implement decisions to change an organization's operations. The basic capacity of the internal auditor has its foundations in the protection of the organization through the prevention and detection of error and of fraud and waste and the monitoring of information systems to ensure relevant information is being provided and transmitted to those who require it.

To fulfil this capacity the internal auditor will need to:

(a) Ensure provision of adequate internal controls and recording systems.
(b) Review the reporting procedures.

(c) Examine records and reports, testing for errors by detailed investigation of transactions and balances.
(d) Report on any fraud or misuse of resources revealed.
(e) Review economy, efficiency and effectiveness of operations.
(f) Review implementation of corporate policies, plans and procedures.
(g) Undertake special assignments.
(h) Support statutory audit requirements as appropriate.

In the context of statutory requirements, the need for internal audit is made explicit in certain cases, notably for local authorities. Here the Accounts and Audit Regulations[9] require the responsible financial officer to 'maintain an adequate and effective internal audit', and grant right of access to all relevant documents and to explanations necessary for the conduct of the audit.

Internal and external audit

The existence of a sound internal audit function contributes to the conduct of external audit, which is defined as 'A periodic examination of the books of account and records of an entity carried out by an independent third party (the auditor) to ensure that they have been properly maintained, are accurate and comply with established concepts, principles, accounting standards, legal requirements and give a true and fair view of the financial state of the entity.'[10] It is usually carried out in compliance with the statutory obligation.

The APC provides guidance on the factors which the external auditor should take into account when assessing the extent to which he/she can rely on the work of the internal auditor. The factors comprise:

'(a) the degree of independence of the internal auditor from those whose responsibility he is reviewing
(b) the number of suitably qualified and experienced staff employed in the internal audit function
(c) the scope, extent, direction and timing of the tests made by the internal auditor
(d) the evidence available of the work done by the internal auditor and of the review of that work
(e) the extent to which management takes action based upon the reports of the internal audit function'.[11]

These factors provide some good indicators of effective internal audit as well as signifying how internal audit can reduce the costs of external audit by its support of that activity. The more the internal audit function is relied upon by the external auditor, the more significant the reductions in the level of tests that must be carried out by the external auditor.

Both internal and external audit are the subject of the CIMA definition[12] of audit: 'A systematic examination of the activities and status of an entity based primarily on investigation and analysis of its systems controls and records'. The reliability of records and adequacy of the reporting and accounting systems are interests shared by both types of auditor.

Coordination and difficulties

However, although the best use of resources should ensure that the work of internal and external auditors should be coordinated to avoid unnecessary duplication, this is not without its disadvantages. Internal audit must not, as a consequence, be seen merely as a service to the external audit. The programming of internal audit work should not be so distorted in order to fit with external audit needs that its own function is materially reduced.

It should not be assumed that internal audit is always a cheaper way of carrying out an external audit function. The internal role extends into many other areas. In the case of Kimco referred to on page 283 the internal auditors provided an important check on the application of transfer prices to the company's internal trading polices. It is unlikely that this would be within the scope of the work of the external auditor. The special position of the external auditor may make him the more effective and appropriate at times and in certain situations.

Differences between internal and external audit

The resolution of these matters is facilitated by an awareness of the major differences between internal and external audit. The principal differences are:

- *Appointment and independence.* Internal auditors are usually employees (although in some cases the management of organizations unable to support full-time internal audit may appoint an external agent to fulfil this role); external auditors are independent of the management and, in the case of companies, appointed by the shareholders.
- *Responsibility.* The external auditors are principally responsible to the owners of the entity; internal auditors are responsible to management.
- *Duties.* The duties of external auditors are determined by statute; those of the internal auditor are not subject to legal restriction but can be extended as determined by management.
- *Principal concern.* The external auditors of companies are principally concerned with the presentation of results and position in the financial reports of the company; the internal auditor should be concerned with the operation of the entity and its internal control.

These differences will have an impact on the working methods of each auditor and on the relationship with management. The external auditor

208   *Control and Audit in Management Accounting*

can be expected to have a more formally defined relationship with senior management than his internal counterpart.

Principles of internal audit

In carrying out their functions internal auditors must pay attention to the key principles, which are paramount in determining the quality of the work undertaken. These principles are independence, accountability, materiality, evidence, and objectivity.

Independence

The CIMA definition of internal audit used earlier in this chapter began with the words 'An independent appraisal activity...' Independence appears in other pronouncements from CIPFA,[13] The Treasury and the Institute of Internal Auditors.[14] Although the internal auditors are part of an organization and report to senior managers, they must be independent of the management they audit and independent of the decision-making functions. Only in this way can they be objective in their critical appraisal of both the work carried out by other people and of the decisions made. Critical comment of their own decisions or of managers on which they depend is likely to be inhibited. Many other influences which would reduce independence must be guarded against. For example, they must ignore undue pressure on their judgement, personal relationships, and conflicting interests.

Accountability

The principle of accountability is that those with the authority over resources and those taking decisions should account for the actions for which they are responsible. This is the basic objective of many of the internal controls which aim to identify responsibility, ensure these are consistent with regulations, job specifications and policies and record and report the actions taken. Management is charged with the stewardship of funds through accounting for the resources it is trusted to control.

Materiality

This principle is important throughout all stages of audit, including planning, testing and review. It may be regarded in simple terms as identifying what is important. In describing this principle the APC stated: 'In an accounting sense a matter is material if its nondisclosure, misstatement or omission would make possible a distortion of the view given by the accounts or other financial information'.[15] It must be recognized that the principle is always applied *relative* to a particular set of circumstances. As a result, no absolute measures can be given as standards for general application. The determination of materiality always depends on the judgement of the auditor.

In carrying out auditing work it is necessary for the auditor to establish what levels of error are tolerable. He or she must set the critical level which determines whether or not those errors are significant. In addition, levels of accuracy must be set, and decisions must be made to identify when nondisclosure becomes significant and when it is sufficient to present information in aggregate form.

The assessment of materiality must be carried out in terms of users who may themselves be unknown at the time, and the manner in which they are to use the information provided may depend on future conditions which themselves are unknown. Rarely is there any opportunity to test to see if correction of error in some cases or inclusion or changed presentation of information in others is significant to any of the many potential users.

The application of the auditor's judgement to the determination of materiality should give consideration to the following properties of an item:

(a) Amount or value.
(b) Nature.
(c) Form or means of disclosure and presentation.

Amount or value

The use of sampling techniques in the audit tests is examined in the next chapter. The design of those tests depends critically on the determination of the levels of materiality of errors. Setting materiality at lower levels will increase the amount of testing but provide more detailed control. The determination of levels should take into account both relative and absolute size.

An error of £100,000 may be critical in a report on a small company but insignificant in a financial report of a major corporation or nationalized industry. If, however, this error related to a cash balance, the possibility of fraud or misappropriation would make such an error potentially significant in an organization of any size.

In addition to error size, materiality considerations are relevant to the rounding and aggregation of reported data. In reporting the results of a company with a turnover of £1,000m or more, it *may* be entirely appropriate to round figures disclosed to the nearest £1m, even though this is large in absolute terms. In the context of such a large company, giving separate disclosure of an activity responsible for a £5m turnover *may* add so little information that it would be preferable to combine the data with that for other activities. The use of the word 'may' reinforces the point that particular cases demand different treatment; no definitive rule is being proposed and judgement still has its place. In exercising this judgement the auditor can turn to a number of sources of guidance. The pronouncements of the APC and the accounting professions must be applied in the light of the auditor's experience and that of other auditors.

In setting materiality in terms of relative size in the context of commercial organizations, reference is very commonly made to one or more of the organization's turnover, total assets or profit levels. A further source of indication of scale is given by values for previous years.

Nature
Just as amounts may be significant in either relative or absolute terms, the nature of an item may be important in determining its materiality, due to the group of items to which it belongs or due to its own special properties. The earlier example in which an error concerning cash was considered material in absolute terms was itself dependent upon the nature of the item.

Errors and levels of accuracy of an arithmetical or recording kind are not the only factors an audit is concerned with, so in turn materiality is a principle which must extend beyond sheer arithmetical accuracy. In relation to accounting, classification of items as capital or revenue has such impact on reported profits and balance sheet values that the methods of achieving classification can be considered of a critical nature to accruals accounting systems.

One particular aspect of nature that has an impact on materiality is derived from legal or other requirements. Where disclosure of a particular item of information is mandatory, this requirement ensures an item is material. An example of this is the inclusion of directors' salary information in published accounts.

Form of disclosure
The form in which information is disclosed also brings in considerations of materiality. The auditor must determine which information should be included in reports from the masses of potential data, with the object of enabling users to be able to interpret the resulting reports in a meaningful manner. Disaggregation of total turnover into elements arising from activities of substantially different types may be essential to give a proper understanding of the results of an organization engaged in a range of markets or products.

In this connection the materiality of an item may be critically dependent on who is to use the information. What may be vital information to one user may be of no significance or even misleading to another. An example is realizable values of the assets of a going concern. To a banker looking for security this may be of prime interest, but to employees of the same company, providing this information as a supplement to financial accounts may be considered of limited significance.

Timing of materiality decisions
It has been suggested that materiality is relevant at all stages of internal audit. Not least is its relevance to audit planning. Of course levels of materiality will determine the extent of internal audit activities, and,

hence, the resources and time to be made available. In addition, the inclusion of materiality determination as part of audit planning will have an impact on the quality of the work. If determination of materiality is postponed until an error is discovered, it will be much more difficult to make such a decision than if the auditor has a predetermined level of significance. If a material difference would cause the auditor extensive further work, he might be tempted to classify an error as immaterial, when his prior view might have set levels to give the opposite result.

Evidence

The major properties of the evidence the auditor obtains in arriving at his opinions are identified in the Auditing Standard,[16] which states 'the auditor should obtain relevant and reliable audit evidence sufficient to enable him to draw reasonable conclusions thereon'.

Attention is directed in this definition to relevance, reliability and sufficiency. Reference may also be usefully made to objectivity.

Relevance
The relevance of an item can only be assessed in relation to the particular audit objective. It is closely related to materiality but is concerned with ensuring that information used in internal audit has a bearing on the opinions, recommendations and controls.

Reliability
Again this is dependent upon circumstances. It will have an impact on the confidence the auditor can place on particular sources of evidence. Some guidance may be offered:

(a) Documentary evidence is presumed to be more reliable than oral evidence.
(b) Evidence obtained from independent sources is likely to be more reliable than internal evidence.
(c) Evidence originated by the auditor would be expected to be more reliable than that obtained from others.

When evidence from one source conflicts with that from another, it casts doubt on both sources. When evidence from different sources is mutually consistent, a cumulative degree of assurance is provided.

Sufficiency
The amount and type of evidence required for the auditor to have enough to enable him to form an opinion will vary, depending upon his prior knowledge and the inherent risk of the situation and upon the persuasiveness of the evidence. The risks will in turn depend upon the nature and materiality of the matter being investigated, as well as the reliability of the personnel and record system providing the relevant

information. The properties of relevance and reliability are brought together in establishing sufficiency.

Objectivity
It is important that evidence is not unnecessarily biased by the individual obtaining it. The need for subjective judgement can never be completely avoided in internal auditing but evidence can be collected in a manner that is independent of the collector of the evidence or other individuals. In this way the elimination of individual bias improves the quality of the information. However, all four properties considered here (relevance, reliability, sufficiency and objectivity) are important, and objectivity should not dominate the others. Generally a trade-off must be made between these properties in selecting the form(s) of evidence to be obtained.

Sources of evidence
Audit tests are carried out to provide and check evidence. Two major types of test are discussed in the following chapter. These are compliance and substantive testing. Compliance testing is defined[17] as 'those tests which seek to provide evidence that internal control procedures are being applied as prescribed'. The same source contains the following definition of substantive testing as those tests 'which seek to provide audit evidence as to the completeness, accuracy and validity of the information.' The greater the extent to which compliance testing indicates problems with internal control, the greater the need to extend the substantive testing.

The approaches to collecting test information include inspection of records and of the reality the records represent, as well as observation of the operation of procedures by computational checks and by enquiry. The last approach seeks explanations and information from individuals. The APC considers the reliability of enquiry to be dependent upon 'the competence, experience, independence and integrity of the respondent'.[18]

A preliminary stage in compliance testing is provided by 'walkthrough' tests. These tests consist of tracing a small number of transactions right through the system, and so they are sometimes referred to as 'cradle-to-the-grave' testing. Not only do walk-through tests provide guidance for recording and understanding the system and associated internal controls in operation, they give an initial indication of any flaw in that control.

It may also be useful at this stage to consider the extension of substantive testing into analytical review. This calls for the study of resulting data to assess how reasonable they are in relation to each other, to past experience and to an understanding of the business, including knowledge of events which should have been reflected in results. The unusual, unexpected or infeasible require further investigation. Ratios, trends and other statistics are particular sources of information utilized in analytical review procedures.

Management of internal audit

Just as any other activity within an organization requires to be managed, the work of an internal audit department must be managed if it is to be effective and efficient. Planning and follow-up are major elements of this. The nature of internal auditing, relying on the efforts of audit staff and being dependent on evidence, give special importance to supervision and to recording.

Planning

The four major functions of audit planning identified by the APC are that it:

(a) 'establishes the intended means of achieving the objective of the audit;
(b) assists in the direction and control of the work;
(c) helps to ensure that attention is devoted to critical aspects of the audit; and
(d) helps to ensure that the work is completed expeditiously'.[19]

It is widely recommended that internal audit planning can be considered in terms of three stages distinguished by the time-scale to which they apply: strategic, tactical and operational planning.

Strategic planning
This is planning in the longer term, usually up to five years ahead. It focuses on the determination of objectives and an assessment of the environment to establish policy. Discussion with senior management will be necessary, for it is ultimately responsible for audit policy and the provision of policy statements. The internal audit function itself is in a good position to suggest and advise on policy development through the generation of proposals.

In carrying out strategic planning it is necessary to identify the fields to be covered and the nature of coverage in terms of the two dimensions, frequency and depth. The form of coverage should reflect the policy objectives, consideration being given to the following six forms:

1. Financial transactions: considering volume of transactions, values of assets, levels of income and expenditure and the associated accounting recording systems.
2. Internal control: evaluation of the system.
3. Regularity and probity: adherence to company policy, rules and regulations; incidence of misappropriation and fraud.
4. Business impact: threats to business survival, use of opportunities, direct and indirect effects across the organization.
5. Operational and management audit: value for money, effectiveness, economy and efficiency.

6 Special investigations: assignments from management, including fraud, major change, contracts.

In providing guidance on the basis of audit planning, the APC[20] point to the need 'to understand the nature of the business of the enterprise [or other entity]; its organization; its method of operating and the industry [or other environments] in which it is involved'. An element of this is the creation and maintenance of permanent fields holding records of the organizational structure, including the positions of individuals within the structure and their authority and responsibilities, identification of locations, operating rules, records and reporting procedures.

Assessment of the purposes, fields and forms of audit in the context of the particular entity is a prerequisite to resource planning. The aim of this assessment is to identify resource needs and resource availability, and to take action to reconcile any difference between need and availability by adjusting purpose and resource provision. Recognition that the major resource requirement is for staff with particular skills and qualities indicates the potential for difficulties in adjusting resource availability. It is a task to be considered over a strategic horizon, even if this time-scale does not permit fine precision.

Tactical planning
This refers to the medium term, representing plans for the coming or current year. It is directed at identifying the programme of audits to be carried out and their objective, specifying staffing needs and probably detailed staff allocations, and dates of commencement and anticipated completion. Tactical plans need to retain a degree of flexibility in order to be able to respond to unidentified needs and problems but must be sufficiently specific to show how the strategic plans are to be implemented.

Operational planning
This provides the details of the operation of each individual audit. Detail is needed to show the stages to be reached and the timetable for each stage. It is in this aspect of planning that the procedures to be adopted must be set out. The selection and design of procedures requires particular skill to ensure they are appropriate to the task. Since the operational plan identifies the work to be carried out, specified procedures provide a valuable check against which the completion of the audit can be determined.

Supervision and staff

It would be all too easy for internal auditing to become so concerned with its assessment of the performance of other managers and members of the organization that it failed to give sufficient attention to performance in its own department. The Institute of Internal Auditors recognizes that 'the Chief Internal Auditor should establish and maintain a quality assurance programme to evaluate the operations of the internal auditing department'.[21]

The management and supervision of the internal audit staff are specially important because their functioning is so dependent upon the quality of the work the staff carries out. Supervision extends beyond monitoring the progress of work carried out, although this cannot be ignored, attention needing to be given to identifying the current status of audit work, evaluating progress and adjusting work programmes and tests as required, and finally ensuring all procedures have been comleted and properly performed. Supervisory action embraces all that goes into ensuring due professional care has been exercised. This depends upon starting with the right individuals. The management of internal audit begins with assigning, to particular work, staff that has the required:

1 Competence and is in possession of the skills and knowledge that are needed.
2 Experience of the industry or other key environmental context.
3 Experience of the special problems of the particular operations or area to be examined.
4 Integrity so that the judgements they might be expected to make can be trusted.

Supervision can take may forms. Some situations require very close personal observations, others permit more extensive delegation. The closeness of supervision will be a function of the complexity and sensitivity of the particular assignment as well as the attributes of the staff assigned to it. The critical attributes here are the same as those which bear on the selection of staff for particular work – their proficiency, experience and integrity.

Demands for competent staff must be supported by education and training. These can be provided in many ways, but should include professional qualifications, audit manuals, communication of technical developments, access to relevant books and journals, and job experience through working alongside experienced colleagues. Allocating work to staff of appropriate quality must be followed up by ensuring that what is required of them is clearly specified. In achieving this there must be good communication of the following:

(a) Responsibilities.
(b) The objectives of the assignment.
(c) The procedures to be followed.
(d) The relevant background through the provision, as appropriate, of well maintained files showing the history of the particular job and other related knowledge.

Item (d) draws attention to a further aspect of control. Work records must be well maintained. Generally this requires the maintenance of working papers that may be reviewed as part of the supervisory process by staff other than those who prepared the papers. Further review of the results and reports must take place before an assignment can be considered complete.

Recording and review

Working papers and internal audit records have many uses. The information provides:

1. Indications of the work that has been done and of its proper execution and discharge.
2. Details of problems encountered.
3. The audit evidence itself and conclusions drawn from that evidence.

It should be remembered that the principles of sufficiency, relevance, objectivity and reliability must apply. 'Audit working papers should always be sufficiently complete and detailed to enable an experienced auditor with no previous connections with the audit, subsequently to ascertain from them what work was performed and to support the conclusions reached.'[22]

Having put forward this statement, drawing attention to the future reference which may be made to audit records, the APC guideline continues by setting down another important principle, i.e. that 'audit working papers should be prepared as the audit proceeds so that details and problems are not omitted'.[23]

Particular requirements within the records of work carried out are indications of errors or exceptions identified and how these are followed up. It should also be clear who did what work, and evidence that the work has been reviewed should show by whom the review was carried out. Significant matters should be summarized, making clear where judgement has been exercised.

The adoption of procedures leading to good working papers should encourage a methodical approach, which may be made more efficient through the use of standardized working papers. Standard forms setting out, for example, space for the reviewer to comment and sign should reduce the likelihood of this stage being omitted by oversight.

What must not be overlooked is the security of records. The appropriate action must be taken to ensure that working papers are kept safe and that due confidentiality is maintained.

Quality control

Emphasis has been placed on quality considerations in all aspects of audit management. Just as the APC provides focus by issuing a guideline devoted to quality control, this section brings together the matters relevant to quality.

- Appropriate procedures should be established and communicated to all relevant staff – in all but the smallest audit functions this would necessitate setting down the procedures to be followed, normally in writing. Manuals and standardized programmes must be regularly updated and staff kept informed of their content.
- Procedures should be designed to achieve adherence to ethical requirements. The statement issued by the accountancy bodies sets out principles relating to independence, objectivity, integrity and confidentiality. Special attention may be necessary to provide guidance on these matters to staff members who are not professional members of accountancy bodies.
- Staff should have attained the skills and competence required – this begins with personnel recruitment and calls for planning the staff resource requirements not only in terms of numbers but in terms of ability to perform the required work. Experience, qualifications and reliability must all be considered.

  Attention must be given to staff training to maintain staff quality, with technical updating through courses and access to publications, including those issued by professional bodies, relevant legislation, books and journals. In addition, on the job training and professional development are required.
- There should be procedures for consultation, and a structured approach to audit file review, including review of working papers is necessary. The means must be made available for technical problems to be dealt with by reference to specialists and for the resolution of matters involving judgement.
- The effectiveness of quality control procedures should be monitored – an element is the independent review of samples of audit files. This differs from the regular review of working papers as part of day to day supervision and monitoring. By contrast, it is intended to assess standards, and procedures should be established so that it is not regarded as ad hoc or casual. The procedures should set out selection for review and frequency, timing, nature and extent of reviews.
- Recommendations for improvement should be followed up, for quality control is not a static matter. It is important to identify weaknesses but insufficient unless recommended responses are implemented.

Performance audits

Operational audit

The appraisal of the performance of organizations is a valuable audit service. Although the classification is not entirely precise, a distinction is sometimes made between management audit, concerned with senior management performance of a particular organizational unit, and operational or operation's audit, concerned at levels subordinate to senior management. At other times operational audit is used as a more general term concerned with the range of audit approaches used to appraise the effectiveness of organizational performance. The terms performance audit, effectiveness audit, efficiency audit and value for money audit are also in use. Concentration, in this chapter, is given to management audit. The principles and methods of this form of audit are applicable to the various forms of performance audit.

Management audit

This has been defined as 'An objective and independent appraisal of the effectiveness of managers and the effectiveness of the corporate structure in the achievement of company objectives and policies. Its aim is to identify existing and potential weaknesses within an organization and to recommend ways to rectify these weaknesses'.[24]

The definition may be taken to indicate that management audit extends the traditional audit scope to examine total organization. By focusing, as it does, on management and organizational performance, it goes beyond those considerations capable of being expressed in financial terms. Mere compliance and propriety may no longer satisfy the demands of audit when extended in this way, so that achievement becomes an object of attention.

The appraisal of effectiveness requires examination of value for money, encompassing the '3 Es': Economy, Efficiency and Effectiveness. Value for money audit was required by statute in local authorities under the Local Government Finance Act 1982. The Code of Local Government Audit Practice for England and Wales, approved by Parliament in 1983, expanded on this requirement, providing definitions of each of the '3 Es'. This built upon an earlier non-statutory Code of Practice 1973, which had directed audit to be concerned with 'the possibility of loss due to ... extravagance, inefficient financial administration, poor value for money...' The added element of 1983 was to ensure that management had made 'proper arrangements to secure economy, efficiency and effectiveness'. Not only the ends but the means come under scrutiny.

During the period 1973–83, a decade in which the concern for value for money developed into a legally backed audit requirement for local authorities, there was considerable attention to management audit in the literature (see, for example, Sayle,[25] Banham and Tristrum[26] and Santocki[27]). Many examples of practical application have also been observed (see Inlogov's *Register of Local Authority Research Projects*,[28] which identifies in excess of 1,000 value for money projects).

Although there are numerous differences between various authors, Jan Santocki provides a definition which includes many of the salient properties: 'Management Audit is an objective, independent, informed and constructive appraisal of the effectiveness of managers/teams of managers... It must be seen as a managerial function and as such must assist management'.[29]

The need for independence is worth stressing if impartial audit judgement is to be maintained. In achieving this the internal auditor must restrict his activities to monitoring, reconsidering and reporting. Responsibility for implementing might affect the auditor's view of performance. Independence is supported when the authority for audit comes from senior management.

Management audit may be carried out on a regular programmed basis or may be introduced ad hoc, as required by particular circumstances. It is not, however, a routine process but an in-depth investigation. Whether programmed or ad hoc, it should start with identification of its objective. The area and problems to be investigated must be defined, and managers to be brought into the scope of the investigation specified.

Central to management audit is examination of value for money by considering economy, efficiency and effectiveness. This must be carried out both in terms of evaluating outcome and in terms of establishing the existence of arrangements made by management itself to secure value for money. Any weaknesses in these arrangements must be brought to light and recommendations made for dealing with them.

Implementing management audit
As with other forms of internal audit, the success of management audit is founded upon good planning. For each area to be given attention it is valuable to consider the scale of resources to be devoted to the task at an early stage. An important consideration is value of, and scope for, financial savings through avoiding waste and other improvements in the particular area. If the cost of resources put into investigation exceeds the potential for any savings, the net impact of the audit must be realized as a loss, and this, itself, cannot give value for money.

In evaluating its potential, we find management audit may be used to fulfil a number of purposes. Through the attention it gives and by taking the perspective of the organization as a whole, it can contribute to motivation of management, control, performance improvement, career development and organization succession, and change.

As a catalyst for change, management audit can provide the channel for crossing responsibility barriers to identify and convey the requirements for resolving problems and for taking advantage of new opportunities. Given that adequate planning should precede implementation, the subsequent steps are:

(a) Examination of the function's objectives.
(b) Identifying weaknesses in management performance.
(c) Evaluation of arrangements to ensure value for money in achievement of objectives
(d) Reporting the audit findings together with any resulting recommendations.

Throughout the investigation the procedures of internal audit must be maintained. Evidence must be collected, recorded and reviewed. Use should be made, when appropriate, of standing files, providing the accumulated background knowledge and formal structure.

To turn to the four steps identified above, the examination of objectives must start with ascertaining the targets limits and requirements of the function. The means by which they are set and communicated to particular managers is a further consideration.

The broad perspective which management audit is able to take is put to good use when these objectives are appraised from the point of view of compatibility with total organizational goals. Similar consideration should be given in relation to the other steps. Specific organizational goals include financial performance in terms of cash flow and return on capital, for example. Closely linked are capital development and asset position. Less susceptible to financial measurement are development of technology and relevant knowledge. Business organizations, in particular, will be concerned with product development and maintenance of competitive position through securing opportunities and developing relative advantage.

Comparison of targets with achievement gives an initial indication of the scope for further investigation. If results are failing to meet targets, the cause must be sought. The problem may lie with the target itself, either because it is being inadequately communicated to managers or because it is unrealistic in relation to the function, its resources and its environment. When the fault is attributable to management, its potential cost and other effects on the organization will be a pointer to the scale of the problem.

Financial performance measures provide an important element in assessing achievement. These may include variance reporting, profit contribution and return on capital measures. Management audit does not have to be confined to these, and in a case of material problems would want to investigate in more depth, extending to areas not readily assessable in financial terms.

The approach to the identification of weaknesses may be guided, in part, by indications drawn from failure of a function to achieve its objectives or failure of those objectives to be compatible with organizational goals. Although it may not be possible to provide an exhaustive list, a number of areas of potential weakness may be particularly important, owing either to their incidence or effect on the organization. A failure to comply with the law or company rules could have significant implications. Although maintenance of professional or company norms may not always be as conclusively established, management audit extends to such considerations.

Since weaknesses represent risks for the organization, the exposure to risks must be investigated. This includes risks through loss of security or confidentiality, and commercial risks.

Managers' responsibility for establishing organizational structure and for planning for the future come under scrutiny in management audit.

Planning weaknesses may be identified by a poor information base, caused either by inaccuracies or limited scope. The latter may well reflect inadequacy of management's perception of factors relevant to their planning. Given the inherent uncertainty of the future, good planning can only be fully evaluated in the light of events, and examination of past success is pertinent.

Both planning and organizational structure require attention to be given to recruitment, training, promotion, management development and organizational succession. A vital element of planning is the provision of finance, and management audit extends to this consideration.

Although management may not be directly responsible for all sources of waste or inefficiency, it must provide the means to ensure sources are pinpointed. Indeed efficiency may require delegation. The system of monitoring and control is a subject for enquiry in the context of the procedures to be followed; it may be necessary to study the manuals which set out the procedures and the extent to which they are being followed in practice. Monitoring creates accountability in those in authority.

The quality of the management information will impact on the quality of monitoring and of decision-making. If follows that management audit needs to give careful attention to the adequacy of the information systems in supporting the arrangements set up to achieve value for money.

Summary

The principles of internal control and audit which have been the subject of this chapter apply equally to performance audits. In this chapter the types of internal controls were discussed, since they are to carry out the monitoring function on a continuous basis.

The work of internal audit has been examined and attention paid to the principles which govern this work. The principles of materiality and evidence are the subject of extensive consideration in the practice of internal audit. The practice itself is taken up in this chapter from the point of view of the management of the internal audit. Although performance audits, including management audits, are considered, details of other particular audit approaches are the subject of the following chapter.

References

1. CIMA, *Management Accounting Official Terminology*, 1986.
2. Auditing Practices Committee, *Auditing Standards and Guidelines*, section 2.4,
3. *Ibid.*, section 4.8.
4. APC, *op. cit.*

5 *Ibid.*
6 *Ibid.*
7 CIMA, *op. cit.*
8 APC, *op. cit.*
9 *Accounts and Audit Regulations*, 1983, HMSO
10 CIMA, *op. cit.*
11 APC, *op. cit.*
12 CIMA, *op. cit.*
13 CIPFA *Statements of Internal Audit Practice – Public Sector.*
14 Institute of Internal Auditors (IIA), *Standards for the Professional Practice of Internal Auditing.*
15 APC, *op. cit.*
16 *Ibid.*, section 2.3.
17 *Ibid.*
18 *Ibid.*
19 *Ibid.*, section 2.1.
20 APC, *op. cit.*
21 IIA, *op. cit.*
22 APC, op. cit., section 2.1.
23 *Ibid.*
24 CIMA, *op. cit.*
25 Sayle, A.J., *Management Audits* – the assessment of quality management systems, McGraw-Hill, 1981.
26 Banham, J. and Tristrum, R. 'Getting the facts for Local Authorities', *Public Finance and Accounting*, November 1983; RIPA, 'Value for Money Audits', 1982.
27 Santocki, J., 'Meaning and Scope of Management Audit', *Accounting and Business Research*, Winter 1976.
28 Inlogov, *Register of Local Authority Research Projects*, Institute of Local Government Studies, University of Brimingham.
29 Santocki, *op. cit.*

Further Reading

Boys, P.G., 'Management Audits', Touche Ross Technical Digest, No. 17, 1985.
Chambers, A. *et al.*, *Internal Auditing*, Pitman, 1987.
Venables, J.S.R. and Impey, K.W., *Internal Audit*, Butterworths, 1985.
Woolf, E., *Auditing Today*, Prentice-Hall, 3rd Ed., 1986.

Questions

1 The concept of 'materiality' is very important in the work of an auditor. However, its interpretation and application in practice rely to a large extent on the exercise of judgement and opinion on the

part of the individual auditor, so that the treatment of identical circumstances may differ between auditors.

You are required to provide an explanation of the concept of materiality and an assessment of the validity of the above statement, illustrating your answer with examples.

2 (a) You are required to
  (i) explain the basic principles on which value for money audits in local authorities are conducted;
  (ii) give three specific examples of methods of analysis which may be employed in practice.
 (b) Discuss the problems experienced with programme planning and budgeting systems and the major differences between PPBS and VFM.

11 Auditing techniques and procedures

Introduction

As described in the previous chapter, the practice of auditing is divided into internal and external, with the latter responsible for the 'true and fair view' of published company accounts. We are primarily concerned with the operation of internal auditing. However, the two activities are of a parallel nature to a considerable degree, as evidenced by the willingness of external auditors to accept relevant internal audit reports as fulfilling certain of the requirements of the external audit, without the external auditor duplicating the examination procedures and tests carried out internally. Naturally before such a situation is reached, external auditors must assure themselves of the competence, procedures and standards of their internal counterparts. Not all organizations as yet boast an internal audit department, though it is now a widely recognized function.

Where it exists, it is likely to carry an extensive range of responsibilities, from what might be termed the 'checking' activities of traditional auditing through to what is really an internal consultancy service. Originally concerned with financial records, the investigative techniques developed are now applied to the analysis of the effectiveness of all parts of an entity's operations and management.

The second part of the CIMA terminology description of internal audit is the key to appreciating the comprehensive nature of today's internal audit practice. The position of the function in the hierarchy of organization varies, but is frequently observed as reporting directly to the managing director and board of directors. At this level the function head reports on the success or otherwise of sectors of a business, as well as on how efficiently and effectively managers within the company have developed and operated its systems and procedures. The operation of internal audit thereby provides an important channel of information and advice not just to departments but also to top management, which is otherwise unlikely to have the time to collect and assimilate the necessary detail. Internal audit's central investigative role, contacts with departments and level of reporting led to a wry self-assessment in one company as the 'accounting mafia'.

In the present chapter we consider further the audit of systems and procedures from the general viewpoint of the types of testing and some of the main tools of the trade which may be employed to assist the process. Elsewhere, the chapter on Budgets and Control briefly discusses the performance evaluation role, whilst that on Systems Evaluations and Audit looks at the technical aspects of objectives of computer-based systems audits. In view of the immensity of the subject and the limited space available here readers are referred to others 1,2,3,4 for a wider, more detailed exposition.

System documentation

For a start any systems audit needs a clear, precise, accurate and up-to-date documentation of the system itself. Depending on the diligence of the proprietor department(s), this may range from being rather less than coherent or complete paperwork to properly produced and maintained manuals. In the former situation the auditor must first of all work out how the system is actually operated. Once he has completed this task, subsequent audits will have the more complete documentation to work on.

Testing internal systems

Systems are used to capture and process information, which in turn is used as the basis for the preparation of accounts. The parallel interests of the internal and external auditors are apparent here: both need to know that the internal systems and control procedures are being operated as planned and that the information they produce is reliable. The two traditional system tests are (i) compliance, and (ii) substantive.

Compliance tests

These tests are defined by the Auditing Practices Committee as, 'tests which seek to provide evidence that internal control procedures are being applied as prescribed'.

Although readily defined, they are not all observed or conducted to the same level by all auditors in all circumstances. Basic of course is testing the sytems, which is done by examining in detail the reports, records and documents, authorizations and so on, to see they have been used, applied and operated as they were designed to be. This procedure could be carried out through or accompanied by walk-through ('cradle to grave') tests, where the auditor follows through a set of transactions as recorded by systems operators to see that proper entries and systems checks have been made.

An 'error' detected by a compliance test is of course non-compliance, which says nothing by itself about its size, significance or seriousness, but nevertheless requires initial recording. Ultimately an assessment has to be made as to how to proceed where non-compliance has been discovered.

Following through records is not the sole type of compliance test. For example, it may be necessary to actually observe how certain systems checks are carried out, say with respect to access to stores and parts of buildings where computer systems are housed.

Compliance tests are concerned with evaluation of the way systems and their controls are operated and implemented. Eight principal categories of internal control were introduced in the previous chapter as:

Organization
Segregation of duties
Physical
Authorization and approval
Arithmetic and accounting
Personnel
Supervision
Management

The nature of compliance tests and their emphasis on systems controls leaves an auditor with many qualitative and judgemental assessments to make, e.g. the number (level) of tests to carry out. There is also the possibility that, because of the interrelated character of systems, proper functioning of a control examined at one point may mean it can be inferred that another must also be functioning properly, i.e. it is not necessary to examine all control points, or at least not to the same extent.

A further consideration is whether a single failure of a control requires investigation or whether a number of failures are tolerable before such a step is taken. Judgement may be guided by anticipating the consequences of a breakdown, e.g. failure in an estimation procedure can affect prices, orders, or the stage in the system at which the failure occurs.

The usual sampling problem of bias has to be covered. However, some difficulties in sample selection, such as it being representative of the type or value of transactions, are not of particular importance here, since it is the operation of the control (by a particular person) which is under test.

Even after completion of tests, the only clear situation is where no compliance failures are revealed, in which case one could conclude that reliance can be placed on the system and its controls. Otherwise a view has to be taken as to whether the degree of compliance/non-compliance

Auditing techniques and procedures 227

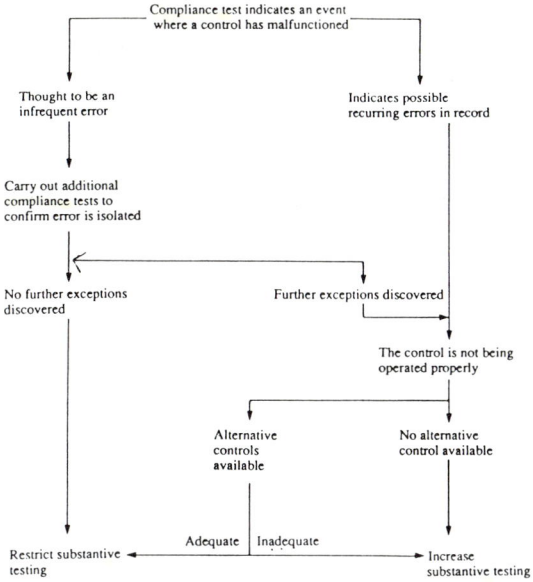

Figure 11.1 *Testing*

recorded is tolerable or not, e.g. if it is not expected to occur other than infrequently. Conversely, if regular occurrence is suspected, further testing may have to be done, which may lead to a review and amendment or redrafting of the control in question.

This point also influences the need and extent to which substantive testing is conducted following the compliance test stage. Venables and Impey[5] illustrate the situation as shown in Figure 11.1

Substantive tests

These follow on from and complement compliance tests as indicated by Figure 11.1 Where compliance tests suggest that reliance on system controls is soundly based, the need for substantive tests is reduced, and vice versa. In themselves substantive tests are comprised of a number of features, principally (i) the verification of transactions and account balances, and (ii) the verification of the existence of assets and liabilities and their valuations.

The definition given by the APC indicates the extensive nature of substantive tests: 'those tests of transactions and balances, and other procedures such as analytical review, which seek to provide evidence as to the *completeness, accuracy* and *validity* of information'[6] in the accounting records or in the financial statements.

As part of the substantive test procedures, analytical reviews enable an auditor to gain a perspective on the accounts, and to see they are coherent and consistent, i.e. 'add-up' to a sensible picture. Analytical reviews follow the substantive tests of accounts to a degree which is likely to be dependent on the auditor's judgement of the reliability of the detail contained in the accounting records: the greater this is, the less the need to conduct these reviews, at least in detail. The reviews are composed of:

1 Analysis of fluctuation in accounts' statements, e.g. debtor to sales ratios. A change here may lead to examination of credit controls and provisions for bad and doubtful debts. Other examples are in the changes in proportions of cost to total cost and turnover.
2 Comparisons of actual and budget in the management accounts.
3 Examination of explanations for noted changes in these items given in accounts' reports.

Analysis of trends where appropriate is an important part of the study. Clearly these reviews could be very extensive and take auditors (internal and external alike) into very wide ranging comparisons, not just within company records but also making use of relevant outside comparator information, say reports and statistics produced in the *Financial Times*, inter-firm comparisons, government statistics, and company reports to insurance companies. The auditor's aim is to find out whether the portrayal of the company's affairs as represented by the accounts is one in which confidence can be placed. Throughout the exercise many general factors condition the auditor's interpretation of the information acquired, e.g. changes in the rate of inflation, government legislation, and such changes in the macro economy as expansion or contraction in trade, competition and technological change. They are factors which supply some of the more obvious explanations for variations in accounts, period-to-period; but the collection of analytical evidence can be seen in principle to be almost limitless, and once again a judgemental approach is likely to determine just how far to go.

Whereas analytical reviews contribute to the understanding and acceptability of accounts records, the fundamental activity within substantive testing is the test of detail. Aimed at the verification of account balances, the objective is to guard against the risk of their misstatement and the further possibility of fraudulent activity. The extent to which these checks are carried out is conditioned, as already noted, by the results of the compliance tests (in the case of the external auditor, the degree of reliance it is felt possible to place on the internal control procedures). Beyond this lies the application of the principle of *materiality* of the item under scrutiny. This relates to its significance and hence the benefit likely to be gained from putting resources into detailed investigations.

The principal substantive tests carried out may be summarized as:

1 Computation – a check on the calculations performed in arriving at an account balance.

2 Inspection/observation – actual counts or observations of counts (associated procedures underlying how they have been carried out), e.g. of stocks, petty cash.
3 Enquiry of third parties to verify the fact of an account balance, e.g. a purchase order or the existence of assets (title deeds held in solicitors' offices, banks, etc.).

It should be noted that names given to these tests vary and the list is not exhaustive.

The determination of materiality is essentially a matter of judgement by the auditor, and is generally to be interpreted as relative to a particular set of company circumstances. Precise rules by which to judge materiality cannot be given, but some guidance can be found in the following considerations:

(a) The absolute value of an error.
(b) The percentage value of an error.
(c) The impact of the item in question on a group of items to which it belongs, and the ultimate effect on a company's final report.

By way of examples for (a) and (b), £0.5m could be seen as quite a large error in the recording of turnover totalling say £10m, but relatively small in the case of £50m turnover, yet in either case £0.5m could be regarded as a significant absolute error; then, with respect to the size of a firm, £0.5m would be of crucial importance in a small/medium-sized firm, but much less important in a large one. These are very similar considerations to those pertaining to the investigation of budget and standard cost variances.

Errors of an arithmetical or recording kind are not of course the only factors an audit is concerned with. For instance, absolute stock of either goods or plant or equipment maintained in the accounts instead of being written off affects both the balance sheet values of the business and the level of reported profit; this situation further affects the assessment of a company's liquidity, its security as judged by suppliers of finance, and its general financial standing. Materiality is thus a concept dealing with situations which go well beyond sheer arithmetical accuracy, relative or absolute, and which have far-reaching consequences for a business.

So some further requirements of the above guidance on deciding materiality may be:

1 Establish a level of materiality, such that smaller size errors are not regarded as material. Since investigations following a judgement that an error is material cost time and money to carry out, some assistance in determining the level might be gained via cost–benefit studies of the situations.

2 Considering the cumulative total of errors, i.e. the individual errors themselves tested against a particular item, may not amount to much, but when the set is aggregated, it may amount to a significant absolute total.
3 The nature of an item, i.e. its influence on materiality, may arise through changes in accounting, for example of depreciation, stock valuation, expensing or capitalization of items, or the way in which items may (or may not) be reported in relation, for example, to statutory requirements.

The level of substantive testing

Materiality is a concept with many facets. As part of substantive testing it also features in the determination of the level of these tests, in particular the degree of statistical sampling which may be employed.

The level of substantive tests is again a matter of choice among several possible approaches, ranging from 100 per cent examination of all items comprising an account balance, through mixtures of 100 per cent examination of all items above a certain amount with a sampling of the remainder, to sampling the entire account balance. Information leading to a judgement here will come from confidence in the internal controls, evidence from analytical reviews and evaluation of materiality.

A full examination of all items obviates any problem concerning sampling, but at the same time can be very costly pursue. On the other hand, sampling schemes based on strict observance of the requirements of statistical theory can also be expensive to set up and maintain and there is the additional problem of having personnel who understand them.

Materiality can play its part in reducing the amount of sampling that needs to be done, e.g. by assessing its level at say £500, all items below this sum being left out of the sampling frame. It could help to cut out the examination of a lot of low value items, which would probably, though not necessarily, produce little benefit in return. It is not essential that sampling should be based on statistical methodology, but to do otherwise prejudices the representative nature of the sample through the possible introduction of bias, even though all the features of a statistical sample – sample size, acceptable error limits, stratification and so on – could otherwise appear to be recognized. Equally, pure reliance on statistical approaches may miss the valuable input of an auditor's experience in detecting the signs, themselves apparently not significant, which lead into a related and significant series of events and results.

Computer assistance can greatly relieve the problems in this area, since a great deal of computation work can be completed very rapidly. Nonetheless, auditors' experience and judgement will always be a major constituent in deciding the best among the options open.

Recording and appraising the system

Before the start of a systems audit, it is obviously necessary to have clear documentation of the system, stating how it should operate. Many companies will probably possess systems manuals for this purpose, but auditors will need to check them out. In other cases they may have to find out how a system works themselves. Reliance by external auditors on the examination of systems carried out by internal auditors obviously depends on evidence that systems are properly recorded and that checks on controls have been completed by the internal staff.

The following are the most widely used techniques for understanding and appraising systems operation:

(a) Flow-charting.
(b) Use of Internal Control Questionnaires (ICAs).
(c) Use of Internal Control Evaluation Questionnaires (ICEQs).

Flow-charting

This technique produces a diagrammatic representation of the system. Completed properly, it provides a comprehensive visual map of how the system operates, how sections/departments interrelate and where internal checks are or should be carried out. The use of symbols may reduce the need for narrative description to provide back-up explanation of the chart, though they may not eliminate it entirely. In any event the language of the symbols has to be learnt.

There are various types of flow-chart, but for present purposes it is the flow of documentation which is usually the main interest. Files and reports should be identified in the sequence in which they are processed, so that there is a complete picture of a system's operation from beginning to end. Activities will generally be grouped by transaction, a separate chart being required for each one, e.g. 'sales' as a generic transaction could be broken down, *inter alia*, into sales of original equipment and sales of spares.

The symbols themselves differ to some extent among individual users, but there is a substantial measure of comparability. Basic ones, not specifically computer application symbols, are shown in Figure 11.2.

The chart is usually joined by horizontal or vertical lines, and flows from top left to bottom right of the chart as the sequence unfolds. A small example follows (Figure 11.3), but the art and detail of flow-charting is quite considerable and readers are referred to other works[7,8,9,10] for futher discussion and examples.

An alternative presentation of systems is to use the logical sequence convention, where yes/no answers are given to questions, indicating a course of action. A very limited example is shown in Figure 11.4.

Internal Control Questionnaires (ICQs)

The use of these may be linked to the flow-chart. Their objective is to provide an auditor with an indication of strengths and weaknesses in

232 Control and Audit in Management Accounting

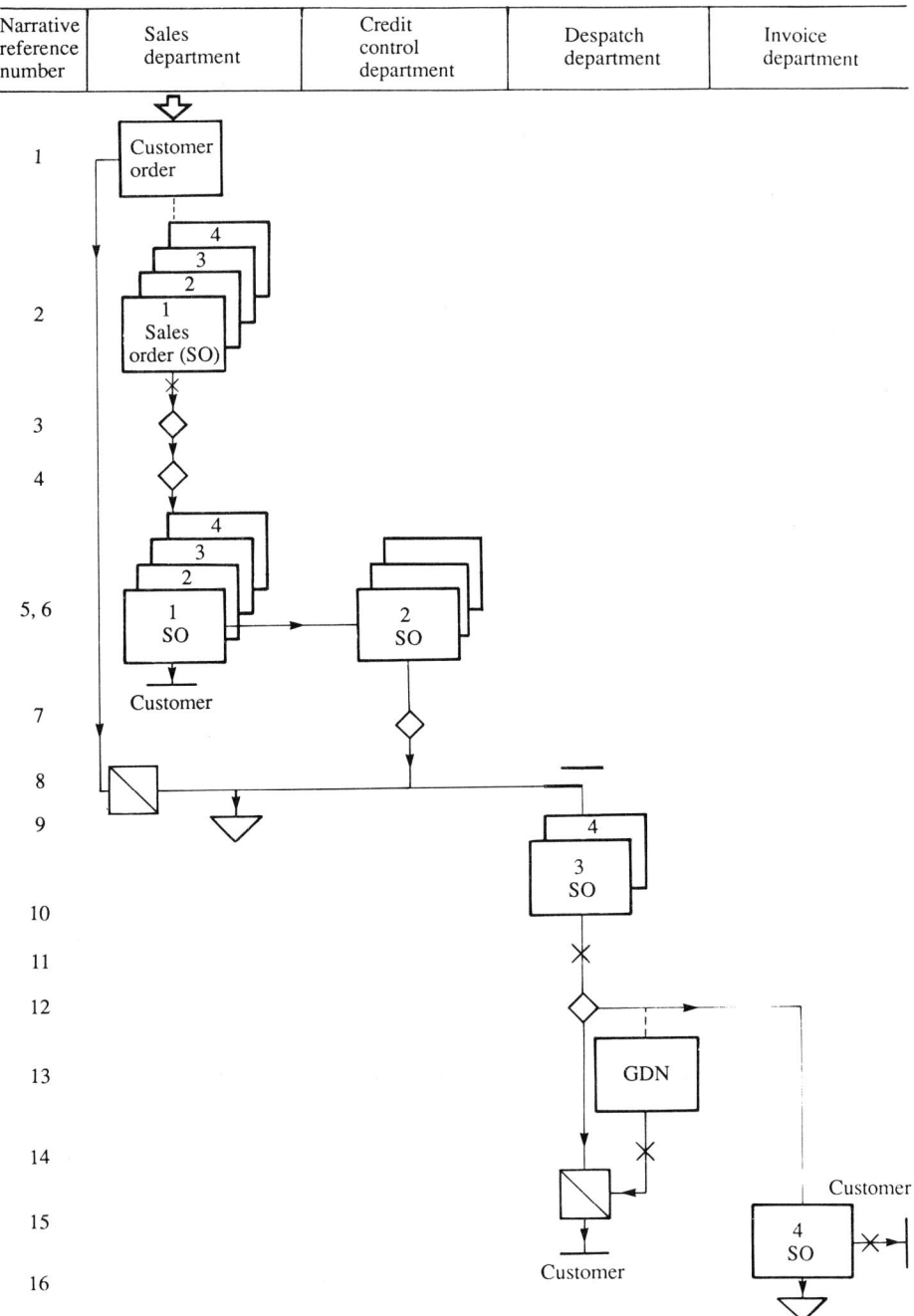

Figure 11.3 *Flowchart examples: recording credit sales orders*

Auditing techniques and procedures 233

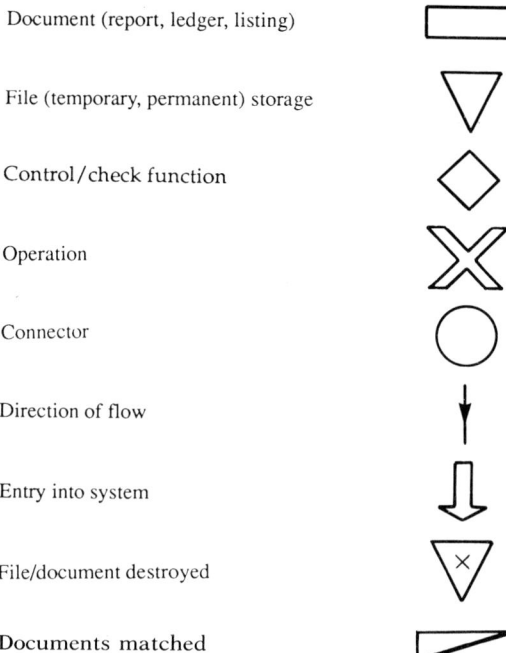

Figure 11.2 *Flow chart symbols*

1 Customer order received
2 Sales order (SO) (4 copies) raised
3 SD clerical check
4 SP supervisor check
5 SO 1 to customer
6 SO copies 2, 3 and 4 to credit control and despatch departments
7 Check by credit controller and report issued
8 Customer order matched to SO 2 in sales department
9 SO 2 filed in sales department and SO 3 and SO 4 sent to despatch department.
10 Despatch department make up order form SO 3
11 Order checked by despatch department manager/supervisor
12 SO 4 to invoice department
13 Goods despatch note raised (GDN)
14 SO 3 matched to goods dispatch note (GDN) and sent to customer
15 Invoice raised from SO4 and sent to customer
16 SO 4 filed in invoice department

Note: In addition to raising the GDN and invoice, there would be further check functions in the despatch and invoicing departments. The invoice routine is not complete.

234 *Control and Audit in Management Accounting*

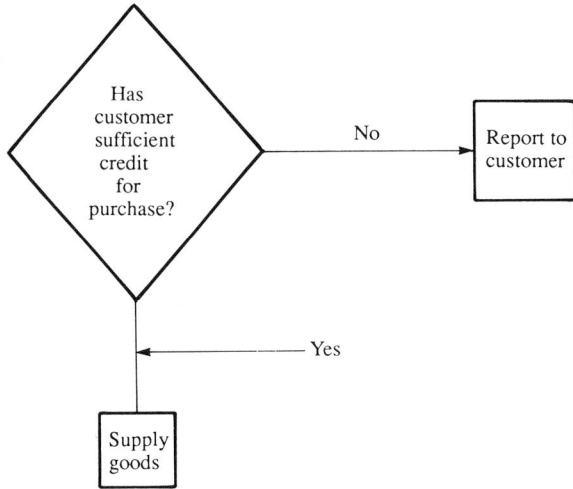

Figure 11.4 *Logical sequence convention*

internal control of systems' operation. These should be comprehensive of a company's systems of processing and control. Questions incorporated in the questionnaire are formulated in a way that a 'no' answer indicates a weakness. ICQs are not standard documents between firms, and they require a regular check themselves to be kept up to date; in addition, they are frequently very detailed and lengthy documents. A brief example is given in Figure 11.5

A 'no' answer to question 2 would be an obvious weakness. The flowchart reference number ties the ICQ to the flow-chart. Provision also has to be made to record the detail of answers requiring a fuller statement than just Yes, No or N/A.

Internal Control Evaluation Questionnaires (ICEQs)

These are prepared principally for senior audit management. They concentrate on key control points, being considerably less detailed than the ICQs. Senior staff are thereby enabled to achieve an overview of the most significant points, but can still find back-up detail where necessary. A further major differences to an ICQ is that ICEQ answers are formulated so that a 'yes' answer indicates a weakness. A brief example from the sales function is shown in Figure 11.6.

Once again, though, there is variety in the way these questionnaires are designed, particularly in their detailed content. However condensed or abbreviated they are, they all seek to highlight the affirmation of weaknesses which exist in key areas and which spell serious problems in the way system controls have been designed (or omitted) and operated.

Reviewer				
Auditee .... Date				
Question	Response			
	Yes	No	Not applicable	Flowchart note ref.
1 How are sales orders recorded?				
2 Is customer credit standing checked before an order is accepted?				
3 Is customer credit checked by a department separate from sales?				
4 Are sales invoices compared with (i) sales orders, and (ii) GDNs?				
5 Is the person responsible for (4) separate from personnel who (i) prepare invoices, and (ii) record dispatches?				

Figure 11.5 *Internal control questionnaire*

Statistical sampling

The purpose of using statistical sampling in internal (and external) auditing is to verify the reliability of accounting records within specified limits of accuracy without examining every transaction. It is

Sales dept Key question	Answer (Yes or No)	Comment/explanation
1 Can goods be supplied to customers without being invoiced? 2 Can goods be supplied to customers with an unsatisfactory credit rating? 3 Can accounts become overdue without immediate detection?		

Figure 11.6 *Internal control evaluation questionnaire*

most applicable where the sheer volume of transactions makes it unrealistic to contemplate the examination of every single item and is mostly used in conjunction with compliance and substantive testing. Although founded on rigorous statistical/mathematical theory, a statistical sampling scheme calls for important judgements to be made with respect to the materiality aspect of errors and the precision limits of the sample. There are many trade-offs between the accuracy of the sample results and the economies of carrying out a sampling procedure, but at least the parameters of the sample can be stated explicitly and accepted or rejected and ultimately interpreted on a common basis.

Not all circumstances lend themselves to statistical sampling: clearly where there are only a few transactions, each one could be material and hence require examination; and other features, such as the degree of underevaluation of items, may render particular types of sampling inappropriate. The volume of literature on the subject is very large and it is only possible to present the fundamental elements of such schemes here, while referring readers to more advanced texts in the references.

Selecting a sample

Random sampling is the basis of statistical sampling schemes. In a random sample each member of a population has an equal chance of inclusion in the sample. There are a number of variants in the approach to collecting sample data which may be adopted in conjunction with random sampling, from simple random sampling itself through to systematic, stratified, and multi-stage samples, with 'variable' or 'attribute' characteristics. 'Variable' relates to measurable parameters such as heights, weights, values, whereas 'attribute' refers to inherent characteristics such as 'heads' or 'tails', 'black' or 'white'. Whatever the nature or detail of the scheme, the aim is to be able to draw inferences about the condition of the underlying total population (which in practice may be either finite or infinite) from the information provided by the sample. The size of the population is not a key factor in determining the validity of sample information, it is the size of the sample itself and the fact that random sampling has been used to select it.

The principal alternative to this approach is the use of judgemental sampling, where, as the name suggests, the auditor uses his experience to decide on how much sampling to do and of what items. The principal danger of proceeding in this way is that it may bias the contents of the sample in such a way that they do not fairly reflect population values; it is also not readily possible for others to judge the adequacy of the sample. However, the contrast between statistical and judgemental sampling is not quite so stark as the foregoing may seem to imply, since, as has already been indicated, various judgements must also be exercised in deciding on a statistical sampling scheme, though they are more overt than in the purely judgemental case.

There are also risks to be recognized in sampling, that a sample may incorrectly indicate that a population is not of acceptable quality when in fact it is and vice versa. Thus a number of conditions need to be determined before a statistical sampling scheme comes into operation, to make sure it is accurate and economic. The main considerations are:

(a) Identify the sampling frame, the population from which the sample is to be drawn.
(b) Define the 'error' which the sample is seeking to identify and which is the objective of the audit.
(c) Ensure as far as possible that the system which generates the information eventually to be sampled is sound.
(d) Determine the *precision limit judged* to be acceptable. (Other terms for precision limit are precision, precision range, and monetary precision (in monetary unit sampling).
(e) Determine the *reliability* that is acceptable. This will normally be expressed as the confidence level required. A commonly chosen level is 95 per cent, which would be interpreted to mean that on 95 occasions out of 100 the sample should reflect the true condition of the population and 5 occasions out of 100 it may not. The latter is the risk of the sample producing inaccurate results.

Both (d) and (e) are related with each other and the sample size. Other factors to be considered will be introduced, along with examples.

Attributes sampling

In auditing, the principal objective is to assess the level of error in a population from the number identified by a sample. 'Errors' are attributes, i.e. the item concerned is either correct or incorrect, an inherent characteristic. Attributes sampling and a form of attributes sampling, monetary unit sampling, are therefore most appropriate and commonly employed in auditing, compared to variables sampling. Monetary unit sampling (MUS) is of special interest, since it provides a result in money values, which can be readily understood and their significance appreciated.

Foundation of attributes sampling
The statistical basis of this type of scheme, apart from the application of random selection, rests on the use of the hypergeometric, binomial and poisson probability distributions. For most purposes the poisson distribution is selected because it is easy to apply and approximates (in the way it is generally applied) the binomial, which in turn approximates the hypergeometric distribution. In the latter case the chance of selecting an error or non-error from a finite population varies as the selection process proceeds. Thus if a population of 1,000 items is known to contain 5 per cent errors, i.e. 50 items, then the chance of successive selections of a sample which would contain no errors varies as each item is selected and the chance of no errors in, say, a sample of 100 would be:

$$\frac{950}{1000} \times \frac{949}{999} \times \frac{948}{998} \cdots \cdots \cdots \times \frac{851}{901} = 0.004475$$

This is referred to as sampling without replacement.

In the poisson distribution, two values are used:

n = sample size
p = expected error rate

'p' is a constant percentage and in terms of the previous example would mean that on average (np) the sample should contain 5 errors.

The poisson formula is

$$\frac{e^{-np} (np)^x}{x!}$$

and gives the *exact* probability of a sample showing x errors when the average number expected is np (np is often abbreviated to 'm' in statistical texts). There are tables for the calculation of these and cumulative values. The tacit assumption of the poisson distribution is that an item once sampled is deemed to be returned to the population and may be reselected; thus the error rate in the population always remains constant. For this example, the chance of finding 1 error in a sample of 100 is 0.0437, compared to the corresponding value for the hypergeometric distribution of 0.0263.

In practice of course the true error rate in the population will not be known. Given that random sampling is used to select a (representative) sample, which in turn produces a number of errors, the latter rate will be assumed to be the most likely rate for the population as a whole. If 1 error was found in the sample of 100, i.e. 1 per cent, it would be interpreted as meaning the population rate would also be 1 per cent; 10 errors would be likely to be present in a population of 1,000, which is referred as the most likely error rate (or projection), MLE.

However, as noted, samples do not necessarily correctly represent the true population error level. It could be either overstated or understated by the sample.

The risk which is used to establish most sampling schemes is the maximum rate in the population which could be considered tolerable, in turn meaning one considered to be a material influence on the auditor's conclusions. This will be referred to as the upper error limit rate (or frequency), UEL.

Examples: Given a UEL of 3 per cent, a 95 per cent confidence level and a sample of 100 items in which no errors are found. A result like this would be interpreted to mean that the population error rate is no higher than 3 per cent.

The UEL of 3 per cent and a sample size of 100 can be shown to meet the desired 95 per cent confidence level as follows:

The risk of drawing a sample of 100 containing no errors from a population which really contains 3 per cent errors is:

$$= \frac{e^{-100 \times 3\%} (np)^0}{0}$$
$$= e^{-100 \times 3\%}$$
$$= e^{-3}$$
$$= 5\%$$

i.e. there is only a 5 per cent chance that a sample of 100 from a population which contains 3 per cent errors could contain no errors. The 5 per cent is the counterpart of the 95 per cent confidence level.

A series of UEL values can be constructed from cumulative poisson probability tables for different sample sizes, number of sample errors and confidence levels. Thus, for example, if one error were found in the sample of 100, then at 95 per cent confidence the UEL rate becomes 4.75 per cent. At 80 per cent, everything else remaining as before, the rate is 1.61 per cent. These variables are linked:

UEL rate × sample size = cumulative values

or UEL rate = $\dfrac{\text{cumulative values}}{\text{sample size}}$

using the earlier example figures

Table 11.1

Balance number	Value (£)	Cumulative value (£)
1	250	250
2	763	1013
3	1029	2142
.	.	.
.	.	.
.	.	.
350	897	75000

$$\text{UEL rate} = \frac{3}{100} = 3\%$$

determined for a 95 per cent confidence level.

Monetary unit sampling (MUS) – a simple example

Let us assume we have a set of stock balances totalling £75,000 to verify. MUS regards these are 75,000 £1 units, each of which, using simple random sampling, would have an equal chance of selection in a sample. Of course it is not the individual £1 units which are to be verified, but the account balances from which they derive, i.e. selection of a particular £1 unit automatically and simultaneously identifies the account balance to which it belongs.

The account balances are listed sequentially, e.g. as taken from the records. Five-figure random numbers would be used, i.e. in effect numbering the £1 units from 00001 to 75000. The account balance sequence may appear as in Table 11.1.

No attempt is made here to stratify the balances or deal with any other difficulties, such as accounts which may be partly right or wrong. For a more advanced treatment of the subject readers are referred to Leslie et al.[11]

With the listing prepared in this way, it is an easy matter to identify the sample required. It is worth noting that this procedure will tend to give a greater representation to higher value balances than would be the case if each balance were given an equal chance of selection. This is because there are, for example, four times as many £1 units in a balance of £400 as in one of £100.

To illustrate the use of random numbers, let us refer to Table 11.2. From a random number table, the following sequence was derived:

06270
62400
00984
50641
etc.

Table 11.2

Balance number	Cumulative value (£)	Random numbers assigned
1	250	00001–000250
2	1013	00251–01013
3	2142	01014–02142
.	.	.
.	.	.
.	.	.
350	75000	74104–75000

The first value is regarded as the 6,270th £1 unit, the second the 62,400th £1 unit and the third, which is within the example, the 948th £1 unit and so on. The third item is within the range of numbers allocated to balance number 2, and hence this balance is selected for examination.

Direct selection of account balances

The principal alternative to MUS would be to make a direct selection of balances. Each one would be numbered and, again, a random number stream used to identify the particular balances for examination.

Thus, in the preceding example, the random number block is 001 to 350, i.e. three-figure numbers. The principal difference to MUS now is that *each balance* has an equal chance of selection and there is no in-built weighting in a simple random sampling scheme towards the larger value balances, as there is in MUS. This difference essentially underlies other important distinctions in the way the two approaches to sample selection operate, distinctions which go beyond the scope of the present book to deal with. Readers are again referred to Leslie et al.[12] for further explanation.

To create a MUS now requires an understanding of the links between the elements of sample size, reliability and precision.

Assume a sample size of 100 is drawn from the 75,000 £1 units and it is found to contain no errors. The UEL value is known to be 3 for a sample of that size at a 95 per cent confidence level and the UEL rate is 3 per cent. In monetary terms this gives a precision gap of 3 per cent × £75,000 = £2,250; the most likely error rate in the population is projected to be 0 per cent.

Imagine now a sample of 100 has been drawn and a single error has been found, i.e. a 1 per cent error rate, which is again projected to be the most likely population error rate. The UEL value is 4.75 and the rate 4.75 per cent, which produces a monetary value of £3,562.5; the precision gap is £3,562.5 − £750 = £2,812.5.

The corresponding values if a 99 per cent confidence level were to be chosen are shown in the Table below:

Sample errors	UEL value (sample size = 100)	Precision limit (£)	Precision gap (£)
0	4.61	3,457.5	3,457.5 − 0 = 3,457.5
1	6.64	4,980.0	4,980.0 − 750 = 4,230.0

Consider now the effect of having a sample size of 200, maintaining the 95 per cent and 99 per cent confidence levels. Taking the 95 per cent case first, to record a 1 per cent sample error rate two sample erros must be found; the UEL value is 6.3 and 6.3 ÷ 200 = 3.15 per cent, which is the UEL rate. Multiplying £75,000 by 3.15 per cent gives £2,362.5, compared to £3,562.5 for the sample of 100. At the 99 per cent confidence level the corresponding value would be £3,153.75, compared to £4,980.0 for the sample of 100.

It can be seen that changes to any of the values of the components of the sampling scheme have consequential effects on the values of others. Viewed in an alternative way, the value of a certain element could be specified and a scheme developed to meet it. In the above example the value of the error may be judged with respect to its materiality; and once the latter is determined, size of sample, confidence level, and sample error rates may all be manipulated to produce a scheme which would keep within the bounds of this material error figure.

By way of a summary of the example, see Table 11.3.

An assessment of materiality requiring a finer precision limit can be met by increasing the sample size, all other things being equal.

A final point concerns the interpretation of the UEL rate. For the population this is an unknown value; the only actual information about the errors is the number recorded in the sample. Using the example data again, with a result of zero errors, at the 95 per cent confidence level, it could be stated that if the population error rate had been 3 per cent, then we could be 95 per cent confident that this would be discovered as a result of the sample containing more than zero errors.

Procedures for applications

An internal auditor's prime duty is to ensure that controls over systems operations are in place and effective. This assessment should be made while bearing in mind an organization's objectives and the broad requirements of economy, efficiency and effectiveness in the utilization of resources. The primary duty requires the auditor to investigate:

(a) The existence of the officially recognized control systems (via documentation etc.).
(b) The way these systems are being operated, compared to how they were intended to operate.
(c) Whether the control systems in place achieve their objectives.
(d) To review and report recommendations.

Table 11.3

Changed variable	Constant variables		Resultant changed variables
Sample size	Sample error rate (%)	Confidence level (%)	Precision limit (£)
100	1	95	3,562.5
200	1	95	2,362.5

As indicated earlier, ICQs will be used to prepare the ground for this activity, the professional standard of the internally adopted procedures greatly affecting their acceptability or otherwise to the external auditor.

The regard for the organization's objectives was referred to above, but this entails consideration of many other factors, such as:

1 The management structure of the organization.
2 Controls specified as required by senior management.
3 The effect of legislation on the organization.
4 The degree of bureaucracy in operating the system.

The controls themselves will not be of uniform significance, some obviously being more important than others. Levels of importance should be clearly designated.

In the following we illustrate the application of basic principles of effective internal control, the types of control and their implementation, to some of the main accounting procedures. These illustrations are intended as such and not as fully comprehensive descriptions.

Purchases

(a) *Aims*, to ensure:
- Purchases are properly authorized and recorded with reference to customer requirements.
- Goods received are properly recorded as such, and are to required specifications.
- Goods failing to be acceptable are properly identified, with controls to ensure appropriate credit is claimed.
- Supplier invoices are properly recorded, checked and approved before payment is authorized.
- Suppliers' accounts are properly maintained.

(b) *Controls*

Purchase authorization
- Through responsible officials in the buying department.
- Order forms properly completed and authorized.
- Use of pre-numbered order forms for purchases of goods and services.
- Commitments-outstanding record maintained.

Goods received
- Proper recording of goods inwards at point and time of receipt, using sequentially numbered goods received notes.
- Proper inspection of goods received at time of receipt for quality and quantity.

Credit notes
- Goods returned to suppliers are immediately recorded in a goods-returned book, covered by sequentially numbered documentation to suppliers.
- Records of reasons for return are made.
- Shortfalls in supply are similarly documented.
- Supplier credit notes should be matched to original claims, showing those still outstanding.

Supplier invoices
- For accuracy: as to terms to agreement, pricing, totals etc.
- No outstanding credit notes exist.
- Evidence that checks have been carried out by requiring signature on documents of responsible personnel.

All the above transactions give rise to accounting record entries which must be checked as to ledger postings, credit control and individual creditor accounts, totals reconciliations and so on. These checks will incorporate the features listed under Types of Control in Chapter 10 and can be carried out against a formal compliance test procedure. It is necessary:

- That there is a proper separation of duties, for instance, in that checking of invoices and credit notes is completed by persons other than those who prepare purchase orders or GRNs.
- That there is supervision of these checks, evidenced by signature.

Sales

(a) *Aims*, to ensure:
- Customer orders are properly recorded, with full sale conditions.
- Goods delivered/services rendered are properly recorded as to date and customer, to trigger invoicing routine.
- Goods returned/credit notes issued are properly recorded, to assess liability.
- Accounting transactions and entries into accounts are properly made and therefore valid.
- Payments and outstanding payments are monitored, and doubtful debts assessed.

(b) *Controls*

Customer orders
- Records of completion of customer orders maintained, using

sequential numbering; regular examination of orders not yet completed.

Goods delivered
- Delivery notes raised or otherwise properly recorded;
- Delivery notes should be sequentially numbered, and matched with invoices.
- Invoices properly raised following delivery note issue.

Goods returned and credit notes issued
- Match with delivery notes/invoices, using sequentially numbered records.
- Monitor outstanding claims.

Accounting entries
- Invoices and credit notes should be sequentially numbered.
- Regular reconciliation of control account with total of customer account balances.
- Procedures for entering details into accounts and ledgers.

Payments routines
- Means exist to determine creditworthiness for both new and existing customers.
- Procedure for identifying and handling overdue accounts.

Income (receipts)

(a) *Aims*, to ensure:
- Cash owing is collected.
- Cash receipts are entered immediately and accurately into the books of account.
- Proper arrangements for cash to be deposited in a secure place such as a bank as soon as possible.

(b) *Controls*
- Cash sales should be recorded on numbered sales notes, completed when sales are made. This applies to all situations: cash registers, tills, and individual hand-completed sales notes.
- There should be a reconciliation of the total of cash and cheques received at frequent intervals, e.g. at least once a day in retailing.
- In the case of credit sales, etc., the receipt should be matched to sales invoices, and again proper procedures should exist to ensure collection is made.
- Receipts of cash and cheques are to be entered into records as soon as mail is opened.
- Persons checking cash and cheque receipts should not be those dealing with initial sales, and proper supervision is required to see checks are made.

That these requirements are complied with can be tested by checking through sales note documents, to examine the evidence of entries into proper records and that supervisory duties have been carried out as required.

Inventory

(a) *Aims*, to ensure:
- Records of all types of inventory – materials, work in progress, finished goods – are accurately maintained. For example, that issues (and returns) of stock from and to stores are properly controlled and recorded; similarly from production into finished goods stock
- Physical stocks are matched with ledger totals
- Stock is properly costed/valued.

(b) *Controls*
- The existence of supporting records for all transfers of stock from suppliers, through the various stock categories and to customers, e.g. sequentially numbered documents backed up by matched recording of transfers in accounting records.
- Cost accounting routines are examined to ensure that cost standards are maintained, variances calculated and investigated, overheads properly attributed to centres, and issues from stock priced accordingly to accepted policy.
- Again there should be division of duty between those responsible for physical stock verification and those dealing with entry and completion of records. Supervision must also be present in the form of personnel with authority and responsibility to see that checks have been made, routines are complied with and so on.

Verification of compliance must be carried out. It is a matter which will vary between firms, depending on the exact nature of their procedures, which of course must be assured to be adequate in themselves. For example, a full annual physical stock count or perpetual inventory procedures are both methods to underpin verification of balance sheet stock values.

The procedures an auditor may use to judge the validity of these records are once more the following:

- Examine the systems procedures and documentation.
- Ascertain the division of responsibility between record-keeping and actual physical stocktaking.
- Following through records.

Trade debtors

(a) *Aims*, to ensure:
- Amounts recorded as owing by customers are accurate.
- Proper provision is made for bad and doubtful debts.

(b) *Controls*
- See 'Sales' above.

Fixed assets

(a) *Aims*, to ensure:
- The physical existence of assets is recorded as on site and that acquisitions and disposals are properly authorized.
- Proper records of purchase cost and depreciation of fixed assets are maintained.

(b) *Controls*
- The existence of proper authorization for the purchases and disposals of fixed assets.
- Enhancements and modifications are similarly authorized.
- Proper records detailing each item acquired are kept.
- A physical check routine at reasonable intervals is specified.
- Actual expenditure is matched with estimates given at the time of authorization.
- In appropriate cases proper title exists to the ownership of assets such as land.

The principal means to ensure the above controls are properly executed is to have a separation of the physical check responsibility from that of recording, and that responsible staff are charged with the task of seeing procedures are duly completed.

The internal auditor will again have to inspect documentation and the existence of proper approval for account entries. Following through records will be an important feature, e.g. the auditor should check the actual existence of assets, and ask for and inspect copies of titles to property and land.

Summary of applications' procedure

There are a number of other areas where procedures of a similar nature will be required, e.g. for wages and salaries, bank reconciliations, petty cash. The obvious essential ingredients are sound and clearly documented systems for recording and verification, the separation of duties as appropriate for checking physical existence (of assets) against recorded amounts and proper supervision. Observance of the demands of relevant statements of standard accounting practice will be needed.

Compliance tests are the ones which have been predominantly referred to, but in a full audit these will be followed up by the application of substantive tests. In the main these latter tests are directed toward balance sheet items, on the argument that if these are correct, then the general set of accounts for the period will also be correct. Substantive tests are directed at the verification of the account balances: in a sense they are not mutually exclusive of compliance tests since they provide additional evidence that control procedures have been observed. It may also be remembered that other tests, such as 'analytical review procedures', form a part of general substantive testing and in turn provide information which helps to bear out the validity of the information given by the accounts.

References

1. Coopers and Lybrand, *Student's Manual of Auditing*, Gee, 1985.
2. Woolf, E., *Auditing Today*, Prentice-Hall International, 1986.
3. Venables J.S.R. and Impey, K.W., *Internal Audit*, Butterworths, 1985.
4. Chambers, A.D., Selim, G.M. and Vinten, G., *Internal Auditing*, Pitman, 2nd ed., 1987.
5. Venables and Impey, *op. cit.*
6. Auditing Practices Committee, PO Box 433, Moorgate Place, London, EC2P 2BJ.
7. Chambers, A.D. and Court, J.M., *Computer Auditing*, Pitman, 2nd ed. 1986, Ch.22 and Appendices.
8. Coopers and Lybrand, *op. cit.*
9. Woolf, *op. cit.*
10. Venables and Impey, *op. cit.*
11. Leslie, D.A., Teitlebaum, A.D. and Anderson, R.J., *Dollar Unit Sampling: A Practical Guide for Auditors*, Copp Clark and Pitman, Toronto, 1979.
12. *Ibid.*

Questions

1. (a) Statistical sampling techniques may be applied in a number of auditing situations.
   You are required to discuss the nature of those situations and the objectives, advantages and disadvantages of applying statistical sampling techniques to them.
   (b) You are given the following information in respect of a particular sampling scheme:

Population size	2 million
Confidence level	95 per cent
Monetary precision	£10,000

   Reliability (R) factor at selected confidence levels:

Confidence level %	63	78	86	92	95	97
R factor	1.0	1.5	2.0	2.5	3.0	3.5

   R factors are based on UEL (Upper Error Limit) rates in the population at the given confidence levels.

You are required to (i) explain the basis of a scheme of Monetary Unit Sampling (MUS), (ii) indicate how it would be utilized in the situation given above; and (iii) state how you would interpret the result of obtaining no errors in a simple random sample derived in the manner you have indicated.

(CIMA, May 1988)

2 (a) You are required to explain the function of analytical reviews with particular reference to the conduct of an internal audit.
  (b) As internal auditor of AB plc you are conducting an investigation of the company's trading results. Your directors believe a further issue of debenture stock is needed to fund both the repayment of the 10% stock due for repayment in 1989 and for investment in new plant and machinery. The industry in which AB plc operates is, and is likely to remain, highly competitive. The following financial information has been provided.

Balance Sheets at 31 December

	1987 £m	1986 £m	1985 £m	1984 £m	1983 £m
Net fixed assets					
Land and buildings	3.0	2.5	2.4	1.6	1.5
Plant and machinery	3.2	2.0	1.2	0.8	0.6
Current assets					
Stocks	5.0	4.7	3.0	2.4	1.9
Debtors	2.6	2.0	1.9	1.5	1.4
Total assets	13.8	11.2	8.5	6.3	5.4
Creditors: Amounts falling due within one year	4.3	4.0	3.5	2.2	2.0
Total assets *less* current liabilities*	9.5	7.2	5.0	4.1	3.4
Creditors: Amounts falling due after more than one year:					
10% Debenture Stock 1989	1.5	1.5	1.5	1.5	1.5
12% Debenture Stock 1995	2.0	2.0	–	–	–
Net capital employed	6.0	3.7	3.5	2.6	1.9
Capital and reserves:					
Authorised and issued £1 shares fully paid	1.5	1.5	1.5	1.5	1.0
Retained profit	4.5	2.2	2.0	1.1	0.9
Shareholders' interest	6.0	3.7	3.5	2.6	1.9
*Includes bank overdraft	1.9	1.3	0.6	0.8	0.9

Extracts from profit and loss account
Net sales   16.4 13.5 10.0 8.5 7.3
Cost of sales   8.9   7.1   6.1 5.5 4.8
Net profit before tax   3.0   1.5   1.4 0.8 0.5

Some average statistics for the industry as a whole in 1987 are given as:

Net profit before tax:Sales	14%
Net profit before tax:Total assets less current liabilities	18%
Working capital (current) ratio	2.2:1
Liquidity ratio	0.75:1
Sales:Fixed assets	3.0
Turnover of stock	2.8
Debtors collection period (based on average debtors)	45 days
Age of stock	120 days

You are required to
(i) present a schedule of data derived from the financial information provided for AB plc which would be used as the basis of an Analytical Review;
(ii) use the data to
   (1) analyse the financing proposals,
   (2) assess the reasonableness of the figures in the five-year statement of results.

(CIMA November 1988)

12 Systems evaluation and audit

Introduction

The concept of a system was introduced in Chapter 2, where attention was drawn to the importance of interrelationships as a key feature of a system. Information has been viewed as an important means for maintaining such interrelationships, which in turn benefit from the application of a systems approach. Chapters 10 and 11 dealt with the audit as a major element in management control, including consideration of internal control systems and the use of flow-charting techniques. Both these methods will be of special relevance to the audit of computer systems.

The rapid growth in the use and provision of computers in business and commerce has had a significant impact on evaluation, audit, and control activities. Although the role of audit may be scarcely changed, computers will change the methods of audit. Response must be made to a number of factors:

- The impact of data storage by means of magnetic devices – security problems may arise, particularly since the updating of data can be carried out in such a way that no audit trail is retained. Furthermore, no record may be retained of how aggregate data has been built up over time.
- The concentration of data from across the whole organization in computer data banks.
- The changes in the costs of information handling as regards the length of records, the use of processing time, etc., will affect the significance of systems development.
- The increased range of controls offered by computers.
- The need for knowledge relating to the technical features of hardware, software and computer 'jargon'.

252 *Control and Audit in Management Accounting*

This chapter will consider evaluation, audit and control as it relates to computer systems, directing attention first to the assessment of performance of systems. Audit and control, which go hand in hand, are the focus of the rest of the chapter. The principles already introduced in this book remain valid. All the elements of internal control apply. Testing, interrogating and assembling evidence continue to be major audit activities. Internal checks have particular significance. The internal auditor may need to give careful consideration to risk assessment and is likely to find his work extending to the examination of efficiency.

Information system evaluation

The importance of control in the success of an organization has been given attention throughout this book. If an organization is to survive in the competitive, dynamic environment of the business world, it will need to achieve more than internal control. Its external relationships will require positive action. Indeed enterprise has come to imply proactive characteristics in its decision-making. The quality of decisions, whether proactive or reactive, and the effectiveness of control will be functions of the information utilized. Information systems, whether computerized or not, must be evaluated in relation to the control and decision-making activities they support.

It is suggested[1] that two approaches are available for the evaluation of the efficiency of an information system – the cost–effective and the cost–benefit approach. The former, which is the simpler, takes the information output as fixed in terms of quality and quantity, and seeks to identify the system which can produce that output at the lowest cost. The cost–benefit approach permits the information output to vary and assesses efficiency in terms of the ratio between the value of the benefits of output and its cost.

Quantification of an information output value may be difficult in part because several sources of information are used jointly in the typical control or decision-making application. The resulting problem is closely related to the joint cost problem, which is all too familiar to the management accountant. In this case the impact of change and uncertainty means that a reliable relation between total inputs and the value of the outputs is elusive, with no opportunity to observe the differences produced by varying inputs.

A number of qualitative factors may be considered good indicators of the value of information and the performance of the system producing it. Suggested approaches to assessing the major factors are set out below:

- Relevance – are the information needs of the users identified? Is the information relevant to the decisions and duties of the users receiving it? Can they act on it?
- Completeness – is the information supplied adequate to enable man-

agement to fulfil its responsibilities and to exercise adequate control? Does it permit established procedures to be carried out? Are there any important omissions?
- Timeliness – is the information received when needed, and based on up-to-date data? Is out-of-date information removed from current files?
- Consistency – is information reported and prepared on a consistent basis from period to period? Are the data utilized mutually consistent? In particular do the time periods to which data relate correspond?
- Security – is the availability of confidential data appropriately controlled? Is there adequate protection for data, and safeguards against its loss?

The product of information systems may be assessed in terms of the quantity and quality of its output, considering its relevance, completeness, accuracy, timeliness, consistency, and the security it offers. In extending evaluation to a cost–benefit approach, attention must be given to additional advantages a system may offer. Improvements in management control and decision-making can result in quicker, more effective decision responses and in savings in management time. Estimating the value of such benefits for a commercial organization is largely a matter of judgement, which would attempt to predict the improved profit resulting from consequent progress in effectiveness and efficiency. Indirect benefits can accrue from better services to customers through, for example, better response to enquiries and shortened delivery times. Again the value of this should be reflected in increased sales or margins and, hence, profits.

Other benefits may result from savings in costs of existing or superseded systems. This may include reduction in clerical costs through savings in employee and employee-related costs, accommodation, equipment costs (including maintenance), stationery and the costs of information processing paid to outside agencies.

Care must be taken to ensure that the savings would be achieved and that those costs would indeed be eliminated rather than merely reallocated. Similar care must be exercised in identifying the costs which would be incurred in providing the information by means of an existing or proposed system.

The evaluation of any given system can proceed by identifying its essential outputs, which can be valued in terms of the cost of producing them by the cheapest alternative means. The value of additional benefits must then be established, taking into account the qualitative factors identified earlier in this section. Performance can be assessed by comparing the benefits with the costs of the system. It may be that the comparison needs to take a long-term view. Technical development is a significant feature of computerized approaches to data-processing. The adoption of a system may be materially affected by the need to acquire knowledge of more advanced technology or by the recognition of impending technological change.

System development controls

Setting up or introducing major modifications to an information system can be a time-consuming process. However, the correction of errors resulting from serious faults in the introduction of a new or modified system can itself be extremely costly, and a great deal of damage can be done before correction is achieved. In this way the development effort does offer rewards.

The design of a management information system (MIS) is by no means an exact science, although a set of nine guidelines have been offered to the systems designer by McCrae.[1] These can be summarized as:

1 The support of top management is essential; the highest decision-taking body should be central to the information network.
2 MIS should concentrate on key areas, not those easily programmed.
3 Design should start with a simplified model of the organization, defining major subsystems and then developing sub-subsystems, etc.
4 Avoid the political problems caused by harnessing MIS to one of the existing departments.
5 Bring in user managers, not just systems experts.
6 Do not let computer problems swamp design problems.
7 MIS should be designed to serve systems rather than departments.
8 Give due attention to the problems of communication between manager and computer.
9 Ensure MIS has the flexibility to enable adoption to changing needs.

The process of development should be one of concern to the internal auditor, not only to provide an input to the control of the development activity itself but also to ensure that the system will contain the controls required to facilitate audit when it is in operation. In this section the former is considered.

In an extended discussion on systems development K.N. Bhasker and R.J.W. Housden[3] identify the major steps as shown in Figure 12.1. Follow-up, testing and evaluation should be carried out at the key points indicated 'test', which may reveal a need to repeat earlier steps.

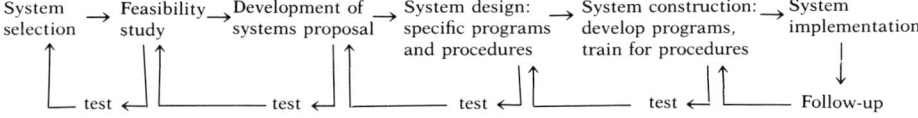

Figure 12.1 *Systems development*

System selection

From this initial stage it is important to ensure that the systems adopted meet the need of the key user departments. A common mechanism employed is to form a computer systems committee, which includes both those who are to be major users of the system and those who have to operate it. The latter will usually include the systems analyst with responsibility for DP aspects of the development and the DP manager or his assistant.

The process of selection needs to define the problem or task to be tackled and consider proposals for schemes. Although it may never be possible to gather all the facts, this activity should not be rushed. Clear formulation of the objectives provides the foundations for the remaining development.

Consideration should be given to the compatibility of proposals with existing and planned hardware and software across the organization. It is rarely possible to consider development in an isolated manner, as very often some has taken place and the concern is to extend this. The related developments need to be identified – part of the general task of establishing the existing position and current system. Examination of records and documents used and produced by the current system are one source of information which must be employed here, and observation and interviews are further useful sources. In recording these systems the use of flow-charts will give precision, helping identify and eliminate ambiguities.

The auditor should hope to get assurance that the users are contributing to this process, and that the needs and implications of any proposals are fully recognized.

Feasibility study

Proposals which appear to warrant further consideration must be investigated to assess their feasibility, before detailed development takes place. This money-saving feasibility stage is usually iterative in nature, short studies often being sufficient to demonstrate the unsuitability of some proposals. Other proposals can then be considered, and if a brief examination does not reveal their unsuitability, more extensive (and costly) examination can be undertaken.

Even for this examination the object is not to explore every detail of the final system. With experience, estimates can be made of the likely costs and benefits which will be sufficiently reliable to enable selection decisions to be confirmed and permit some commitment to development of the proposal.

The internal auditor should be concerned to ensure that the feasibility report has been completed, showing that attention has been given to all relevant matters. He needs to assure himself that the assumptions included are reasonable. Before commitment to development is made the acceptance of the proposal by key user departments should be verified.

Development of the proposal

The first stage in implementing a proposal is to construct a detailed specification of the systems structure. This should identify what is to be performed by the system and set out the responsibilities of the various contributions, showing where information is to be obtained and where supplied.

It is important to estimate volumes of work at this stage in order to judge capacity needs and potential bottlenecks. Opportunities for subsequent developments or needs should be recognized, with the acknowledgement that by the time the system is implemented changes may have occurred elsewhere in the business which impact on it. The indirect effects of introducing the system are also a relevant consideration. This is analogous to considering the broader changes in travelling behaviour brought about by the introduction of a new motorway. Planners who failed to consider this would rightly be open to criticism.

The test function at this stage would continue to examine feasibility and acceptability from the point of view of users of the proposed system. Throughout there should be control activity to ensure development work adheres to the standards required and that good documentation is maintained. A major contribution to this is to have predetermined standards for the forms and items of documentation to be maintained. Independent verification that these are being followed should be included, a point that the auditor would want to check.

The information system evaluation described earlier in this chapter is applied at this stage, so that more detailed quantification of the costs and benefits is obtained. Approval of this evaluation and budgets for the implementation and operation of the proposed system will require authorization. Again the process may require further iterations, possibly modifying the proposal in order to proceed.

System design and construction

At the first of these stages the work is extended to specifying computing needs, producing:

(a) Specification of the systems.
(b) Identification of program requirements and file designs.
(c) Design of the procedures and documentation of inputs and outputs.

Network analysis may facilitate provision of a clear schedule of the work to be carried out in the second of these stages.

The program requirements may be met by purchasing externally produced software which may require adaptation. This approach may offer significant savings in development costs, but care must be exercised in establishing what the software does and does not do, so that its functions meet the requirements of the proposal. Where external programs are not the source of software, it will be necessary to write in-house programs.

The link between specification and development of the programs must be carefully managed. Once again clear documentation is vital.

The details of these stages are technical aspects of information technology management, and not within the scope of this chapter.

What are important from a control and audit point of view are the standards of work recording and testing carried out. Data-processing standards are set up to ensure uniformity and quality of practices and documentation. It is useful, particularly in reviewing systems, if standards are collated in a manual, covering standards for documentation, file organization, form, presentation and notation for systems design and programming flow-charts, testing procedures and operating procedures.

Attention has already been drawn to the need to record the work completed and to ensure this is properly attested. Programs, file designs and systems should also be prepared following standard techniques and standard notation, as this facilitates their subsequent use by others both in checking what has been done and possibly adapting it, which may occur long after the original work.

Testing takes on a special role here. A number of standard testing procedures should be laid down and followed before any program is considered ready for implementation. This will comprise running the program with test data and checking to ensure it has correctly processed it.

Review and audit of controls to ensure these standards are being followed is essential. The standards themselves should also be the subject of periodic review.

At this stage the auditing needs of the system when it is in operation must be given attention. These are discussed in more detail later in this chapter and will include consideration of physical security and control of data, and control of computer operations to ensure audit functions can be performed.

Systems implementation

The planning and control efforts that are needed in creating a new system must be extended to the implementation stage. Adopting a new system will have many implications and require a number of changes in the organization to support its operation. It is essential that, if these are to be prepared for the start-up phase, adequate planning is carried out. This will need to be given attention before the systems are produced if unnecessary delays are to be avoided, and must coordinate the timings of the various elements. Network analysis may offer a useful facility here.

Although programs may have been tested with test data in nearly all cases, further testing is carried out with live data in the implementation phase, which comprises:

1   The provision of stationery, equipment and other needs.
2   Training and, if necessary, appointment of staff.
3   Setting up channels to provide inputs.

4   Creating opening files or converting existing files to required new formats.
5   Live testing.

The last two may require further explanation. File creation and conversion lay down the foundations of all future historical records and, as a result, must be treated with great care. For some situations this will mean substantial manual effort, so that attention must be given to ensuring staff time is available to meet these needs as well as to check the accuracy of the work. The computer itself may be capable of carrying out the conversion, but this will also need to be checked.

Live testing can be carried out in two ways: either parallel running or pilot testing. In the former both the old and new systems are operated for the test period and comparison of outputs is used to verify the adequacy of the new system. It is of course possible that differences may arise because of limitations in the old system, but in each case testing will produce explanations which reconcile differences, so that any necessary corrective action can be applied to the system. Parallel running is time-consuming and may be the source of some frustration from the apparent duplication of effort. It does permit the correction of errors and system failures before the company becomes entirely dependent on the new system. The longer it is carried out, the less chance there is of failing to identify a source of error, but this must be viewed in the light of the considerable extra costs it imposes.

Pilot testing comprises live running, usually in parallel to the old system but on only a limited range of activity. It may be that the system is to be applied to a number of different sites or regions. One region may be selected by the pilot test, limiting the full cost of a total parallel run. This may follow but a shorter period of parallel running may be adequate to enable the system to be tested.

Follow-up procedures should ensure that testing is adequate and that all system errors have been adequately dealt with. Once the system is running, post-implementation reviews should enable the performance of the system (and those who produced it) to be assessed. This is considered in the following section.

Computer systems efficiency audit

Not only does this process enable the system selection, development and implementation to be reviewed, it may also be useful in identifying the causes of poor performance which might arise from inefficient operation of the system or from the effects of other changes. In turn this may provide a trigger for necessary updating of the system.

In addition to being able to take a broad view to establish whether or not the system and the facilities it uses are appropriate for the current purpose, the efficiency audit will aim to identify any of the system's weaknesses. In attempting to identify weaknesses, the auditor may find it useful to examine a number of specific indicators. These may include:

(a) User department comments and complaints.
(b) Error rates – for inputs and outputs identifying how often special exercises have had to be undertaken to carry out correction.
(c) Records of delays and failure to meet normal production dates.
(d) Growth in levels of processing and file size.
(e) Increase in operating costs.
(f) The existence of queues for access to the system.

This evaluation may also be assisted by the existence of data-processing standards. Instances of nonconformity with standards can provide the potential for inefficiency; they could be indications that systems are not capable of being conducted in accordance with the standards, which might suggest a weakness in the standards or in the system.

Efficiency is assessed in terms of the relation between the outputs from the system and the inputs provided to operate the system. The major criteria for efficiency evaluation have been set out already when considering information system evaluation. They are equally applicable here but, with the system running, the auditor can evaluate how well they are being achieved in practice.

Specifically he/she can examine the relevance and completeness of the outputs. He/she can seek to identify where users are receiving information they do not use and consider unnecessary, and where users are unable to act on the basis of the information supplied. The needs for additional information or additional receivers can be sought. The timing of the receipt of information can be established, and improvements brought about by the system calculated.

Although measuring benefits may continue to pose difficulties, identifying savings achieved will be less subjective than measures of prospective savings. Of course the possibility of further savings should not be ignored, and the potential efficiency should remain a target.

The measurement of the cost of operating the system is also more readily measured once it is in place. Once again efficiency audit should extend beyond this to consider if there are more cost-effective ways of operating, while recognizing that these may have become available subsequent to the adoption of the existing approach.

Follow-up of this nature should not just be a one-off event. When applied to computer systems, it is a valuable addition to the regular internal audit procedures to which this chapter now turns.

Computer security and protection

Computer systems are able to handle and store volumes of data of giant proportions when considered in terms of equivalent manual systems. Security considerations become equally large, owing to the speed at which data can be amended and the form of storage, usually electromagnetic disc, which lacks visible evidence and can allow data to be modified or erased to leave no record of the change or of the original data. It must be recognized that data are valuable resources which may be vital to the survival of the organization. The value of data may arise from their contribution to the operation and management of the company when used, for example, to record sales ledger details or the costs of production of a product line. Data may be valuable for competitive reasons when a competitor could use data to the organization's disadvantage. A lack of protection exposes the organization to fraud. The Data Protection Act 1984, the Financial Services Act 1986 and the Consumer Credit Act 1974 have drawn attention to the need for organizations to protect data on behalf of others.

Uncontrolled disclosure of personal data not only risks the reputations of both individuals and organizations supposedly managing the information, it can also open up legal liabilities. It is not surprising that of three Information Technology statements issued by ICAEW, two are directly concerned with computer security.[4]

In assessing needs for protective measures it is valuable to assess the threats to the data and system security. Some of these may arise accidentally; others may be deliberate. The former category includes:

- Human error – the most common source of risk. IT Statement No.1[5] identifies, as examples of this, entering incorrect transactions, failing to correct errors, using wrong data files during processing and failing to carry out instructions in respect of security procedures.
- Hardware malfunction – although electronic processors are normally highly reliable, even these can develop faults. Peripheral equipment is often more dependent on mechanical devices and more likely to break down. A further source of malfunction can arise from the various communication links supporting the system. The functioning of the hardware depends upon external support, including power supply and environmental controls. Extremes of temperature, humidity or dust pollution can seriously harm the performance of equipment.
- Software errors – these can arise from program errors that had not been revealed during testing, and errors in the system.
- Natural disasters – the most common natural threat is from fire. Flooding, explosion, radiation and impact from a vehicle or aeroplane are all possible. Depending on the particular location, earthquake can even be a material risk.

The major, almost exclusive, deliberate threat is human. Malicious damage may be directed at the hardware, while vandalism may attempt to corrupt the data. Data are also susceptible to fraudulent manipulation and 'theft' or commercial espionage. A further threat arises from industrial action.

A risk which has more recently come to light is from computer viruses. These are elements of software which, once introduced to a computer system, corrupt much of the existing software and continue to impact on other systems that are introduced later. Software transferred to other systems then introduces the 'virus' to that system.

Data security encompasses many aspects. The ICAEW Information Technology (IT) Statements include reference to the physical security of hardware, software and files, transmission controls, user and personnel controls, back-up and disaster arrangements, and operational controls.

Physical security

A major contribution to reducing the risks of a computer system can be made by physical means. Protection can be provided by creating a secure area in which computer hardware is stored and extending the same approach to security of files and software. A secure area requires a suitable structure, such that access can be strictly controlled. The aim is to keep out unauthorized individuals in order to reduce fraud, espionage and vandalism, and to shield the hardware from external environmental threats, especially fire hazards. The threat of fire is further reduced by the use of fire-resistant materials within the secure area.

Despite taking these precautions, security is enhanced by installing alarm systems and organizing satisfactory emergency procedures. For protection against fire these include smoke alarms, the provision of fire extinguishers or other equipment, regular fire prevention inspection and ensuring all personnel are aware of procedures in the event of a fire.

The proliferation of personal and micro computers and terminals throughout an organization offers wider, more convenient usage of computer facilities. However, ease of access can generate security needs. Devices such as keyboard locks associated with assigning responsibility for machines to individuals can be useful.

The physical techniques used to provide files and software security are not dissimilar to those for hardware. In considering how to store these, attention must be given to access control and to guard against a hostile environment, using, for example, fireproof lockable cabinets. It may be important to control the humidity temperature and dust content of the environment for the protection of not just files and software but hardware also. Files and programs stored in this way should be returned immediately after use; to leave them exposes them to all the threats, including accidental damage.

Safeguarding hardware requires a routine of attention, which should be extended to inspection and maintenance. Equipment malfunction can be very expensive, since a breakdown may deprive an organization of the service it provides at a most vital moment. Potentially more damaging, faulty equipment may destroy data files or other software. The costs of inspection and regular maintenance may be small in relation to the costs of data loss.

User and personnel controls

The principles of personnel controls have been referred to earlier (see Chapter 10). They apply equally to computer systems, where the quality of staff is critical to security. Quality requirements include proficiency, experience and integrity, plus special education and training.

Reference has been made already to identifying which staff are authorized to have particular access to areas or files. This is closely related to providing supervision and assigning responsibility, and extending the latter to information-handling systems may be unfamiliar. A valuable contribution to achieving security can be achieved by making individuals responsible for software and for data, even though they lack physical form.

Back-up and disaster procedures

Even when all the steps discussed earlier have been taken, the possibility of something going wrong can never be completely ignored. In anticipation of this, back-up arrangements should be planned. It is too late to take action after some calamity has occurred. Back-up comprises both the provision of alternative resources to permit continuity of information-processing, as well as the facility to recreate data destroyed by some action. The loss of data, which might be catastrophic, becomes a relatively minor problem if a copy is available. Similarly back-up copies of software should be available.

Standby facilities may be provided by having additional hardware available, by access to a computer bureau or other external resource, or perhaps merely by the predetermination of alternative clerical routines which can be brought in to meet short-term interruptions. A further measure to alleviate hardware breakdown problems is provided by an emergency repair service. Contracts for such a service must be agreed in advance, to guarantee maximum response times between call out when the service organization is informed of the need to attend to a breakdown and the arrival of an engineer on site.

Data and software back-up require that the copies made are sufficiently up-to-date to permit files to be reconstructed with enough detail to allow system operation to continue. Attention should be given to their storage. Not only must this also be the subject of security procedures but the location and access must be separate from the primary data source. The function of the back-up file fails if it is lost at the same time as the primary file, e.g. if they are both kept together in the same cupboard.

A system of security copying must be adopted. One approach is the grandfather–father–son system, keeping generations of master files and transaction files. An effective system can be operated by a three-file system, calling the files A,B,C, for example. At the start of each major update, or periodically on a regular basis, the oldest file, say C, is overwritten by copying the up-to-date file, A, on to it. In the ensuing period C becomes the active file and is updated and all updating transactions saved. At the next major update the remaining file, B, is overwritten by the updated C. B becomes the active file and the transactions used to update C

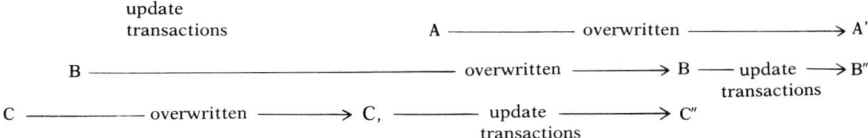

Figure 12.2 *Security copying*

need to be retained no longer. The cycle is continuous, as shown in Figure 12.2.

Faulty overwriting of B on to A could destroy both files. However, the current file could be reconstructed by updating C by the most recent transactions. If there was a subsequent destruction of the new active file, A, this could be reconstructed by updating the copy B by the new set of updating transactions which are retained. It may be important in protecting confidentiality to ensure that saved update transactions from earlier periods are destroyed.

In the event of loss of a data file and the need to resort to the back-up file, the first step is to copy that back-up. This must be carried out with great care, recognizing that this has become the sole source of the data it contains.

A final expedient in protection from the impact of breakdowns and disasters is to insure against the potential losses. While this does not prevent the mishap from occurring, it cuts down on the scale of the consequences.

Operational controls

This refers to the range of procedures which function to give protection during the conduct of the system. These include the internal controls discussed in Chapter 10, and take in the special controls available when using computer equipment. The latter are related to the hardware, files and the update systems.

The hardware controls include personal security measures, such as keyboard locks, which help prevent unauthorized use of equipment and machine operation controls. Additionally, there are parity checks, which operate automatically to ensure that processing is not faulty.

In protecting files both physical and electronic means are available. Removable files usually offer a physical device which is capable of preventing a user from either writing to a disc or both writing to and reading from a disc. This may take the form of a clip or self-adhesive strip.

Electronic protection can restrict access from writing and/or reading only to users with particular activity software, to those using particular terminals or to those quoting a required password. Some combination of these may be employed, as in the case of the use of automatic cash dispensers, which require a machine-readable bankers' card and a code number to operate the system. Where passwords are used, these must be kept secret and changed periodically to avoid them being the subject of espionage. Password systems can operate in guarding data files and operating software.

The quantity and ease of processing data makes this activity one meriting special control attention. A number of controls are available, mainly directed at ensuring that the correct data are processed and that all data are loaded, without unplanned duplication.

Control totals are used to ensure completeness. Usually with batch data a hash total is calculated by adding some number (e.g. invoice serial number); the system then checks that the same aggregate is achieved for the data processed.

Programs can incorporate file identification checks which verify that the file loaded for updating is the appropriate one. In addition, programs can include data validation, to check that data to be loaded or output are potentially valid or eligible for processing. These checks can test the number and nature of the digits to be entered. Non-feasible data or that representing quantities outside the expected range are not processed but identified as an error. Of course it is important that such errors are not ignored. The procedures needing to be set down and followed identify the nature of errors, correct them, ensure the corrected data is processed and initiate action to investigate and prevent repetitive errors.

Some systems operate on a real time or on line basis. These present special problems for security and control, since there is often wide access, both to read and to add data. Further the regimes which can apply to periodic update, including back-up procedures, are more difficult to enforce. Audit techniques can play an important role in this case, and it is to audit that attention is now turned.

Computer audit

In the previous section of this chapter the particular security problems of computer systems were introduced and approaches to provide protection presented. These matters have a clear bearing on audit. The special security problems lead to actual and potential difficulties for the audit process; at the same time audit itself provides a valuable instrument of protection.

Efficiency audit has been considered earlier but the emphasis here is on its safeguard and control functions. The notion of 'cradle to grave' tracing of transactions was identified as a major source of audit evidence in Chapter 10. There is a fundamental need in audit to be able to identify what has led to the production of a particular record in order to consider its validity. This identification and tracing is facilitated by the audit trail.

Auditability and audit trails

The audit trail refers to the evidence which allows transactions to be tracked forwards or backwards through each intermediate stage of processing to or from its final location. The production of an audit trail in a manual system results from the hard copy that is created as part of the processing. In order to maintain the audit trail the documents representing that hard copy must be preserved and stored.

Computerized systems do not automatically create such a hard copy as a by-product of processing. There may be suitable sources of audit trail data provided in computer readable form but in this form special attention needs to be given to its preservation.

The major problems in maintaining an audit trail in computerized systems can be listed:

- Lack of hard copy – particularly for the intermediate stages of processing, where the only routine output may be highly aggregated or merely exception reports.
- The volume of data and the speed of processing increase the scale of the tracking task substantially.
- The efficiency of data-processing may be improved by reducing the quantity of data retained on files being processed – often only current transactions and accumulated past data are used.
- Systems often use computerized sorting – while this may facilitate processing, it may remove data identification and the original sequence of input entry is lost.
- Updating on computer storage media is achieved by overwriting updated records.
- Common data bases may be used to serve many departments to avoid duplication of effort and storage capacity – this removes the possibility of cross-checking against the different sources and may make identification of the department which brought about the data input impossible.
- There may be no record of prime entry, particularly for data input directly from on-line terminals.

One approach to overcoming the problems of lack of audit trail may be to design the system to produce all the hard copy which would result from a comparable manual system, including full printed ouput showing every initial entry and its contribution to every aggregate. This would result in substantial additional cost and time and could counteract many of the advantages of computerization.

As a stopgap, in the absence of a full audit trail, a 'round the computer' approach has been employed. This is operated by performing the full audit routine on the elements of the system up to and including entry of data into the computer system, and on those procedures dealing with the output from the computer. Internal control over input data is important. The operations internal to the computer are examined manually in sample form by checking selected output with the source inputs. The complexity of computer procedures, often combining data from very many sources, makes this approach either too large or too superficial for many systems currently in operation.

An alternative which utilizes the computer itself to construct an audit trail is not confined to using hard copy but stores the trail in a computer-readable form. This may be achieved by the labelling of data entries contained in the active file or by creating a special file for the sole purpose of providing a trail. In this manner processing can focus on current data, while past data can be 'dumped' to a back-up file in disaggregated form. In addition, the computer programs can be directly analysed by those with appropriate programming expertise to check the system itself and identify if it is designed to carry out the task intended.

Computer-assisted audit techniques (CAATs)

Other audit procedures make use of the ability of computer methods, for example:

- Audit test data can be entered into the system to check that they result in the correct output; the composition of the test data can be designed to assess the system's reaction to errors by deliberately including data containing invalid elements.
- Audit programs can be employed to check the system. These may be used to process input data to check that the results at each significant stage are consistent with those produced by the system in operation.

Other CAATs have software that includes procedures to select and test data. Although the selection of tests has traditionally been regarded as the prerogative of individuals, the power of expert systems enables testing criteria to be translated into selection policies. The systems are capable of accumulating the testing criteria in an adaptive manner, so that they 'learn' over time.

On-line systems and interrogation

On-line and real time systems have already been identified as setting special problems for audit. It is here that the construction of audit trails using computer labelling has particular relevance. Since it is essential that labelling is carried out as part of the data-processing itself, the adoption of this approach must be planned and built into the system before data are entered. The technique is to create labelled records of all transactions as they are entered. A transactions file can then be examined at a later date.

Available software can use a variety of approaches to interrogate these transaction files. In addition to periodic estimation, the software can be permanently installed, selecting data to be checked on what is effectively a real time basis. It is feasible to install computer-operated vouching, checking all transactions that find their way into the final output. Continuous checking for completeness and acceptability forms part of the audit procedures.

'Tagging' is a computer-aided sampling method. It operates by attaching a computerized label or 'tag' to sampled transactions, and checks the presence of these inputs in final output either continuously or as part of a periodic review procedure.

One development in CAATs in on-line systems is the use of audit terminals to perform 'eavesdropping'. This represents on-line interrogation, permitting the auditor to observe the entry of transactions which may be taking place at a remote terminal elsewhere in the system.

Conclusion

The power that computer facilities bring to information systems adds a dimension to the tasks of evaluation and audit. Procedures which recognize the special attributes of computerized systems must be developed. As with manual systems, the audit manual can play a major role. However, with the speed of development of the technology, the manager and auditor must maintain flexibility, adapting to developments in the operating technology and audit facilities. Attention must be given to efficiency and audit requirements at a very early stage in the development of a system. Omissions and mistakes at this stage may be costly to put right.

In addition to the needs created by the nature of storage and amendment of computerized data, the much increased volume of data handled imposes further requirements. There is a particular need to provide a sound system of internal control to safeguard the data inputs. Manual systems generally incorporate a series of edit functions designed to identify, question and correct the unusual and irregular. It is not yet possible to simulate these functions fully within a computer. Expert systems and continuous computer interrogation may have slightly tempered the 'garbage-in: garbage-out' criticism of computer systems. Input quality remains a major determinant of output quality.

References

1 McRae, T.W., *Computers and Accounting*, Wiley 1978.
2 *ibid.*
3 Bhasker, K.N. and Housden, R.J.W. *Accounting Information Systems and Data Processing*, Heinemann/CIMA, 1985.
4 ICAEW, 'Security and confidentiality of data' (2.301) and 'Control and Management of Information' (2.303), *Information Technology Statements*, 1986.
5 *Ibid.*, IT Statement, No. 1.

Further reading

Chambers, A.D., *Computer Auditing*, Pitman, 2nd ed., 1986.
Jenkins, B.G., Perry R.C.L. and Cooke, P.J., *An Audit Approach to Computers*, ICAEW, (Revised edition), 1986.
Jones, G. and McNamara, T., *Information Technology and the New Accounting*, McGraw-Hill, 1988.
Thomas, A.J. and Douglas, I.J., *Audit of Computer Systems*, NCC Publications, 1981.

Questions

1 (a) Given that cost and revenue classification vary from one organization to another, draft a general scheme of headings under which an analyst can set out to evaluate the costs and benefits of the introduction of a computer-based, accounting information system.
(b) Discuss the effect that the introduction of a computer-based accounting information system is likely to have on the procedures required to perform the internal audit function.

2 The following data have been collected as part of a feasibility study covering the introduction of a new accounting information system:

COSTS Years	0 £000	1 £000	2 £000	3 £000	4 £000	5 £000
Computer and support equipment lease		10	25	25	25	25
Other equipment purchases		15	15	2	2	–
Maintenance		5	5	5	5	5
Supplies		2	2.5	2.5	2.5	2.5
Re-layout of room		4	1			
Direct charges, including personnel		25	30	30	30	30
System design, test and implementation	15	15				
Training		2	10			
Total costs	15	78	88.5	64.5	64.5	62.5

BENEFITS Years	0 £000	1 £000	2 £000	3 £000	4 £000	5 £000
1 Reduction in clerical costs of previous system		10	30	30	30	30
Sales of software development		5	20	25	25	25
2 Improved management decision-making		10	20	25	25	25
3 Improved customer services		5	15	20	20	20
Total benefits		30	85	100	100	100

The company concerned seeks a 20 per cent internal rate of return. Ignore tax.

You are required to:
(a) Carry out the appraisal and calculate the sensitivity of the re-

sults to the following factors: reduction in clerical costs, system design, test; the required DCF return.
(b) Explain the purposes and limitations of the sensitivity tests.
(c) Explain, with respect to the items listed as 1, 2 and 3 under BENEFITS, how you might approach the problem of obtaining quantitative information.

3 You are required to:
(a) Discuss the process of designing and developing a computer-based management information system, using as an example a proposal to enhance the present system by adding a cost estimation module.
(b) Describe a procedure for appraising and evaluating such a proposal.
(c) Discuss the role of the internal auditor in the operation of these systems and the service he could provide.

4 (a) Distinguish between systems development controls and procedural controls and state the objects of each.
(b) State with reasons, in which of the above categories each of the following falls:

   (i) An installation rule that the systems of control for all applications have to be reviewed before the work of programming is started.
   (ii) A program control in a wages application that the net wage payable to any weekly-paid employee shall not exceed £25.
   (iii) An installation requirement that each system of processing shall be tested by the operations staff, and by those in the user departments, before being run 'live'.
   (iv) Arrangements for checking the accounts codes entered in input documents in the accounts department of a company before the input documents are passed to the data preparation section, in which the data is transferred to punched cards.
   (v) Arrangements for retaining and updating systems and program documentation in a computer installation.

5 The audit of an EDP system can be achieved either by reconstructing or retaining the so-called 'audit trail' so that final results can be checked back to original documentation, or by the 'round the machine' approach, which assumes that if valid input has been processed by the correct program, the resulting output must also be correct.
   What are the main points of internal check to which an auditor should direct his attention on first undertaking an audit where no 'audit trail' is provided?

6 Your company is currently considering the installation of a computer. The chairman is an elderly graduate manufacturing chemist who has become alarmed by reading of a number of substantial frauds perpetrated (mainly in the USA) by the misuse of electronic computers.

Bearing in mind the status, education and background of its recipient, you are required to write a memorandum to your chairman setting out the real nature of the risks of such a thing happening and what can be done to reduce them.

13 Investigations and special audits

The basic themes of this book concern control and audit. These two interrelated activities have been interpreted broadly. The full control cycle has been considered from budget setting to performance assessment. The positive aspects of control have been emphasized, recognizing that they include the encouragement of desirable action as well as the prevention of counter-productive actions. The contribution of audit to control has extended to quality and performance audits; and the treatment of systems and computers to include efficiency considerations.

The inclusion of this chapter presents an even further expanded role for management accounting in control and audit. It considers the extension to producing reports on special situations. Management structures are set up to cope with the tasks it expects to face in the accomplishment of its function in relatively normal conditions, but the very nature of special situations means that management is unlikely to have much experience of the type of decision-making to be faced. The management accountant's familiarity with financial control information from across the organization, and his expertise with appropriate techniques, are advantages in meeting the demands of a range of situations. The internal auditor's independent position may make him particularly suited to such tasks.

The subjects considered relate to major decisions, including substantial acquisitions and disposals, and the raising of debt. Other special audit tasks are also considered. The techniques employed in connection with the major decisions are the subject of the fields of decision-making and financial management. These techniques will not be given lengthy treatment here, where emphasis is placed on the production of reports. When carrying out an investigation of any of these types, the management accountant should adopt a broad perspective. In decision-making, benefits, costs, risks and the impact of other relevent changes need to be established, even when they are indirect or are not obvious.

The format and structure of reports will vary with their purpose, but some basic principles apply to most reports. Requirements include:

- Clear indication of their purpose and standing – title, date, sender and distribution list should all be given.
- Precision, relevance and comprehensiveness – managers' time is limited and valuable; the content of reports should address the matter in hand, giving it comprehensive treatment without excessive length.
- Understandable – a manager gets little help from a report he cannot understand, either because the presentation is ambiguous and confusing or because it uses unfamiliar technical language and methods which are not explained.
- Identification of assumptions and sources – recommendations may be critically dependent upon the underlying assumptions and/or the data utilized; clear statements of these permit managers to assess their validity.
- Conclusions and recommendations – these should not be hidden in the body of the report.

Long reports may need to provide the reader with further assistance, including a list of contents, an introduction giving terms of reference, objectives, etc., and a summary or synopsis.

Acquisitions of businesses

Although some companies conduct their business by frequently acquiring and disposing of other businesses, for most such activity is rare. The scale of such decisions is invariably large, justifying thorough investigation.

There are a number of forms in which an acquisition can take place. These include:

1. Acquiring a controlling interest in the shares of a private company or a public company.
2. Acquiring all or a section of the assets, together with an ongoing business from a company.

The consideration can take the form of cash or of shares (or other securities) issued by the acquirer, or a combination of these.

In the case of acquisition of a controlling interest in shares, the acquirer needs to make an offer to existing shareholders. The Bank of England convened a Panel on Takeovers and Mergers which produced the *City Code on Takeovers and Mergers*.[1] It covers all such bids for public companies. Takeover tactics can play a very important part in the success or failure of a bid, and it is usual to seek independent assistance from city experts in such situations. Stock markets tend to react strongly even to a rumour of a takeover bid, so that maintaining confidential information can be vital. However, the City Code requires certain disclosures to be made with the intention of protecting the investing members of the public, and these would need to be followed.

The existing management of a company considered for takeover is likely to feel threatened by the possibility of loss of independence and status and even its posts. Any hostility it shows could make a takeover more difficult, not only because of their influence over shareholders during the bid. Its cooperation in the subsequent management and possible reorganization could be of significant value.

An investigation of a proposed bid would need to establish the purpose of the acquisition. This may be to secure or expand supplies, sources or markets; to move into new markets; to expand facilities or applications of technology; or for many other reasons. Whatever the purpose, a major factor will be the determination of the price to be paid for the acquisition and comparison with its value. In this chapter valuation of businesses is considered in general before some attention is given to the specific factors relating to shares.

Valuation of businesses

All valuations are of necessity based upon forecasts and to that extent are uncertain and subject to the same limitations as any other forecast. A range of values rather than a discrete amount can be estimated. Value will depend on the stream of future income, or benefits, and the risks associated with it.

The theoretical approach requires this income to be estimated, discounted and aggregated to give its present value, expressed in terms of cash flow. Therefore the income stream is not concerned with the distinction sometimes made between capital and income. This may be estimated from the existing earnings of the business, though these may have been so low in the past that the use of assets in a different combination, and possibly by different users, would produce a higher income stream. These two general alternatives lead to a valuation based upon 'earnings' or 'assets', although it must be remembered that the assets are ultimately based upon the earnings expected from their use.

If the earnings could be expected to be constant over time, the calculation on an earnings basis would be simple. Having decided upon the maintainable earnings, a purchaser merely has to divide this amount by the rate of return that is required. For example, if the maintainable earnings are £240,000 and the required rate of return is 25 per cent, then £960,000 (i.e. £240,000 ÷ .25) would be the value to the purchaser.

To capitalize earnings at 25 per cent is the same as multiplying the earnings by a factor of 4, and this is similar to use of the traditional price–earnings ratio (market price divided by earnings) as a factor. The price–earnings (P/E) ratio is usually applied to the purchase of a number of shares in the market, e.g. if maintainable earnings are £240,000 and a P/E ratio of 4 is appropriate, then the maximum value is 240,000 × 4 = £960,000.

An alternative approach sometimes used in practice is the super profits basis, which uses two different rates for capitalizing earnings, depending on the quality of those earnings. The 'quality' of earnings becomes very important when considering conglomerate businesses, or any where there are significant differences in the various sources of earnings. Calculation begins with an estimate of maintainable earnings. Next, the current buying price of the assets of the business must be estimated to give a normal going-concern value. The required rate of return is applied to this value to determine the normal level of earnings, and this amount is deducted from the estimate of maintainable earnings (the difference represents 'super profits'). In the long run such 'super profits' are likely to be competed away, and are considered less certain than normal profits, so that a higher required rate of return, or lower P/E ratio, would be appropriate to value the stream of super profits. The total value is then found by adding together the value of the normal profits and the value of the super profits. For example, a business has maintainable profits of £240,000 and a going-concern value for the assets of £800,000. A 25 per cent return is required on 'normal' profits and a 40 per cent return on 'super' profits.

25 per cent return on £800,000 is	£200,000
and deducting this amount from	£240,000
leaves 'super' profits of	£40,000

which, capitalized at 40 per cent, have a value of £100,000, so that total value would be £900,000. The effect of capitalizing at 40 per cent may be expressed as 2½-years purchase of the super profits.

The determination of maintainable earnings is a particular problem. If conditions in the future are estimated to be similar to those in the past, then it would not be unreasonable to expect the same profits as had been earned in the past. However, it is usual for many of the conditions which have determined individual items of revenue and cost to change, and the effect of these on the profit must be estimated. The detailed examination of the past trading and profit and loss accounts depends to some extent on the nature of the business and the records available, but will include an analysis of:

1. Trend of sales and gross profit percentage and their relationship.
2. Sales and gross profit percentage by product lines/departments/ geographic areas.
3. Proportion that individual items of expense bear to the total unusual fluctuations.
4. External conditions which have affected the business and the likeli-

hood that they will continue, considering, for example, the effect of an economic downturn, pollution control, inflation, changing interest rates, changing technology, changing tastes.

It is only after an examination of this nature that 'maintainable' earnings can be estimated.

The alternative approach to the earnings basis is the assets basis, which may be used either as the main method of value determination or to confirm the value arrived at on an earnings basis. When the ownership of a business changes, the buyer is acquiring a collection of assets. Possibly the management of these assets has not been very efficient, or the business may have experienced peculiar circumstances, so that recent income is not representative of the assets' potential. In such cases an earnings basis is not appropriate. In fact the value of any asset is determined by the cash flow that is expected to be derived from it, but the recurrent flows are not necessarily those obtained by the vendors. It is important to determine the basis of valuation: those in common use include current open market, existing use, alternative use, depreciated replacement cost, and going concern. There is clearly a distinction between a value based upon cost and one based upon the cash flows attributable to the ownership of an asset.

Often the information is provided by accounts which only contain book values, but the net assets basis disclosed by the most recent balance sheet provides a readily available figure. It may not be very relevant to current values, but trends in book values may provide useful indications of changes. An analysis of each type of asset may offer valuable information. The age, state of repair and technological obsolescence of equipment are relevant considerations. Others include the condition and usefulness of the stock, the location of sites, and the period of any leaseholds remaining.

It may be more appropriate to obtain current values. Current open market value can usually be applied to a standard asset for which there is an active market, since market prices will provide the necessary information. However, this is not appropriate when assets of a business are not acquired for disposal. Here existing use value is of more value. This is based on the use of the assets (property, plant and machinery) for the same purpose as it is used at present, which may be particularly suitable by reason of the assets' nature, location and character, and as a consequence the assets are able to command a premium.

If a prospective purchaser can see that there are ways in which the assets can be used to produce a higher cash flow, then the assets will have a higher value to him than to anyone else who has not seen such a profitable use for them. This *alternative use* may be in the existing combination or in separate uses by himself or when sold piecemeal to further purchasers. For example, for several years a business has produced profits of £100,000 and this is expected to continue indefinitely. In view of the stability of earnings a 20 per cent discount rate is appropriate, and that leads to a value of £500,000. A prospective purchaser knows that he can sell some of the assets for £300,000, and estimates that the remaining assets could produce a steady income of £50,000. Capitalizing £50,000 at 20 per cent, assuming that is still the appropriate rate, gives a value for the retained assets of £250,000. Together with the £300,000 from the sale of assets, there is a total value of £550,000, £50,000 more than before.

This is the classic argument of the 'asset stripper', and freehold property is often an asset which can be sold without reducing earnings significantly.

Acquisition of shares

This is very similar to acquisition of businesses and the same considerations apply. However, this section provides an opportunity to highlight the factors particularly associated with share values. The availability of market prices for quoted shares can provide valuable information, and use can be made not only of the share price of the potential acquisition but also of similar companies.

As indicated in the previous section, the price–earnings ratio (P/E) is often used in valuation by applying a suitable P/E to maintainable earnings. In the case of share purchases the stream of earnings is represented by the stream of future dividends. It can readily be shown[2] that if constant growth g is expected in a dividend stream which commences at a level D_1 at the end of the current period, then the theoretical value of the share at the beginning of the period is:

$$P_o = \frac{D_1}{r - g}$$

where r is the required rate of return or discount rate.

This formula can be modified to express price in terms of earnings. Making the simplifying assumption that growth results from reinvesting retained earnings at the rate r

$$P_o = \frac{E_1}{r}$$

where E_1 are earnings of the current period.

$$\therefore \frac{P_o}{E_1} = \frac{1}{r}$$

The requirement for valuation is to identify a P/E that reflects the earnings growth and risks of the earnings stream. Many factors provide indications of risk. A number will be considered, but the industry in which the business operates is usually of particular importance. Economic changes tend to have a similar impact on all companies in an industry; and in selecting a suitable P/E ratio it is usual to begin by finding the P/E ratio of a company of similar risk in the same industry.

Adjustment needs to be made for the impact of gearing (the debt–equity ratio). This impact is most readily apparent when considering the interest ratio (earnings before interest as a multiple of interest payments). Since interest is a fixed annual commitment, any percentage fluctuation in pre-interest earnings will produce an amplified change in after-interest earnings. For example, a company paying £1m interest out of £3m earnings before interest has a cover of 3:1. If these earnings halve to £1.5m, earnings net of interest will fall from £2m to only £0.5m. Halving of the pre-interest figure produces a reduction to a quarter in net earnings in this case.

Other factors which affect riskiness must also be borne in mind. Indications can be found in the company's accounts. Working capital ratios (e.g. the current ratio, current assets to asset liabilities) will provide information on liquidity.

Cash flows are of particular importance in most cases. If a business is unable to generate sufficient cash to meet its operating costs, it is likely to fail. Past records may point to future problems but direct estimates through cash budgets will permit attention to be given to the elements of cash flow.

The ability of a company's earnings to meet dividends as well as interest is another indicator of capacity to continue successfully. The dividend cover gives some measure of security by measuring the adequacy of the earnings to meet the ordinary dividend. Its calculation is illustrated below:

Share capital	50,000 shares of £1 each
Dividend	10 per cent
Earnings	£10,000
Dividend	£ 5,000
Dividend cover	2 times

The lower the dividend cover, the more of the earnings the shareholders are receiving but the less is being ploughed back into the business, probably resulting in lower profits and dividends in the future. High dividend cover may indicate a good policy of ploughing profits back into the business, particularly if associated with a consistent growth in earnings and dividend.

In assessing risk, you will find that the quality of the underlying assets will be relevant, as with business valuation.

Disposals of businesses and management buy-outs

Just as companies may consider acquiring a business from another company, companies may have the opportunity of selling part of their operations. Complementary considerations apply here to acquisitions.

278 Control and Audit in Management Accounting

The purpose of such a sell-off should recognize any potential strategic impact on product, lines, markets, etc. Valuation may present less problems, in that access to information is easier than for an outside buyer. Management buy-outs have been a growing method of facilitating the sell-off of parts of companies.[3] They occur when a number of existing managers of a company are active in putting together a financial package to acquire part of that company and intend to continue in the management of the acquisition.

From the point of view of the management team contemplating the acquisition, the considerations are similar to external purchase. They will be aiming to obtain benefits from their financial and career investment. The particular advantages to them of management buy-outs are:

- They have access to internal information and may be expert at evaluating it from their experience in operating within the existing structure
- The company will not face the difficulties of management change to the extent that existing managers continue.
- Interrelations with other business activities are not a concern if a separate entity is to be created.

However, in most buy-outs existing managers do not have sufficient capital of their own to finance the transaction. New capital is needed. The new company has no track record and may not be able to raise large amounts of share capital by public issue. Financial help is available from a number of specialist institutions, though these will tend to provide much of the capital in the form of debt, producing new companies with high debt and consequently the high risks of having to meet substantial interest charges. The advantage to the managers is that they will be able to retain a controlling interest in the company's share capital, although the debt-providers may include a condition on their loan that they can appoint a director to the board. Redemption requirements may impose substantial burdens on cash flow, and this would require special attention.

Raising debt finance

The effects of gearing and redemption applies whenever debt is considered. The principal need is to be able to generate funds to redeem the debt, and provide a worthwhile surplus over the life of the debt. It is important to match the period of borrowing with the purpose. Financing a long-term need from a short-term source exposes the company to the possibility of having to raise new finance, in order to repay in the short term, at a time when this is very difficult. Conversely, a company may not wish to have to continue to pay interest on a debt it can afford to repay. It follows that the amount borrowed should be carefully calculated, allowing for any other internal sources the company may wish to utilize.

Evaluation of borrowing will centre on its cost. The direct cost will be the interest payment, together with any premium payable on redemption. A recent practice has been to issue debt at a substantial discount, so that the lender can expect to be repaid much more than originally provided. In such circumstances the interest rates may appear low but the total cost of the debt to the borrower includes the amounts repaid in addition to the amount borrowed.

The security offered by a borrower will have an impact on costs of borrowing. Companies with marketable assets which can be offered as security will be able to borrow at lower rates, reflecting the reduction in the lenders' risks. Loans may be secured by granting the lender a charge on specific assets or on the assets of the company in general. While this is very useful in getting debt, it must be recognized that this can limit a company's future flexibility. A specific charge on an asset may prevent the company selling it, and certainly restricts its use as security for other loans.

Investigation of fraud

More directly linked with the control activities of the management accountant is the investigation of fraud. The objective is to establish if fraud has taken place, and, if so, to provide evidence to prove its occurrence and identify those responsible. This can lead to disciplinary action, including criminal proceedings so must be handled with extreme care.[4] The detection of fraud is an element of internal audit, and the foundations of any investigation will need to follow the relevant procedures and principles set out in Chapters 10 and 11.

Of course it is preferable to prevent fraud through the provision of good systems of internal control and suitable personnel policies. If fraud is suspected and an investigation is instigated, the systems of internal control will need to be well understood by the investigator.

The first steps should be taken cautiously. Facts should be checked before any allegations are made, since if the facts are proved false, there could be serious implications. At the same time, it is necessary to introduce procedures to ensure no important records disappear. It may be appropriate to introduce as soon as possible additional procedures to give protection for the company's assets against the effects of future fraud.

The investigation will need skill at detecting fraudulent activity, including examination of records and interviewing personnel. It is important that good records of the investigation are maintained. Interviewing will require particular care. In criminal cases this is subject to provisions of the law, and the investigator should acquaint himself with the current legal position[5] before any interview is undertaken. CIPFA has laid down the need to include the police in such cases, 'If as a result of the Audit Investigations, the Auditor concludes that in addition to possible disciplinary action, there is prima facie evidence that a criminal offence has been committed...'[6]

As in all cases of investigation, the work of the management accountant will be largely assessed by the quality of his report, and this chapter has drawn attention to the requirements of good reports. Although the range of special investigations a management accountant may be called upon to carry out can extend beyond those considered in this chapter, the examples chosen illustrate some of the major factors to be borne in mind. The particular area is likely to require expertise extending to areas outside the normal scope of accounting controls. Acquisitions draw upon the field of finance; fraud upon knowledge of criminal law. The information to be gathered is often dependent on the breadth of perspective taken, and may stretch beyond the immediate accounting data. Good records of the sources and values of raw data and clear statements of the underlying assumptions are part of the procedures to be followed by the thorough investigator. These skills are not easily acquired, but are developed alongside the understanding of a range of disciplines and experience of their application.

References

1. Stock Exchange, *City Code on Takeovers and Mergers*, (5th ed.), 1981.
2. See, for example, Van Horne, J.C. *Financial Management and Policy* Prentice-Hall, 7th ed., 1986.
3. Wright, M. and Coyne J., *Management Buy Outs in British Industry*, Croom Helm, 1985.
4. Criminal Law Act 1977; Police and Criminal Evidence Act 1984.
5. *Ibid.*
6. 'The Role of Internal Audit and the Police', published February 1983 by Hampshire County Council, is reproduced in Venables, J.S.R., and Impey, K.W., *Internal Audit*, Butterworths, 1985.

Further reading

Auditing Practices Committee, 'Fraud and other Irregularities', Draft Guideline 1985.
Bentley, T., *Report Writing in Business*, CIMA, 1978.
Pearson, B., *The Successful Acquisition of Unquoted Companies*, CIMA, 1983.
Samuels, J.M. and Wilkes, F.M., *Management of Company Finance*, VNR, 1986.

Questions

1. Major plc is investigating the possible aquisition of Minor Ltd. The following general financial details have been obtained:

Major plc
Issued and paid-up shares	10 million @ £1 nominal value
Current market share price	£4.20
Previous year's earnings per share	£0.60
Earnings per share forecast for current year	£0.80

Minor Ltd
Issued and paid-up shares	250,000 @ £1 nominal value
Previous year's earnings per share	£0.50
Earnings forecast for current year (This forecast was made by analysts acting on behalf of Major plc)	£185,000

You are required to:
(a) Advise the management of Major plc on the proposed acquisition of Minor Ltd.
(b) Explain why it is not necessarily possible to arrive at a 'correct' buying price.
(c) Indicate the main additional information you would require in conducting a full investigation of the proposed acquisition.

2 The owner of ABC Ltd has established a business in the manufacture of high value-added parts for computer and office equipment systems. He is now looking for a buyer to take over the business. The plant site and building have been leased from the local authority, but all other assets have been acquired, using a mixture of share capital and loans.

The price asked for the business is £280,000. The current balance sheet can be summarized as follows:

	£000	£000
Plant, machinery, fixtures and fittings at cost	400	
Less: Accumulated depreciation	100	300
Current assets:		
Stocks	100	
Debtors	200	
Cash	20	
	320	
Less: Current liabilities	180	
Net current assets		140
Total assets *less* current liabilities		440
Less: Loans (short- and medium-term)		300
Net assets		140
Share capital and reserves		140

The business has been in operation for four years. Its turnover and pre-tax earnings (after deduction of operating costs and interest) during this period have been:

	Year 1 £000	Year 2 £000	Year 3 £000	Year 4 £000
Turnover	150	750	1,200	1,400
Earnings	10	40	65	70

You are required, as adviser to a potential purchaser, to give a reasoned opinion of the asking price, setting out relevant calculations. Explain clearly any assumptions used in this evaluation and state any further information you consider necessary.

3 An opinion has been expressed that 'Apart from their purchasers' origin, management buy-outs scarcely 'differ at all from the purchase of one company by another. In both cases, it is necessary for the purchaser to investigate the same factors to determine whether an acquisition is likely to prove sound.' You are required to discuss the above opinion, detailing the common factors and the factors which may be different between management buy-out and external acquisition.

(CIMA November 1988)

14 Conclusion

It is well recognized that the business environment of many organizations today is changing both substantially and rapidly. In order to contribute efficiently and effectively to an organization's survival and success under such conditions, management accounting must adopt a proactive strategy towards the generation of information for management and the way that information is utilized. The continuous introduction of new ideas, requirements, methods and techniques for the development and processing of information currently taking place certainly puts in question the passive acceptance and perpetuation of long established routines even in companies experiencing only limited change in their business circumstances.

Studies carried out within companies by the authors[1,2,3] reflect, as might be expected, a very wide range of actual practice and views about the future within management accounting and among accountants. A particular feature was the need for accountants to be active in the capture of information, so that the control of an organization – using the term in its broadest sense – was placed in the position of anticipating events rather than merely reacting to them.

The Stapylton company[4,5] provides a good example of a company accountant taking a positive lead in the creation of information necessary to enable it to meet the challenge of competition both by securing external intelligence and by the quantification of responses needed from within the organization. Lynnfield, the competitor company to Stapylton, was the subject of a detailed examination by Stapylton's accountant as to every aspect of its business, from its technology through its cost structure to its pricing policy. The intelligence used for this purpose came from a variety of external sources, such as customers, suppliers and company reports, as well as members of Stapylton's staff, using their own knowledge and experience to piece together a picture of their competitor's business:

> ... an estimate of Lynnfield's prime costs could be made, which, although not based on actual information about the Lynnfield operations was considered sufficiently accurate as a starting point. The cost structure identified by this process of what may be termed simulating the activities of the competitor was checked out in the first instance by an analysis of Lynnfield's company accounts.

As part of the response to the competitive threat, Stapylton itself had to formulate its own marketing strategy. Here the accountant made the following observation:

> My problem as the accountant was to pin down the marketing man to having to quantify the various options. Accounting played the right part and made them quantify. I would ask 'if you want £1 million for advertising what will you give us in sales volume? What would be the effect of a price cut of 2%, 4%, zero?' These questions I made them answer so it was capable of quantification, but it was up to me to work them out.

In neither of the above illustrations did routine, readily available internal accounting information play a significant role. There is no implied diminution of the value of such information by this, merely that on its own it only constitutes a part of what management accountants should be aiming to secure in their role of prime suppliers of information to top management in their running of the business.

As an example of the more intelligent analysis of information than would be gained by slavish adherence to simple cost classification, the same study contains the cases of the 'Quadratic', 'Waterloo' and 'Midlands Metals'. In the former, how cost and volume of activity are related was the subject of the investigation. Simple linear relation models abound in the accounting literature, suggesting there is perhaps some automatic mechanism whereby a certain volume of activity naturally produces a predictable amount of expenditure: the accountant can only sit back and let it happen, apart from quantifying the relationship in the first place. As many would at least intuitively recognize this cannot be the case; even in the very short run the exigencies of the state of the business, however caused, need expenditure to be managed. The fact that much financial thinking is perhaps distorted by trying to fit information and effects into precise time periods may well contribute to rather inflexible and stereotyped responses to issues such as the way costs behave and how they may be managed. The time horizon over which an objective has to be achieved is a continuous variable, and this removes many problems from the arena of simply utilizing budget data, produced for a specific and different purpose, for a decision problem.

In the case of Waterloo the budget information itself was generated on the principle that 'costs are matched to the underlying level of business rather than, in part at least, being expected to change more or less immediately and in direct proportion to changes in business activity'. There is a substantial difference between these two approaches in the context of cost management.

A degree of psychology was also observed in the practice of the accountant at Midlands Metals. In what might be taken for a fairly standard budget report format, with expenses classified as to whether they were regarded as fixed or variable costs (though even this is an advance on the commonly observed budget–actual–variance presentation), the subtlety lay in keeping the fixed cost elements as few as possible, on the grounds that calling a cost 'fixed' tended to produce the reaction on the part of managers that they could do little to manage it effectively.

In a further study, entitled 'Kimco', the question of the real independence of divisions in a situation where they were regarded as autonomous, conducting 'arms length' trading with each other, was addressed. In this case the role of the internal auditor became critical in ensuring that the benefits of autonomy were not completely lost through the individual divisions producing potentially damaging goals of their own in conflict with those of the group. The internal auditor was able to utilize his own information system to provide top management with the checks and balances needed to keep group and divisions working toward the same goals without the former seeming to interfere too obtrusively into the latter's affairs.

These and other cases cited[6,7] are mainly aimed at illustrating the need for management accounting to provide a positive lead in the generation of information and its application in facilitating the processes of business decision-making and control. The common feature is not to rely on existing records alone, but to be constantly aware of emerging needs as business demands change.

There is of course, a well documented body of literature in management accounting, generally referred to as contingency theory,[8] which has pointed out, largely in a non-specific way, how various factors may influence the design and development of accounting information systems (AIS). Four major factors are cited as having the greatest impacts, namely: environment, technology, organization and decision-making style. A continengy theory is also applied to organizations.

The objective of contingency theory, put rather superficially, may be thought of as being to project the information needs of an accounting information system at all stages of its design or re-design. For instance, as regards the environment, there are varying degrees to which it is dynamic and therefore demanding of information beyond the normal requirements of a stable market. Each factor in turn exerts varying degrees of influence on the design of the AIS. As a matter of logic, it may appear possible to synthesize a range of situations and draw up an AIS to match at least the basic requirements of each. Even this relatively limited objective for the production of tailor-made systems appears unattainable; there is little evidence so far to suggest that the 'theory' can be turned into practice in this way.

It is possible that the best which can be expected of contingency theory is that it heightens awareness of the variables which should be addressed in the design of a system (or its revision). Beyond this, it has to be recognized that management accounting information systems, like many other internal systems, depend for their actual configuration on what the company management perceives as being needed. Its collective opinion would carry at least as much weight as its accountant's clearly diagnosed appraisal of a business's information needs.

It is not suggested there is a need to categorize everything into neat AIS packages. The main point of the argument is that systems should not be allowed to atrophy to the stage of becoming an irrelevance to the circumstances of the business whose interests they are supposed to serve. The danger of continuous perpetuation of outdated systems, for whatever reason, is well illustrated by the study of Crossways,[9] where information output had reached the point of being largely ignored within the plant.

Kaplan[10] debates the issue, while in a recent study carried out for CIMA,[11] and referred to early in Chapter 4, the whole purpose of the investigation was to look at the question of how firms were responding to changes brought about by being in new and high technology industry. The study used detail with respect to the traditional features of a management accounting system, such as its budgeting/standard costing system, performance measures, and capital expenditure appraisal measures, principally as a touchstone against which to contrast change. Of major interest was the impact of information technology in improving the information collection and processing capability, and the views of company accountants as to how they saw change affecting their responsibilities in the provision of information. As such, much of the work deals in effect with the technology and environmental variables of contingency theory.

The range of industry covered by the investigation was substantial, taking in what would be recognized as many of the most important of the new technologies, such as the production of silicon chips, printed circuits, office automation systems and so on; it also incorporated the change to high technology manufacture now being extensively experienced in many long established industrial firms. It was felt that the substantial diversity of influences on the development of management accounting was well represented by the study. The following repeats most of the main findings of the enquiry in order to illustrate the breadth of issues which must be faced proactively rather than reactively.

1 The general requirement of the AIS in new and high technology industry was for the provision of 'higher quality' information: its scope, content and availability must be aimed at the anticipation of events rather than forcing the firm into the relatively passive stance of reacting to them as events unfold and their effects become known.
2 A central requirement for the achievement of 1 was seen to be in most cases the deployment of information technology systems which facilitated the necessary capture, storage and analysis of information, if the proactive vision is to materialize.

3 Coordinated evolution of company strategies for product and process development was emphasized as a factor needing significant support from within management accounting.
4 The implementation of a strategy almost invariably commits a company to significant investment expenditures. Apart from underlining once more the importance of 1, this commitment is frequently very specific to the extent that a company's options as to its operation either in volume terms or product variety are narrowed down. Together with the level of finance invested, this throws emphasis on to the control activity in particular: the investment, once made, has to succeed. Short-term cost analysis is relatively downgraded in significance.
5 Absorption costing remains the principal accounting routine for providing information on department and product cost. This is of course a very 'traditional' process, and, paradoxical as it may seem, reference to it was generally accompanied by statements on the need to improve the 'accuracy' of product cost. This is perceived as very important in respect of product profitability and the ability to react effectively to change in the competitive environment – all this in spite of the well documented problems arising in respect of cost allocation and apportionment. However, it is a challenge to the ingenuity of accountants, under conditions where a high proportion of cost is at least short-term fixed and jointly determined over several lines of business, to attempt to produce cost analyses in such a way as to disaggregate them effectively to individual product groups. One observed approach was to analyse separate elements of the businesses to determine what its requirements for resources would be in order to operate independently, but recognising the effects of economies of scale.
6 The comments in respect of 5 may give the impression that contribution analysis was rarely encountered. In the sense of being by product it rarely was in detail, but was part of the build-up to identifying and directly attributing cost to business sectors.
7 A variety of developments in the modern manufacturing scene impact on management accounting: material requirements planning, just-in-time supplier systems, and total quality (which incorporated in large measure, the previous two concepts). However, it is interesting in respect of 'quality' on its own that this did not necessarily emerge as a factor which should be 'accounted' for in the normal sense; it was rather an attitude of mind to be generated throughout an organization. It was observed to be rather illogical to design a product to certain specifications and then to make it almost an issue for congratulation if the standard were achieved; achievement should be the expectation without a need for an expensive panoply of cost measurements to record how far off target actual results were. Accounting would still play a role in helping to determine where quality problems might lie, though much reliance is now placed on quality groups established throughout a plant.

8 As regards the question of whether management accounting needs a new array of methods and techniques in the sense of acquiring new algorithms for data manipulation in order to meet new industrial environments and technologies, the answer appeared to be that it did not. What was required was a more active and intelligent use of what is available, coupled with a willingness to change.

The points made above may read as though they represent a widely accepted statement of general tendency. This was not the case: reactions to questions posed were frequently very different for all kinds of reasons, but they added up to the fact that uniformity in the detail of management accounting practice is unlikely to be realized.

The best that probably can be hoped for is that accountants are alert to the information requirements of a business and are willing to implement change in so far as they are permitted to do. In this context perhaps the ultimate observation came from one or two companies where accountants themselves were reporting to management on the value to the company of their own activities – no more daunting a problem than the same type of measurement applied to other activities, but seldom contemplated.

References

1 Coates, J.B., Rickwood, C.P. and Stacey, R.J., 'Examination of the Differences Between Academic Concepts and Actual Management Accounting Practices', Report to ESRC, British Library Document Supply Centre, August 1987.
2 Rickwood, C.P., Coates, J.B. and Stacey, R.J., 'Managed Costs and the Capture of Information', *Accounting and Business Research*, Vol. 17, No. 68, Autumn 1987.
3 Coates, J.B., Longden, S.G. 'Management Accounting in New and High Technology Growth Companies'.
Report to the Chartered Institute of Management Accountants. November 1987.
4 Coates, Rickwood and Stacey, *op. cit.*
5 Rickwood, Coates and Stacey, *op. cit.*
6 Coates, Rickwood and Stacey, *op. cit.*
7 Rickwood, Coates and Stacey, *op. cit.*
8 Emmanuel, C. & Otley D. T. Accounting for Management Control. Van Nostrand Reinhold. 1986
9 Coates, Rickwood and Stacey, *op. cit.*
10 Kaplan, R.S. 'Measuring Manufacturing Performance: A New Challenge for Managerial Accounting Research'. The Accounting Review. Vol. LVIII. No. 4. October 1983.
11 Coates and Longden, *op. cit.*

Appendix: Linear programming

Consider this very simplified situation.

LP Processes Ltd manufactures two grades of washing-up liquid, Brand X and Brand Y. Brand X requires 320 litres of Solvin, 100 litres of Tergit and 80 litres of Peroma, while Brand Y requires 400, 40 and 160 litres respectively of the same constituents, per 1,000 bottles. Both grades are produced by the same process equipment, which can deliver 5,000 bottles of X and 4,000 bottles of Y per hour. A total of 1,920 production hours are available next year. Contributions per bottle of X and Y are budgeted at 9.5p and 12p respectively. Supplies of Tergit and Peroma are only available from RB Ltd, a fellow subsidiary, for whom these supplies are waste products. Due to contractions in RB's outputs, Tergit and Peroma will be in limited supply in the coming year and are estimated at 750,000 and 1,250,000 litres per annum respectively.

LP Processes believes it can sell all it can manufacture, and wants to know what the optimal sales/production volumes would be, and how 'robust' such a decision would be to changes in 'circumstances'. In particular it is aware that the price differentiation between the two brands could well change from that budgeted if market conditions experienced over the year are even slightly different from that assumed in the budget.

Using a simple LINDO package the inputs to the model expressed in units of thousands of bottles, £ and litres would be:

Maximize the objective function representing contribution
$95X + 120Y$ subject to constraints:
TERGIT $100X + 40Y \leq 750,000$
PEROMA $80X + 160Y \leq 1,250,000$
PRODUCTION HOURS $0.2X + 0.25Y \leq 1920$
Computer output would be:

OBJECTIVE FUNCTION VALUE 921600.00

VARIABLE	VALUE	REDUCED COST
X	0.000000	1.000000
Y	7680.000000	0.000000

ROW	SLACK OR SURPLUS	DUAL PRICES
TERGIT)	442800.000000	0.000000
PEROMA)	21200.000000	0.000000
PRODN)	0.000000	480.000000

RANGES IN WHICH THE BASIS IS UNCHANGED

OBJ COEFFICIENT RANGES

VARIABLE	CURRENT COEF	ALLOWABLE INCREASE	ALLOWABLE DECREASE
X	95.000000	1.000000	INFINITY
Y	120.000000	INFINITY	1.250000

RIGHT-HAND SIDE RANGES

ROW	CURRENT RHS	ALLOWABLE INCREASE	ALLOWABLE DECREASE
TERGIT	750000.000000	INFINITY	442800.000000
PEROMA	1250000.000000	INFINITY	21200.000000
PRODN	1920.000000	33.125000	1920.000000

Under the assumptions of the model, LP Processes Ltd would maximize contribution and profits if they made no Brand X and the most their limited production facilities would allow (7.68m bottles) of brand Y!

It may be useful for the reader to identify terms used in the computer output:

1 *The objective function* value is the value of the variable to be optimized (either maximized or minimized). In this case it refers to a maximization of the contribution to be earned. Fixed costs have still to be deducted before net profit is found.
2 *Value*. The values of the outputs of the product variables.
3 *Reduced cost*. The loss which would be realized by introducing a unit of product not included in the optimal plan (X in this instance). The objective value would fall by £1 for each unit of X brought into the solution at the expense of certain losses in Y (due to the effect of the constrained resource).
4 *Slack or surplus*. These values show how much of a variable remains unutilized. In the case of Tergit and Peroma we have 442,800 and 21,200 litres respectively which would still be available. The production constraint is fully utilized. Had there been any limits on de-

mand for the products, a similar set of values would describe unfulfilled demand.

5 *The dual (or shadow) values* express the value in £ to be gained by relaxing the constrained variable by one unit. Thus if one more production hour were available, total contribution would rise by £480. Conversely for a reduction in hours. This also exemplifies the linearity of the problem.

6 *The ranges in which the basis is unchanged.* Given the uncertainty of the business situation in general, a single variable optimization, assuming complete certainty of values, is clearly unrealistic. The information provided under this heading is for purposes of assessing the sensitivity to change of each of the values stated in the initial formulation of the problem. Thus:

(a) For the objective coefficient ranges we consider the sensitivities of contribution values given in the initial objective row and the range within which these could move (either through cost or price changes) before the initial solution changes (though the objective value will of course change).

(b) For the right-hand side ranges, which represent the initial constraints, information is provided on the range within which these values could move before the solution changes. An existing resource variable which is in surplus in the original solution may be reduced until it becomes binding, but can be increased by an infinite amount without effect.

It is important to remember that these changes are for the individual variable under examination, assuming no change in any of the others. In this particular case, even if such a sales/production policy would be acceptable to LPP, only relatively small changes in the prices of X and Y would change that optimal level, i.e. an increase of the contribution of X from 9.5p to 9.6p or a decrease of Y's contribution from 12.0p to 11.875p.

Suppose, for example, that the contribution of X is increased from 9.5p to 10.0p per bottle. Then the LINDO objective function would become 100X + 120Y and the tableau would be:

OBJECTIVE FUNCTION VALUE 47647.063

VARIABLE	VALUE	REDUCED COST
X	6511.764648	0.000000
Y	2470.588135	0.000000

ROW	SLACK OR SURPLUS	DUAL PRICES
TERGIT)	0.000000	0.058824
PEROMA)	333764.718750	0.000000
PRODN)	0.000000	470.588226

RANGES IN WHICH THE BASIS IS UNCHANGED

OBJ COEFFICIENT RANGES

VARIABLE	CURRENT COEF	ALLOWABLE INCREASE	ALLOWABLE DECREASE
X	100.000000	199.999985	4.000001
Y	120.000000	5.000001	80.000000

RIGHT-HAND SIDE RANGES

ROW	CURRENT RHS	ALLOWABLE INCREASE	ALLOWABLE DECREASE
TERGIT	750000.000000	209999.984375	442800.000000
PEROMA	1250000.000000	INFINITY	333764.718750
PRODN	1920.000000	443.281281	420.000000

Maximum contribution would now be obtained by producing 6,511,756 bottles of X and 2,470,588 bottles of Y. In fact this is only a slightly more robust decision than before, as a change in contribution of 0.4p down of X or 0.5p up of Y would change the 'optimum' point. What has changed, however, is that while in the first scenario only production hours were limiting further improvements in contribution, under this second scenario both production hours and the limited supply of Tergit put a stop to further improvements in contribution levels (although even in Scenario 1 only 21,200 litres of Peroma were surplus/slack to the optimal level).

In practice, even using simple LP software packages such as LINDO, management is able to observe the effects of different planning decisions on profitability/contribution levels and, in particular, understand the sensitivity of their plans to changes in variables. There is no need for managers or accountants to understand linear programming at a sophisticated mathematical level, but simply to have enough knowledge to interpret the output 'indicators'.

In real life, situations would be much more complex than in the simple example. However, the principles remain relevant and applicable.

Index

Absorption costing, 285
Accountability, 208, 220
Accounting conventions, 120–3, 129–33
Accounting information system, 283, 284
Ackoff, R., 10, 22
Acquisition, 270 et seq.
  of businesses, 270
  of shares, 274
Added value, 142
Alchian, A., 18, 23
Amey, L.R., 137, 149
Amey, L.R. and Eggington, D., 136, 137, 149
Analytical review, 212, 227, 228
Anderson, R.J., 284
Annuity depreciation, 126–9
Anthony, R.N., 67, 75
Anthony, R.N., Dearden, J. and Vancil, R., 158, 165
Argyris, 27, 42
Aspiration levels, 22
Assessment – criteria, 115 et seq.
Assets – valuation, see Valuation – asset
Attributable – performance, 26
Audit:
  commission, 82–5, 95, 181 et seq.
  internal, 8–9, 51, 52, 202 et seq. 277
  internal compared to external, 206
  internal defined, 205
  management, 213
  manuals, 215
  planning, 211, 213 et seq.
  programme, 264
  tests, 212
  trial, 249, 262, 263 et seq.
  value for money, see Value for money audit
Auditing:
  Practices Committee (APC), 202–12, 221, 225, 227, 248, 274, 278
  techniques and procedures, 224 et seq.
Auditor general, 187

Back-up, 200–62
Banham, J. and Tristram, R., 218, 222
Barnard, C., 17, 22
Becker, S.W. and Green, D., 22, 27, 42
Beer, S., 11, 22
Beeton, D., 188, 190
Behaviour, 20 et seq.
  and budget, 21
Bentley, T., 278
Bhasker, K.N., 252, 265
Bierman, J., 56, 65
Birmingham City Council, 184
Birnberg, J.G., 56, 65
Boys, P.G., 222
British Rail, 172
Budget:
  aspiration levels, 22, 28–30
  behaviour, 21, 26 et seq.
  centre, 25 et seq., 117–18, 145–6, 165

centre selection, 25–7, 118–20
and change, 39–41
constraints and limiting factors, 32–3
control, 30–1, 47, 48
coordination, 29–30, 31–2
negotiation in, 27, 62–4
planning, 30–1, 47, 48
resources, 32–3
revision, 36 et seq.
rolling, 37, 38
variances, 33
Burgess, T., 95
Butt, H., 94
Buy outs, see Management buy-outs

Cambridgeshire experiment, 93, 94
Central government, 187
Centre for interfirm comparisons (CIFC), 87
Chambers, A.D., 222, 247, 248, 266
Chandler, A.D., 9
Chartered Institute of Public Finance & Accounting (CIPFA), 87, 182, 208, 222
City code on takeovers and mergers, 270, 278
Coates, Rickwood and Stacey, 9, 42, 65, 105, 148, 149, 165, 285
Committed costs, 158–9, 161–2
Competitor – assessment, 103 et seq.
Compliance tests, 212 et seq., 225
Comptroller and auditor general, 187
Computer:
  assisted audit techniques (CAATs), 264 et seq.
  audit, 249 et seq., 267 et seq.
  cost benefit, 250
  cost effective, 250
  eavesdropping, 265
  labelling and tagging, 264–5
  software and hardware, 249 et seq.
Consumer Credit Act 1974, 258
Contribution, 50, 51
Control, 11
  and behaviour, 8
  internal definition, 202 et seq., 261, 277
  mechanisms, 7, 8
  and performance, 52
  and plans, 7
  process, 8

Controllable:
  cost, 134 et seq.
  performance, 26
  profit, 134 et seq.
Cooke, P.J., 266
Coopers & Lybrand, 247
Cost:
  apportionment, 49, 50
  attributable, 51
  centre, 26, 116, 158 et seq.
  controllability, 49, 50
  current, 132
  direct, 49, 51
  fixed, 50, 51
  historic, 132
  indirect, 50
  managed, 50
  responsibility for, 49, 50
  variable, 50
Court, J.M., 248
Coyne, J., 278
Criminal Law Act 1977, 278
Cusum, see Variance analysis and variances
Cybernetics, 12 et seq.
Cyert, R.M., 17, 23, 63, 65

Data Protection Act 1984, 258
De Rooven, Edler, 9
Debt, 276–7
Decentralization, 19, 109 et seq., 118–19
Decision:
  programmed and non-programmed, 16, 19
  theory models, see Variance analysis and variances
  units and packages, see Zero based budgeting
Decoupling, 16
Demsetz, H., 18, 23
Demski, J., 57, 65
Department of Energy, 173
Direct cost, see Cost
Disposals – of businesses, 275
District Audit Service, 185, 190
Dividend cover, 275
Division of labour, 19
Divisionalization, 18, 20, 120 et seq.
Dopuch, N., 57, 65
Douglas, J. J., 266
Drinking Water & Sewerage Corporation, Nepal, 175

Economy effectiveness and efficiency, 157–8, 170, 213, 218, 251
  audit, 218
  of computers, 256 et seq.
  definitions, 81, 82
Electricity Council, 173
Emmanuel, C.R. and Otley, D.T., 23, 63, 137, 149
Energy costs, 89
Engineered costs, 158–9
Environment, 12
Evidence:
  audit, 211, 220, 262
  objectivity, 211
  recording, 216
  relevance, reliability, sufficiency, 211
  sources, 212
Exception report, 13
Expert systems, 264

Feasibility study, 253
Feedback:
  definition, 115
  loop, 14
  negative and positive, 15, 22
Feedforward, 16
File creation and conversion, 256
Financial:
  management initiative, 188
  performance, 22
Financial Services Act 1986, 258
Flow chart, 231
Foster, G., 65
Fouraker, J.C., 57, 65
Fraud, 204, 258, 277

Garbage-in-garbage-out, 265
Gearing, 275–6
Glendinning, R., 174, 189
Glynn, J.J., 81, 95
Goal:
  congruence, 96 et seq., 140
  organizational, 17 et seq., 220
Grandfather-father-son system, 260
Green, D., 22, 27, 42

Hash totals, 262
Hatch, J., 174, 175, 189
Hawthorne studies, 20
Henley, D., 172, 189
Herzberg, F., 20, 22, 26, 27, 42
Hire of assets, 133–4

Hofstede, G.H., 27, 42, 63
Hopwood, A.G., 23, 63
Horngren, C.T., 1, 65
Housden, R.J.W., 252, 265

Impey, K.W., 222, 247, 278
Independence:
  audit, 208, 219
Inflation, 60, 61
Information technology statements (ICAEW), 258, 265
Inlogov (Institute of Local Government Studies, Birmingham), 218, 222
Institute of Internal Auditors, 208, 222
Inter-firm comparisons, 99 et seq.
Internal:
  audit see Audit – internal
  control evaluation questionnaires, 231
  control questionnaires, 231, 232
  systems, testing, 225
Interrogation of computers, 264
Investigations – special, 214
Investment centre, 26, 117 et seq., 137–9, 160

Jaedicke, R.K., 57, 65
Jenkins, B.G., 266
Johnson, H.T., 9
Jones, G., 266
Jones, R., 69, 73, 76, 77, 81, 94

Kaplan, R.S., 9, 57, 284
Kayartha, A., 174, 189
Key results analysis, 146–8

LAMSAC, 87
Leslie, D.A., 239, 241
Lewis, C.D., 58, 65
Life-cycle costing, 87
Limiting factors, 32–3
Loan capital, see Debt
Local authorities, 181
  budgeting in, 68, 69
Local government audit practice code of, 218
Local Government Finance Act:
  1972, 81
  1982, 80, 218
Longden, S.G., 65
Lupton, T., 36, 42
Lyden, F.J., 94

296 Index

McClelland, Atkinson, Clark and Lowell, 27, 42
McCrae, T.W., 252, 265
McGregor, 21, 23
McNamara, T., 266
Managed costs, 158–9, 162–4
Management accounting:
  definition, 1–4
  development, 4–5
  origins, 4–5
Management audit – definition, 218 et seq.
Management by objectives, 52
Management buy-outs, 275 et seq.
Management information systems, 13, 252
Manager – as entrepreneur, 11
March, J.G., 17, 23, 63, 65
Maslow, A.H., 20, 21, 23, 27, 42
Materiality, 208 et seq., 228, 229, 242
Mayo, E., 23
Mayston, D., 189
Meyer, H.H., Kay, E. and French, J.P.R., 148, 149
Miles and Vergin, 42
Miller, E.M., 94
Model building, 13
Monitoring, 220
Motivation:
  budgets, 20, 26 et seq.
  congruence, 96–7

National Audit Act 1983, 80, 93
National Audit Office, 187, 190
National Coal Board, 173
Nationalized industries, 172–81
Neilson, A., 190
Nepal Electricity Authority (NEA), 175
Network analysis, 254, 255
Not-for-profit (NFP) organizations, 67–95, 164

Objectives and goals, 13, 17
Objectivity, 212
On-line systems, 262–4
Operational:
  audit, 217
  controls, 261
Organization:
  chart, 12, 19
  control, 202
  definition, 17
  structure and budgets centres, 17, 26
Otley, D.T., 17, 23, 63

Palmer, R., 94
Parallel running, 256
Parity checks, 261
Parsons, T., 17, 22
Participation in budget setting, 22, 26 et seq.
Passwords, 262
Pearson, B., 278
Pendlebury, M., 69, 73, 76, 77, 81, 94
Performance:
  audit, 217 et seq.
  centre, 26, 27, 165
  evaluation systems, 96 et seq.
  indicators, 88–91
  inter-firm comparisons, 99 et seq.
  short vs long term, 140
Perks, R., 174, 189
Perry, R.C.L., 266
Personnel controls, 203, 259–60
Physical controls, 203, 259
Pilot testing, 256
Planning:
  budgetary, 5, 6
  budgets and standards, 25
  management, 5, 6
  operational, 6
  strategic, tactical, 5, 6, 47
Plans and controls, 7
Police and Criminal Evidence Act 1984, 278
Precision limit see Statistical sampling
Presthus, R.V., 17, 22
Price/earnings ratio (P/E), 271–5
Procedures for audit, 242–7
  fixed assets, 246
  income, 245
  purchases, 243
  sales, 244
  trade debtors, 246
Profit centre, 26, 27, 117 et seq., 141 et seq.
Programme, planning, budgeting systems (PPBS), 69, 75–9, 81
  categories, elements, 76–7
Public sector:
  central statistical office data, 169

significance of, 169
and SSAPs, 174

Quality control, 216

Ratio analysis, 100 et seq.
  profit to sales, 142–4
  public sector, 170–2, 174 et seq.
  ROI/ROCE, 120 et seq., 173, 220
Rayner scrutinies, 188
Real time, 262, 264
Recording, see Evidence
Redwood, J., 174, 175, 189
Relative advantage, 220
Relevance, 211
Reliability, 211
Reports (for management), 269–70
Required rate of return, 173
Residual income, 124 et seq.
Responsibility – centres, 26, 115 et seq.
Revenue centres, 116–17, 164–5
Reward systems, 96
Rickwood, C.P., 9, 42, 65, 105, 148, 149, 165, 285, 286
Risk, 220, 275
Round the computer audit, 263

Sample size, see Statistical sampling
Samuels, J.M., 278
Santocki, J., 218, 220
Sayle, A.J., 218
Scapens, R.J., 64
Schiff and Lewin, 27, 42
Scott, W.G., 17, 23
Security (of systems), 251, 255, 257 et seq.
  for debt, 277
Segmentalization, 111 et seq.
Segregation of duties, 202
Selim, G.M., 247
Severn Trent Water Authority, 196–201
Share valuation, see Valuation – of shares
Shillinglaw, 136, 137, 149
Simon, Guetzkow, Zrozmetsky and Tyndall, 27, 42
Solomons, D., 4, 9, 47, 136, 137, 149
Span of control, 19
Speculation, 18, 19
Stacey, R.J., 65, 286
Standards:

costing, 34, 47
and change, 39
data processing, 254 et seq.
definition, 33–4
engineered, 34
expectations and estimates, 35
historical, 34
revision, 36
Starbuck, W.H., 63, 65
Statistical control, see Variance analysis and variances
Statistical sampling, 234
  attributes, 237–9
  monetary unit, 239–42
  precision limits/gap, 241–2
  sample size, 241
Stedry, A.C., 21, 23, 27, 28, 42
Substantive tests, 212, 226, 230
Superprofits, see Valuation
Supervision, 203, 214, 215, 260
Systems:
  boundary, 11
  closed/open, 12
  definition, 10 et seq.
  design, 254
  development, 250
  documentation, 225, 231
  evaluation and audit, 231, 249 et seq.
  hierarchy, 11

Tait, G., 48
Taylor, F.W., 19, 23
Teamwork, 18
Teitlebaum, A.D., 248
Terotechnology, 87
Test data, 255, 264
Thames Water Authority, 180, 181, 190–6
Thomas, A.J., 266
Timeliness, 251
Tomkins, C., 95, 169
Transfer prices/pricing, 118–19
Transport Act 1962, 172

Upper error limit (UEL), see Statistical sampling

Valuation:
  asset, 273
  of businesses, 271 et seq.
  earnings basis, 271

of shares, 274 *et seq.*
superprofits, 272
Value analysis (and cost reduction), 87
Value for money audit (VFM), 69, 80–93, 164, 170, 218
Van Horne, J.C., 278
Variance analysis and variances, 14, 53–62, 220
  ad hoc rules, 54, 55
  controllable, 61
  cusum chart, 57
  decision theory models, 58, 59
  experience in, 54, 55
  price, 61
  revisions, 61
  statistical control, 55, 56
Venables, J.S.R., 222, 247, 278
Vintner, G., 247

Virus-computer, 258–9
Vouching, 265

Walk through tests, 212
Weaknesses, 220
Whitehead, C., 187, 190
Wilkes, F.M., 278
Woolf, E., 220, 247
Wright, M., 278

Young, G.W., 75, 95

Zero based budgeting (ZBB), 69, 70–5, 78, 81
  decision packages, 72, 73
  decision units, 72
  incremental, 73
  mutually exclusive, 73